Richard Lassels

An Italian Voyage, Or, a Compleat Journey Through Italy. In Two Parts.

With the Characters of the People, and the Description of the Chief Towns, Churches, Monasteries, Tombs, Libraries, Pallaces, Villa's, Gardens, Pictures, Statues and Antiquities.

Richard Lassels

An Italian Voyage, Or, a Compleat Journey Through Italy. In Two Parts.
With the Characters of the People, and the Description of the Chief Towns, Churches, Monasteries, Tombs, Libraries, Pallaces, Villa's, Gardens, Pictures, Statues and Antiquities .

ISBN/EAN: 9783741151217

Manufactured in Europe, USA, Canada, Australia, Japa

Cover: Foto ©Andreas Hilbeck / pixelio.de

Manufactured and distributed by brebook publishing software (www.brebook.com)

Richard Lassels

An Italian Voyage, Or, a Compleat Journey Through Italy. In Two Parts.

AN ITALIAN-VOYAGE,

OR,

A Compleat Journey

THROUGH

ITALY.

The Second PART.

With a Character of the People, and the Description of the Chief Towns, Churches, Monasteries, Tombs, Libraries, Pallaces, Villas, Gardens, Pictures, Statues, Antiquities:

AS ALSO,

Of the Interest, Government, Riches, Force, &c. of all the Princes.

By *RICHARD LASSELS*, Gent.

The Second Edition; with Large Additions, by a Modern Hand.

LONDON,

Printed for R. *Wellington*, at the *Lute* in St. *Paul's*-Church-Yard, MDCXCVIII.

Part II.

A
JOURNEY
Through
ITALY.

PART II.

BEING arrived at *Rome*, we Lodged in an *Inn* for three or four days, till we had found out, and furnished a House to our satisfaction. That done, I began presently my *Inquest*, and made *Hue* and *Cry* after every little thing which time seemed to have robbed us of.

But as we approach not to great Persons in *Italy*, without informing our selves first of their *Titles*, that we may know how to *Stile* them: So before I bring my Reader acquainted with *Rome*, I think it not amiss to tell him how this great City is commonly called.

And although *Rome* were anciently stiled *The Head and Mistress of the World*; *an Earthly Goddess*; *the Eternal City*; *the Compendium of the World*; *the common Mother and Nurse of all Virtues*;

tues; (while she was yet *Heathen*;) Yet since her Ladyship was Baptized and became *Christian* (though she have had great Elogies made of her by the Holy Fathers) I find no Title so honourable to her, as that of *Roma la Santa*, Rome the Holy; which is given her by the *Common Proverb*, and common Proverbs are nothing else but the observations of common Sense: For whereas the other Cities of *Italy* are *Proverbially* called, either *Fair, Gentile, Rich, Proud, Fat* or *Great*; as *Florence, Naples, Venice; Genua, Bologna, Milan*; *Rome* only is stiled *the Holy:* and this deservedly, for many Reasons.

How Rome is stiled.

Roma la Santa.

First, for being the Episcopal Seat of St. *Peter* and his *Successors*, to the number of 240 and odd *Popes*.

2. For having been watered at the roots, by the Preaching and blood of the two Glorious Apostles St. *Peter* and St *Paul*, which made St. *Leo*, speaking to *Rome* of these two great *Apostles*, make her this *Apostrophe*. *Hi sunt qui te ad hanc gloriam provexerunt, ut gens sancta, populus electus, civitas Sacerdotalis, Regia, per sacram Beati Petri sedem caput orbis effecta, latius præsideres religione divina quam dominatione terrena.*

Serm. 1. de Natal. Apost. Petri & Pauli.

3. For having been looked upon in all Ages, as the *Center of Catholic Communion*: and the place where the *Matrix* and *Radix Ecclesia*, the *Mother Church* and the *Radical Church* (as St. *Cyprian* calls her) did flourish always.

4. For having been washed and purged in the blood of so many thousand *Martyrs* in the Primitive times, which even baptized *Rome* a new, and made it be called by Holy Fathers *Nova Sion*, a New Sion.

5. For

Part II. A Voyage through Italy.

5. For having so many *Saints Bodies* lying in its *Churches*; and so many *Churches* within its Precincts, which are above three hundred in all.

6. For having been the happy occasion of Converting most of the Nations of *Europe*, and many others out of *Europe*, unto the Faith of *Christ*, by Preachers sent from thence.

7. For having been the *Depositary* (as St. *Irenæus* calls her) *of the Holy Apostolical Traditions* and *Doctrine*, which have always been conserved in her *Church*.

8. For having always *conserved the Symbole of the Creed inviolably* (saith St. *Hierome*.)

Besides these foresaid Reasons, *Rome* may deservedly be called *Holy*, for the many and singular acts of *Charity* which are done there daily, more than in any other place. *Charity* is the Queen of *Vertues*, and if ever I saw this *Queen* in her Throne, it was in *Rome*. For there I saw no evil, either of *body* or *mind*, but it had its remedy, if curable; at least its comforts if incurable. *Great Charities in Rome.*

For the *first*, to wit, *Evils of Body*, it hath its *Hospitals*, and those many, and many of those are *Hospitals in Folio*. Besides no *Pilgrim* comes to *Rome*, but he finds *Rome*, as *Adam* did *Paradise*, with the Table covered, and Bed made ready for him. *Poor young Girls* find Portions either for Husbands or Nunneries, according to their choice; *Infants* whom cruel and unlawful Mothers, like Wolves, expose to death, *Rome* receives to life, and thinks it but a suitable *Antipelargesis* to nourish *Wolves* Children, seeing a *She-Wolf* nourished her *Founder* being exposed by Men. *Fools* too and *Madmen*, so much the more miserable, as not being so much as sensible of *Remedies for evils of the body.*

Meretrices lupas vocabant unde Luparia. Augustin. de Civit. Dei. l. 18. c. 21.

A 3

Quint. Curt.

of their Condition (for *sæpe calamitatis solatium est nosse sortem suam*) have here those that take care of them. *Poor Men* find *Hospitals* when they are sick; and *Gentlemen*, whom Nature hath not exempted from common *Miseries*, *Rome* exempts from common *Hospitals*; and not being able to give them better health she gives them at least better accommodation in their sickness. Here you shall find an *Apothecaries-shop*, founded by *Cardinal Francis Barberin*, with a yearly revenue of Twelve Thousand Crowns, and this for ever; to furnish the Poor with Physick *gratis*.

Here you shall find the *Hospital* of the *Holy Trinity*, which in the *Jubile* year of *Clement the* VIII, is found to have treated at Table, in one day, Fifteen Thousand Pilgrims. And in the whole *year* Five Hundred Thousand. The last *Jubile year* 1650. I my self was present one day, when the said *Hospital* treated Nine Thousand Pilgrims that day: The *Pope* himself (*Innocent the X.*) and many of the *Cardinals* having been there to wash the feet of the Pilgrims, and to serve them at Table. Add to this, that every *Nation* hath here its several *Hospital* and *Refuge*, with *Church* and *Churchmen* to serve it. As the *English Colledge*, once an *Hospital* for the *English*: That of the *Anima*, for the *Germans*: That of St. *Lewis*, for the *French*: That of St. *Iacomo*, for the *Spaniards*; That of St. *Antony of Padua*, for the *Portuguese*: That of St. *Julian* for the *Flemmings*: That of St. *Ambrose* for the *Lombards*: That of St. *Juo* for the *Britans*: That of St. *Hierom* for the *Illyrians*: That of St. *Mary Egyptiaca* for the *Armenians*: That of St. *Stephano*

Almost every Nation hath an Hospital in Rome.

Part II. A ~~Voyage through Italy.~~

Stephano for the *Hungarians*: That of St. *Stanislaus* for the *Polonians.* Besides a world of others. Nay almost every *Corporation* or *Body of Artisans* have their Hospital among themselves, which they maintain. In the *Church* of the Twelve *Apostles* they chuse yearly Twelve Noblemen and one *Prelate*, who is called their *Prior*: These go into every corner of *Rome* to seek out poor Men who are asham'd to beg, and yet are in great want. These bashful poor Men put their names into a Coffer well lock'd up, and standing in a publick place, by which means these Charitable Noblemen find them out, and relieve them.

What shall I say of the publick Charity of the *Pope* himself, well known to all; besides a world of private Charities which he gives by his *Secreto Limosimero* to those that are asham'd to beg publickly.

The like do many *Cardinals* by their own hands; and in that high measure, that *Cardinal Montalto* (to name no more) is found by his Books of *Accounts*, to have given away above a Hundred and Seven Thousand Crowns to the Poor. Of which pious *Cardinal* I cannot omit to write this following Story, as I have learned it from very good relation.

"A poor Widow of *Rome*, Mother of one *An ingeni-*
"only Daughter both young and handsome, *ous piece of*
"got her Living honestly by her own, and her *Charity.*
"Daughters Labour; and rub'd out poorly, but
"yet honestly: Now it happened that this Wi-
"dow falling Sick, and her Daughter having
"enough to do to tend her, their work went on
"so faintly, and their gains came in so slowly,

"that

"that at her recovery, she found her *Purse* as
"much spent as her *Person*. Whereupon be-
"ing called on for the quarters Rent of her
"Chamber, and not knowing what to do, she
"was advised by her *Confessarius* to go to *Car-*
"*dinal Montalto* (who gave publick Audi-
"ence thrice a Week to all the Poor in
"*Rome*, and to beg as much of him, as would
"pay her little debt. Pressed therefore by her
"great necessity, and emboldened by the fame
"of the Charity of this good *Cardinal*, she en-
"tred the Palace, and found him in his great
"Hall, giving Ear and Alms to all those that
"could give him a good account of their wants.
"In her turn she and her young Daughter ap-
"proached unto him, sitting at his Tables End;
"and expressing modestly her wants caused by
"her three Months Sickness, she humbly be-
"sought his *Eminence* to give her *five Crowns*
"for to pay the Rent of her Chamber, and pa-
"cifie her Landlord, who otherwise threatned
"to put her out of Doors. The *Cardinal* see-
"ing as much modesty in her looks as Sickness
"in her Countenance; and liking well, that she
"did not go about to fright him into Charity,
"by urging the danger of being forc'd one day
"to expose her Daughter to lewd Courses (a
"common Rhetorical figure of Beggars in all
"Countries) wrote down in a little Paper, Fifty
"Crowns to be given to her; and folding up
"the Paper, he bid her carry it to his Servant
"below at the entrance of the Palace, who
"kept the *Cardinals* Bills, and payed the
"contents of them. She did so with humble
"Prayers of thankfulness; and the Servant up-
"on

Part II. *A Voyage through* Italy.

"on the Sight of the Paper, presently threw her
"fifty Crowns, and bid her make an acquittance
"for it. The poor Woman seeing fifty Crowns
"counted out for her, who had asked but five;
"and fearing lest the Servant upon sight of
"her handsome daughter, might have done
"this by way of Bribery, told him smart-
"ly, that tho' she were Poor, yet she was
"honest, and that she scorn'd to go by one
"Corruption to another. The honest Servant
"civilly replied, that he understood not her
"words: nor I your deeds, said she, I asked
"the *Cardinal* five *Crowns*, he granted me my
"request, and why then do you offer me fifty
"*Crowns?* The honest Servant to shew his In-
"nocency, shews his Masters hand writing, im-
"porting fifty *Crowns*. Then your Masters
"hand, said she, for haste outshot his Intenti-
"ons. I asked him for five *Crowns*, and more
"in Conscience I cannot take. The Servant,
"though he knew his Masters Generosity, yet to
"take all scruple from the poor Woman, locked
"up his Money and Papers, and desired the
"poor Woman to go up with him to the *Car-
"dinal* again to clear this doubt. The *Cardi-
"nal* hearing from this Servant the whole paſ-
"sage, and that the poor Woman was afraid
"his hand had been mistaken in writing fifty
"*Crowns* instead of five; 'tis true, said he, my
"hand was mistaken indeed; and calling for
"his *Pen* again, as if he would have corrected
"the *Cypher* which made the Bill fifty, he put
"in another *Cypher*, and so made it five Hundred
"*Crowns*; reading it now aloud to his Servant
"and the poor Woman; commanding her to
"bestow

"bestow her Daughter with that Money; and "if it were not enough, to come again to "him, and he would make it up. *A true Ro-* "*man Charity.*

Remedies for Evils of the Mind.
Osmundus apud Herodot.

As for those *Charities* which concern the *Mind*, if a great King of *Egypt* wrote over his Library-door, *Medicina Anima*, *Physick for the Mind*, here in *Rome* I find store of such Physick in *Libraries*, *Colledges*, *Monasteries*, and devout *Companies*. And first for *Libraries*; you shall find here (besides the *Libraries* of every *Religious* house) the incomparable *Library* of the *Vatican* (of which more below) those also of Cardinal *Barberin*; of the Duke of *Altemps*; that of *Sapienza*, and that of the *Augustins*; the last two being open to all Men every day, with a courteous Gentleman to reach you any Book, and a learned *Manuscript* in *Folio*, addressing you to the Authors that treat of any Subject you desire to be informed of, which affords great help to the painful Student. Then the *Colledges* and *Seminaries* of almost all Nations where youths are both fed and bred up in Learning for nothing.

Publick Libraries.

Colledges.

Monasteries.

Add to this the variety of *Monasteries* and *Convents*, both of Men and Women, where they may hide themselves securely, *donec transeat Iniquitas*.

Houses for young Girls.

Then the taking away of *young Girls*, at ten or twelve years old from their poor suspected Mothers; and the bringing them up vertuously, under careful Matrons of known Vertue, till they either chuse the *Nuptial Flammeum*, or the *Sacred Velum*.

Then

Part II. *A Voyage through Italy.* 11

Then the *Remedies* for *ill Married Women*, whose unadvised choice (Marriages being often made for Interest) or incompatible humours force to a Corporeal separation; and lest such unfortunate Women should either live incontinently indeed, or give suspicion of it, they are provided here with a House where they live retiredly under *Lock* and *Key*, till they either reconcile themselves again to their Husbands; or upon just occasions, leave them for ever. Over the door of this house is written, *Per le donne mal maritate.* *Remedies for ill married Women.*

Then the *Convent* of *Penitent Whores* (that none may perish in *Rome* who have a mind to be saved) called *Sancta Maria Magdalena in Corso*; where many of those poor *Magdalens* have led such penitential Lives, (as the bloody Walls of their *Cells*, caused by frequent disciplining, shewed to all *Rome* in a conflagration of that *Monastery*) that *Paulus Quintus* himself being informed of it, would needs be carried thither, to see those Bloody Chambers from the Street, and having seen them, wept for Joy; and I can scarce hold from crying out: *O felix culpa.* *The Convent of Penitents.*

What shall I say of the *Congregation* of *Advocates* and *Attornies*, instituted in *Rome*, where they meet once a Week to examine poor mens *Law-Suits*; and either dehort them from proceeding in bad causes, or prosecute good causes for them at the cost of this *Congregation*. *Charity of Lawyers in Rome.*

What shall I say of several pious *Clergy-men* (especially the good *Priests* of the *Oratory*, happy in this employment) who make it their task to reconcile disagreeing Families, and *Broken Friend-setters.*

A Voyage through Italy. Part II.

and with great zeal and piety, exhort firſt the one, then the other of the parties, intervene between them, ſpeak well of the one to the other, clear and take away jealous miſunderſtandings, and in fine, piece again broken Neighbours?

Four Sermons daily in one place in Rome.

What ſhall I ſay of the *four Sermons* daily in the *Chieſa Nova*, by the moſt learned and good *Prieſts* of the *Oratory*, who being moſt of them learned Men, as *Baronius*, *Boſius*, *Juſtinianus*, *Renaldus*, &c. and able to fly high, yet in their Sermons ſtoop to a low pitch, and a Popular facile way, which aims rather at converſion, than oſtentation; and doth great good, though it make little noiſe; *Dominus in leni aura*.

Weekly Sermons to the Jews.

What ſhall I ſay of the Weekly *Sermon* to the *Jews*, upon *Saturday*; where they are bound to be preſent to the number of three hundred: where the *Pope* entertains a learned *Preacher*, to convince them out of their own Scriptures; and thoſe that are converted, are provided for in the *Hoſpital* of the *Catechumens*, till they be throughly inſtructed? I have ſeen divers of them baptized.

The Schola Pia.

What ſhall I ſay of the *Scholæ piæ* in *Rome*, a company of good Religious Men, who look like *Jeſuits*, ſave only that they go bare-foot in Sandals? Theſe good *Fathers* make a profeſſion to teach poor boys *gratis*, their firſt *Grammar Rudiments*, and to make them fit to be ſent to the *Jeſuits Schools*; and having taught them thus in the *Schools*, they accompany them home in the *Streets*, leſt they ſhould either learn waggery as they go home, or practiſe it. Nay theſe humble Men make it their profeſſion not to teach

higher

Part II. *A Voyage through* Italy.

higher *Schools*; where there might be some profit and honour, at least some satisfaction and pleasure: but they content themselves to go barefoot, and teach only the *lower Schools*, and *first Rudiments*; by which they neither grow wiser nor richer: A strange mortified trade; but *Beati pauperes spiritu*.

What shall I say of the *Fathers* of the *Agonizants*, whose Vocation is, to be the *Seconds* of those who fight against death it self; that is, whose profession is, to assist those that are in the *Agony of Death*; and to help them to make then those pious *Acts*, which *Christians* should most of all then rouze themselves up to? *The Fathers of the Agonizants.*

What can be said more; yes, *Rome* not content, to have fed, to have bred, to have converted, baptized, reconciled the living; and assisting the dying; she extends her *Charity* even beyond death it self, and hath instituted a pious *Confraternity*, called *La compagnia de Morti*, whose office is to bury the Dead, and to visit those that are *Condemned*, and by praying with them, exhorting them, and accompanying them to the Execution, help them to dye Penitently, and bury them being Dead, and Pray for their Souls being Buried; after which, *Charity* can do no more to Man, and therefore I will conclude, that seeing such singular Acts of *Charity*, both for *Body* and *Mind*, are practised no where so much as in *Rome*, its true which I assumed above, that *Rome* deserves to be call'd *the Holy*. *La Compagnia de Morti.*

Having said thus much of the *Title of Rome*, I will now make my Reader better acquainted with her, by describing the Particuliarities which I observed here. And that I may not ramble

In

in writing of *Rome*, as most men do in visiting of it, I will begin at the *Bridge* called now *Ponte Angelo*, and from thence take the whole *Gyro* of the *City* in Order.

Ponte Angelo.

Arriving then at the *Bridge* called anciently *Pons Elius*, because it was built by the *Emperor Elius Adrianus*, but now called *Ponte Angelo*, because it was upon this *Bridge* that *S. Gregory* the Great saw an *Angel* upon the *Moles Adriani*, sheathing his Sword after a great *Plague*: here we saw the stately new decoration of *Iron*-work with the twelve Marble Statues set upon it by this present *Pope Clement* the Ninth, and looking down into the River on the Left-hand, we saw the ruins of the *Triumphal Bridge*.

The triumphal Bridge.

This Bridge was called the *Triumphal Bridge*, because over it *Triumphs* were accustomed to pass anciently to the *Capitol*. This made it so proud, that it scorn'd that any rusticks, or Country-Fellows should pass over it; and got a *Decree of the Senate* for that purpose. But pride will have a fall; and the proud *Triumphal Bridge* hath got such a great one, that there's but just so much of it left, as to shew, where it was once; so true is the saying of *Ausonius*,

Mors etiam Saxis nominibusque venit.

At first the *Romans* were modest enough in their *Triumphs*, as in all other things: Hence *Camillus* was content with four *white Horses* in his *Chariot*; but afterwards luxury and excess banishing out of the City old modesty, they began to strive who should be the most vain in this point. Hence *Pompey* was drawn in Triumph by *four Elephants*;

Mark-

Part II. A Voyage through Italy.

Mark-Antony, by *four Lyons: Nero* by *four Hermophrodites*, which were all four both Horses and Mares: *Heliogabalus* by *four Tygers*; *Aurelianus* by *six Stags*; and *Firmicus* by eight *Ostriches*.

Vanity in Triumphs.

At the end of *Ponte Angelo* stands the *Castel Angelo*, so called, because, as I said before, *S. Gregory* in a solemn *Procession* during the Plague, saw an *Angel* upon the top of *Moles Adriani* sheathing his Sword, to signifie, that Gods Anger was appeased. Before this *Miracle* happened, it was called *Moles Adriani*, because the *Emperor Adrian* was buried here. It was built anciently in a round form of vast stones going up in three rows or stories, lesser and lesser, till you came to the top; where stood mounted that great *Pine-apple* of *Brass guilt*, which we see now in the Garden of *Belvedere*. Round about it were set in the wall great *Marble Pillars*, and round about the several Stories stood a world of *Statues*. This *Moles* being found a strong place, *Bellisarius* put Men into it to defend it against the *Goths*, and they defended themselves in it a great while, by breaking the *Statues* in Pieces, and throwing them upon the Heads of the *Gothes* that besieged them. Since that time divers *Popes* have turned it into a formal *Castle*. *Boniface* the VIII, *Alexander* the VI, and *Urban* the VIII, have rendered it a *Regular Castle*; with five strong *Bastions*, store of good *Cannons*, and a constant Garison maintained in it. From this *Castle* I saw divers times these Fortifications; and below divers great pieces of Artillery, made of the Brass taken out of the *Pantheon*; and they shewed us one great *Cannon* which was made of the brazen Nails only, that nailed that Brass to the walls of the *Pantheon*; the length

Castel Angela.

A Voyage through Italy. Part II.

length and form of those Nails, is seen upon that *Cannon*, to shew unto posterity how great they were, with these words upon it; *ex clavis trabialibus Porticus Agrippæ*. In this *Castle* are kept *Prisoners* of *State*; the five Millions laid up there, by *Sixtus Quintus*; the *Popes* rich *Triple Crowns*, called *Regni*, and the Chief *Registers* of the *Roman Church*. From the top also of this *Castle*

The long Corridor from the Palace to the Castle.

you see distinctly the long *Corridor* or *Gallery*, which runs from the *Popes Palace* of the *Vatican* to this *Castle*, for the *Popes* use in time of danger. It was made by *Pope Alexander* the VI. and used by *Clement* the VII. who by it got safe into the *Castle*, from the fury of the *German Soldiers*, who being many of them *Lutherans*, swore they would eat a piece of the *Pope*.

From hence entering into the *Borgo*, we went towards *S. Peters Church*, and in the way stept into the Church of the *Carmelites*, called *Santa Ma-*

Santa Maria Transpontina.

ria Transpontina, where, in a Chappel on the left hand as you enter, are seen two Pillars of Stone enchased in wood, to the which *S. Peter* and *S. Paul* were tyed when they were whipped before their death, according to the *Romans* custom. Here's also the Head of *S. Basil* the *Greek* Father surnamed the Great. Here's also a curious Picture of *S. Barbara* in the Vault by *Cavalier Gioseppe*.

Going on from hence, we came presently to the Palace of *Campeggi*, so called, because it belonged to Cardinal *Campeggi*, the Popes Legat in *England*, to whom *Henry* the VIII. gave it.

The English Embassadors Palace.

Heretofore it belonged to the *English* Embassadors, and was one of the best in *Rome*, both for being near the Pope's Palace, and also for that

it

Part II.

it was well built by famous *Bramante*. It belongs now to Cardinal *Colonna*.

Over against it stands a little *Piazza*, with a fine Fountain, and joyning to it a little Church called *San Jacomo Scozza Cavalli*, in which, under an *Altar* on the right hand, I saw the Stone upon which *Abraham* offered to sacrifice his Son *Isaac*, and under another *Altar* on the left hand, the Stone upon which our *Saviour* was placed, when he was presented in the *Temple*. Both these were brought, or sent to *Rome*, by *Helen* Mother of the *Emperor Constantine the Great*.

S. Jacomo Scozza Cavalli.

Presently after, you come to the *Piazza* of St. *Peter*, built round about with a noble *Portico* of Free-stone, born up by four rows of stately round Pillars, under which, not only the Procession upon *Corpus Christi* day, marched in the shade; but also all People may go dry, and out of the Sun in Summer or Winter, unto St. *Peter's* Church, or the *Vatican Palace*. This *Portico* is built in an oval form, and fetcheth in the great *Piazza*, which is before St. *Peter's* Church, and therefore can be no less than half a mile in compass. This noble Structure was begun by *Alexander* the VII, and half of it finished, and the other half is now almost finished. I never saw any thing more stately than this. The number of the Pillars and of the Statues on the top, I do not justly remember. In the midst of this *Piazza* stands the famous *Guglia*; which was brought out of *Ægypt*, in the time of the old *Romans*, and dedicated to *Augustus Cæsar* and *Tiberius*, as the words upon it import. It lay hid long in *Nero's Circus*, which was there where now St. *Peters Sacristy* is, and at last, *Sextus Quintus* having proposed

The Portico of the Piazza of St. Peter.

The great Guglia before St. Peter's.

B b

proposed great rewards to him that would venture to set it up here without breaking, it was happily undertaken by *Dominico Fontano*, a rare Architect of *Como*; and so placed as you see it now. The manner of bringing it out of *Ægypt*, and of erecting it here, are both painted in *Fresco* upon the walls of the *Vatican* Library: This *Guglia* is all of one stone except the *Basis*; and it hath no *Hieroglyphes* upon it. The stone is a *Granate*, or *speckled Marble*, which together with its *Basis*, is a hundred and eight foot high. It rests upon four Lyons of Brass gilt; and at the top of it is planted a Cross of Brass mounted upon three Mountains, with a Star over them (the Arms of *Sextus Quintus*, whose name was *Montalto*.) Within the Cross, is a piece of the Holy Cross of our Saviour, included here by *Sextus Quintus*. The whole *Guglia* is said to weigh 956148 pound weight. I wonder what Scales they had to weigh it with.

[The Fountains.] On each side of this *Guglia* is to stand fair Fountains, one whereof is that which is seen there now; which throweth up such a quantity of water, that it maketh a Mist always about it, and oftentimes a Rainbow when the Sun strikes obliquely upon it.

The Piazza. This *Piazza* is capable of two Hundred Thousand Men, and delivers you up to the Stairs which lead you up to the Church of St. *Peter*.

St. Peters. Coming therefore near to St. *Peter's* Church, I was glad to see that noble structure, where greatness and neatness, bulk and beauty are so mingled together, that its neither neat only, like a spruce Gallery; nor vast only, like a great blast; but it's rather like a proper Man, and so well proportioned.

Part II. A Voyage through Italy.   19

portioned. You mount up to this Church by an *The Marble* easie ascent of four and twenty Steps of Marble *Steps up to* Stairs, as long as the Frontispiece of the Church *St. Peters Church.* is wide; these Stairs were those of the old Church of St. *Peter*; and *Baronius* observes, *Baron ad* That when the Emperor *Charlemagne* mounted *an. 774.* up those Stairs first, he kissed every step as he went up.

These Stairs lead you up to the Frontispiece of *The Fron-* the Church, which hath five doors in it, letting *tispiece.* you into the Porch; and these doors are cheeked with vast round Pillars of free-stone twenty four foot in compass, and eighty six in height. Over these Pillars runs the Architrave, and over it the Lodge or great Balcony, where the Pope is Crowned, and where he gives his Benediction upon *Easter-day.* Over this Lodge runs a continual Baluster or row of Rails, upon which stand Thirteen vast Statues of our Saviour, and his Apostles cut in stone.

Entring into the Porch, you will admire the *The Porch.* length, breadth and height of it. For the length of it; it's two Hundred Eighty nine Foot, the breadth forty four foot, the heighth a Hundred Thirty three foot. It's adorned on both sides with great Marble Pillars, and a curious gilt Roof. In fine, this Porch any where else would *The Church* be a handsom Church. *is self.*

Over against the five Doors of this Porch, stand the five Doors of the Church; one whereof is called the *Porta Sancta*, and only open in the *Porta San-* Jubile year: The others are daily open; and the *cta.* two principal doors are called *Valvæ Sancti Petri*, *Valvæ St.* and are covered with Brass, by the command of *Petri.* *Eugenius* the IV. whose memorable actions, to

B b 2   wit,

A **Voyage through** Italy. Part II.

wit, the Crowning of the Emperor *Sigismond*, and the reunion of the *Greek* Church with the *Latin*, are expressed in them. These *Valvæ* are thirteen Foot wide, and forty five high; and to them all Popes Bulls are nailed at their publication.

The inside of the Church of St. Peter.

Entring into the Church, I found it to be built in Cross-wise; containing in length five hundred and twenty foot, and three hundred eighty five in breadth. So that it passeth in greatness, the famous Temples of Antiquity, to wit *Solomon*'s Temple, long Threescore Cubits: The Temple of *Diana* in *Ephesus*, long four Hundred Twenty five foot; and the great *Moski* at *Fez*, long a Hundred and fifty Cubits.

The Roof.

The Roof or Vault of this Church is arched with great squares, and each square is adorned with a great gilt Rose, which almost fills the square. This Roof, is born up by great Pillars of Freestone, of a square form, whose *Capitelli* are curiously wrought, after the *Corinthian* order, and joyned to one another above, by Arches and a perpetual *Cornice*, over which are cut in stone, the Statues of several moral Vertues. These Pillars are a Hundred and five Foot in compass, and distant Forty foot one from another. On that side of them which looks towards the Body of the Church; they are to be over-crusted with white Marble, with two rows of niches in them, for great Statues of Brass gilt. The other sides of these Pillars are already adorned with a neat overcrusting of a reddish Marble, beset with the Heads of the primitive martyr'd Popes, held up by two Angels, and with the Pigeon of *Innocent* the X (who made this decoration) and all these

Part II. **A Voyage through** Italy.

these are in *mezzo rilievo*, and of pure white Alabaster. Behind these Pillars is a large Isle, or passage, and behind that Isle immediately, stand fair Chappels, which flanck up this Church notably, and each Chappel is graced with a little *Cupola* of its own.

In the midst of the Cross building of this Church is mounted the great *Cupola*, which looks like a great Crown, wherewith this Queen of Churches is Crowned. It rests upon four *Pilastri* or great Pillars, which make the corners of the Cross of this Church, and from them it riseth into such a high Vault, that it seems to walk into Heaven. Its full as round as the Pantheon in *Rome*, that is, it carrieth the compass of an hundred and seventy Paces, as you may easily measure upon the circle of white Marble in the Pavement which environeth the Altar of St. *Peter*, and is made there on purpose perpendicularly under the *Cupola* to shew its greatness, the inside of this *Cupola* is curiously painted with Pictures in Mosaick work, representing a Heaven, indeed nothing but Heaven it self can be finer or higher. So that I may say truly to *Rome* with *Rutillius*.

Non procul a cælo per tua Templa sumus.

In a word, this *Cupola* is the boldest piece of Architecture that perhaps the World hath seen; and it was the last and greatest work of *Sextus Quintus* his Purse.

The four Pilastri upon which this *Cupola* resteth, are vast square Pillars, a Hundred and twenty foot in Compass, and capable of Stairs within them, and large Sacristies above, for the holy re- *The four great Pilastri.*

licks

A Voyage through Italy. Part II.

licks that are kept in them; to wit, the Volto Santo or Print of our Saviours Face, which he imprinted in the Handkerchief of St. *Veronici*; The piece of the holy Cross; the top of the Launce wherewith our Savior's Side was pierced, and the Head of St. *Andrew* the Apostle translated hither into his Brothers Church by *Pius Secundus*. Hence in these great Pillars are cut Niches, and in them plac'd four vast Statues of white Marble. Under the Relick of the *Volto Santo* stands the Statue of the *Veronica*, under the piece of the Holy Cross, the Statue of St. *Helen*. Under the top of the Launce, the Statue of *Longinus*: under the Head of St. *Andrew*, the Statue of St. *Andrew*. These Statues are of *Colossean* greatness, and made by Masters as great as themselves.

The high Altar.
In the midst of the Cross of this Church, and perpendicularly under the very *Cupola*, stands the high Altar of this Church. This Altar may well be called the high Altar, (*Altare quasi alta ara*) or the *Altare Majus*, being the noblest Altar in the World, both for matter and form. The Altar it self stands over the Tomb of St. *Peter*, half whose Body, together with half of St. *Pauls*, lies buried here; and the other half of their Bodies in St. *Pauls* Church. Over this Altar four stately Pillars of Brass bear up a Canopy of the same Mettal, wrought about the Edge like a Canopy indeed, with Vallances and a gilt Fringe, yet all of Brass. Over the corners of this Canopy, stand four great Angels of Brass gilt, and in the midst of it is mounted high a round Ball of Brass gilt, and a fair Cross upon it of the same mettal.

The Tomb of St. Peter.

These

Part II. *A Voyage through* Italy. 23

These four Pillars are as great in compass (I *The four speak by experience, having taken the measure of* *Brass Pillars of the them upon their model) as three ordinary men* *Altar.* are thick. Their Form is Serpentine, wreathed about with Vine-trees and Leaves; but all of Brass; as also adorned with little Angels of Brass clambering up those Leaves and Branches, and with Bees here and there also, relating to Pope *Urbans* Arms, who made them. These Pillars are fifty foot high from the ground. Every one of them weigheth five and twenty Thousand Pound weight, and all of them together make this Altar, the Altar antonomastically, as this Church is the Church of the World. So that if the Climax be true (as true it is) that Churches are for Altars, Altars for Priests, Priests for God, I know no Religion which payeth such honourable tributes of Worship to God, as the Roman-Catholick Religion doth, which hath the noblest Church, the noblest Altar, the noblest Priest, the noblest Sacrifice, and all this to the noblest God. *Deus Deorum Dominus.* Hence the Pope may say *2. Paralip.* with *Salomon: Domus quam ædificare cupio mag-* *c. 2.* *na est, magnus est enim Dominus noster super om-* *nes Deos.*

Behind this Altar (not in respect of him that *The Con-* comes into the Church by the great door, but in *fessio St.* respect of him that stands at the Altar) stands *Petri.* the Confession of St. *Peter*; so called, because that in the Primitive times, the place where the Bodies of Saints and Martyrs were kept, was called *Confessio,* and in the *Greek* Church *Martyrium.* For in ancient Writers the word Confessor was taken often for a Martyr, who had confessed Christ so far as even to die for him: So that Mar-

Bb 4 tyrs

tyrs are sometimes called Confessors, and Confessors Martyrs, though they did not actually die in Torments; as you may see plainly in the Annotations of learned *Pamelius* upon *Tertullians* Book *ad Martyres*. Now this place because it conserves the Body (at least half of the Body) of St. *Peter*, is called the Confession of *Peter*. As for this Confession, it's made like a hollow Cave, open above, and railed about with low Rails, so that the People kneeling may look down to the Iron door and grate, behind which the Tomb of St. *Peter* stands, under the Altar; for these Rails fetch in a demi-circle from one corner of the Altar to the other. There are also a double pair of open Stairs, of some twelve steps a-piece, for those to descend by who officiate, and there are two little half doors which let them in to those Stairs. And I conceive at the bottom of these little doors, the *Limina Apostolorum* to be. For though I know it's generally held, that to visit the *Limina Apostolorum* (which Bishops by their Canon Law are oblig'd unto) is to visit St. *Peter*'s Church; and that divers learned Authors think the *Limina Apostolorum* to be the very steps of the entrance of the great door of the Church; yet I am of opinion, that these little half doors and the steps about the Altar, are most properly the *Limina Apostolorum*, because I found these very words written in Golden Letters in the bottom of the like little doors, which stand about the high Altar in St. *Paul*'s Church, where the other half of the Bodies of St. *Peter* and St. *Paul* are intomb'd.

Num. 1.

The Limina Apostolorum.

Cubicularil St. Petri.

Round about this Church stand Side Chappels, some six and twenty in all, called anciently *Cubicula,*

Part II. A Voyage through Italy. 25

bicula, and those whom we call Chaplains were anciently called *Cubicularii*: Hence the title of *Cubicularius* S. *Petri*. Now these Chappels have for the most part some remarkable thing in them. In one of them is always reserv'd the B. Sacrament for the daily use of Pilgrims that desire to communicate in St. *Peters* Church, and other devout People. In that of St. *Gregory Nazianzin*, is the Body of that Saint translated hither out of the Church of the Nuns of *Campo Marzo*. In the Chappel of the Canons, reposeth the Body of St. *Chrysostome*. In the Chappel called the *Clementina*, reposeth the Body of St. *Gregory* the great, who being Pope of *Rome*, and moved by Godly Instinction (as *John Stow* saith) sent *Augustin*, *Justus*, *Melitus*, and other Monks living in the fear of God, to convert the *Angles*, or *English*, to the Faith of Christ; and therefore I took particular notice often of his Tomb, as being (as venerable *Bede* calls him) our Apostle. In a Chappel at the very farther end of the Church is set up the Chair of St. *Peter*, held up by four Doctors of the Church, all cast in Brass in a stately Posture. This Chair is of Wood, but much spent with old Age; and therefore Pope *Alexander* the Seventh caused it to be set up here, and enchafed curiously to preserve it. I once saw it near at hand, being expos'd to publick view in the middle of the Church upon the Feast day of St. *Peter*'s Chair in *Rome*. In another Chappel is the Crucifix made three hundred Years ago by rare *Pietro Cavalini*. In another Chappel you see cut in white Marble the History of St. *Leo*'s meeting *Attila* out of *Rome*, and his hindering him from coming any nearer to the City. As

Vid Ana-staf. Bibli-oth. in Marcello. Paulin. Epist. 12. ad Sever.

St. Greg. Nazian-zens Tomb.

St. Chrisostom's Tomb.

St. Gregories Tomb. vid in his Chronicles in Kenulph Saxons.

The Chair of St. Peter.

The chief Relicks.

As for the Relics and Bodies of Saints which are in this Church, besides those mentioned already, there are the bodies of *SS. Simon* and *Jude*, of *S. Petronilla*, of *SS. Processus* and *Martinianus*, of ten first Popes after *St. Peter*; with a world of other precious Relics kept in the Sacristy.

Some Tombs.

As for the Tombs which are in this *Church* above ground, they are these. That of *Sextus* IV. of *Paulus* III ; of *Urban* the VIII ; of *Leo* the XI. of *Innocent* the VIII ; of *Gregory* the XIII ; of *Innocent* the X ; and lastly that of the Countess *Matilde*, the only secular Person that I find to have a Tomb in this *Church* above ground. Indeed she deserves well to lye in St. *Peter*'s Church, who deserved to be called St. *Peters* Daughter ; and she deserved this surname, for having defended the Church so gallantly in its greatest conflict, against *Henry* the IV. Emp. and having endowed it with a good part of its Patrimony. Her Body was translated from *Mantua* hither, in the year 1633. by the command of Pope *Urban* the VIII.

Near the Confession of S. *Peter*, is an old brazen Statue of S. *Peter*, sitting with his hand up as giving his blessing; and holding his right foot a little out, to be kissed. At first, some wonder to see devout People flocking thither, and kissing the Foot of that Statue, and putting their heads under that Foot, when they have done ; but when they are well informed, that all this is done, only to testifie that they submit themselves to the Authority which was given by our Saviour, to S. *Peter* and his Successors, they rest satisfied.

Part II. A Voyage through Italy.

Over the Holy-water-pot, on the left hand, as you enter into the Church, is seen, fastned to the wall, an old Inscription upon a square Stone, importing, that that was the very stone upon which the Bodies of St. *Peter* and St. *Paul* were divided, when half of their Bodies were buried here, and the other half in St. *Paul's* Church, by St. *Silvester*.

As for the prime Pictures that are in this Church; they are these: That of St. *Michael* in *Mosaick* work, is of the design of *Cavalier Gioseppe*: As also the design of the *Mosaick* work in the *Cupola*. That of St. *John* Evangelist, and St. *Luke* just under the *Cupola*, are of the hand of *Giovanni de Vecbi*. The Picture where *St. Peter* cures the lame man, is of the hand of *Ludivico da Civoli*. That of the fall of *Simon Magus*, is of the hand *Vanni* of *Siena*. That where *St. Peter* is painted with *Annanias* dead before him, is of the hand of *Cavalier Rancalli*. That of the Altar of *St. Gregory*, is of the hand of *Andrea Sacco Romano*. That of the Creation of the World, is of *Pietro Berettino de Cortona*. That of *Medicæ fidei*, is of the hand of *Lanfranco*. *Some prime Pictures.*

Having thus seen the Church, I went to see the Sacristy of this Church, where by express leave from the *Monsignor*, who hath the chief care, as well as the Keys of it, I saw the Holy Relics, and neat Church-plate belonging to this Church. The Relics are many, and richly enchased in Gold and Silver. The Church Plate is both plentiful and of great value, as many Chalices of pure Gold set with Jewels, huge Silver Candlesticks, with a Crucifix of the same, as heavy as a Man can lift, with a world of other *The Sacristy of St. Peter.*

such

such like Plate. But that which pleased me most here, was the ancient Picture of St. *Peter* and St. *Paul*, which St. *Silvester* shewed to *Constantine* the Great, to confirm the truth of his Vision. The Picture is very old, yet the faces are perceivable, and that is all. It's set in a frame of Silver. The History of it is both long and known: And if any man be ignorant of it, let him read it in *Baronius*. There is also in the said Sacristy, another Picture nailed high upon the wall, which was made by *N. Carpi* with his Fingers, instead of a Pencil.

An ancient Picture.

Being now in the Sacristy, I got leave to go down into the Grot under this Church, with a practical Clericus, with a lighted Torch to shew me and explicate unto me the most considerable things that are there: As the Tomb of St. *Peter* with an Altar over it, at which any Bishop or Priest may say Mass: a world of ancient statues (set in the low Chappels, and in the wall of this Grot) which belonged to the old Church of St. *Peter*, and shewing the Antiquity of Pictures in Churches: The Tomb of the most honourable Churchman of our Nation, Pope *Adrian* the IV. the only English Pope that ever was: The Tomb of the Emperor *Otho* the second, in a great Porphiry Shrine: The Tombs of divers other great Popes and Cardinals: And in fine, the Tombstone of *Charlotte* of *Lusignan*, Queen of *Jerusalem*, *Cyprus* and *Armenia*, who having been driven out of her Kingdom by her Bastard Brother, came to *Rome* in *Sixtus Quartus* his time, and there died. She transferred before her death her right to the Kingdom of *Cyprus*, to the Duke of *Savoy* her Brother-in-law; which makes that Duke

The Grot under St. Peter's Church.

Adrian the IV. an English man.

Part II. *A Voyage through* Italy.　　29

Duke give a close Crown over his Arms, and be stiled by his Subjects, *Altezza Real*, Royal Highness.

　　Having thus seen this Church both within and under ground, I was desirous to see it also above. Ascending therefore by a fair Stair-case I arrived at the great Terras over the Lodge, and there saw the Thirteen Statues of our Saviour and the Twelve Apostles, near hand, which seem below, a little taller than the Statue of our tallest Men, and yet here above are eighteen Foot high. There also I saw the several little *Cupola*'s, which give light to the side Chappels of this Church, and look like the issue and spawn of the Great *Cupola*. Then mounting a little higher, I beheld a rare Fabrick of the Mother *Cupola*, both within and without. The Stairs to mount up into it, the double Vault in it, and stairs between the two Vaults: The Lantern upon the *Cupola*: The narrow Stairs in one of the Pillars of that Lantern, up to the Ball: Lastly, the straight neck of the passage into the Ball, and the Ball it self, are all worth particular observation, as being the height of Architecture. The Ball it self of Brass gilt, is capable of thirty Men, though from below, it looks only as big as twice a Mans Head. We were eight in it at once, and I am sure we could have placed thrice as many more. Upon the round Ball is mounted a great *Cross* of Iron gilt, to signifie, that the vertue of the *Cross* by our *Saviour*'s passion, hath triumphed over the World, of which this round Ball is the express Emblem. From this *Cupola* we had a perfect view of *Rome* under us, and of all the Villas about it. But nothing was so wonderful,

St. Peter's Church above.

The round Ball capable of 30 Men.

Praise of St. Peter's Church. as to see S. *Peters* Church and Palace, look like a Town under us, which we knew to be but one Church and House.

You will wonder perchance too, when you shall hear that this Church is the eighth wonder of the World, that the *Pyramids* of *Egypt*, the Walls of *Babylon*, the *Pharos Colossus*, &c. were but heaps of Stones compared to this Fabrick: That it hath put all Antiquity to the blush, and all posterity to a *Non-plus*: That its several parts are all incomparable Master-pieces: Its Pictures all Originals: Its Statues perfect models: That it hath a revenue of above Twenty Thousand Pounds a year, only for the Fabrick: That it hath cost till the year 1654. (The accounts being then summed up) Forty Millions of Crowns: That most of the Popes since *Julius* the II. his time (and they have been twenty three in all) have encouraged and advanced this work: That the prime Architects of the World, *Sangalla*, *Bramante*, *Baldassire*, *Buonarota*, *Giacomo della Porta*, *Giovani Fontana*, *Carlo Maderno*, and now *Cavaliero Bernino*, have brought it on to this perfection: That the whole Church it self is nothing but the Quintessence of wit and wealth, strained into a religious design of making a handsome House to God, and of fulfilling the Divine Oracle which promised; that, *magna erit gloria domus istius novissimæ, plus-quam prima.*

Aggai 2. 9.

The revenue of St. Peter's Church.

Going at last out of this Church, and summing up in my thoughts all the Rarities I had seen in it, I began to think of *Ammonius* (a holy primitive Saint, and afterwards Bishop in the Council

Part II. A Voyage through Italy.

cil of *Sardis*) of whom its written, that coming to *Rome* with S. *Athanasius*, he desired to see nothing there but S. *Peter*'s Church, and knew not the way to any place else; I think, that if this good man had seen S. *Peter*'s Church as it is now, he would never have cared for seeing any thing else in the World, and would even have forgot his way home too.

Baronius an. 390. n. 5.

Near to the Church of S. *Peter* stands the Vatican Palace, where the Popes use to Winter. To describe it to you all at length, would take me up too much time; nor indeed is it fit for me to dwell there. I will therefore pass thro' it quickly, and rather point you out what's to be seen there, than paint you out in words what I saw there.

The Vatican Palace.

1. From the Church of St. *Peter* you ascend into this Palace by an easie and stately pair of Stairs, capable of ten Men a Breast. These Stairs render you up at the great Hall called *Sala Regia*, because the Pope receiveth here Embassadors of Kings in their Embassies of State. It is beautified with rare Pictures in a great volume: as that of the Emperour *Frederick* kissing the Popes Foot, of the Hand of *Gioseppe del Salviati Garsagnino*. That of the *Ligne* in *France*: that of *Coligni*, that of the Pope condemning Heresie, that of the Pope returning from *Avignon*, are all of the hand of *Georgio Vassaria*. That of the Emperor *Charles* the Great, signing the brief of the Donation, is of the hand *Thadeo Zuccare*: that of the battel of *Lepanto*, with the Picture of Faith at the side of it, is of the hand of *Donato Formello*.

The Sala Regia.

2. This

2. This great Hall stands between two Chappels, the *Paulina* and the *Sista*. In the *Paulina* is seen a rare Picture of the Crucifying of St. *Peter*, by *Michael Angelo*. The roof of it also was rarely painted by *Fiderico Zuccari*, but the smoak of the Candles upon *Maunday Thursday*, when this Chappel serves for the Sepulcher, hath so defac'd these Pictures, that a far worse Hand would have serv'd there.

The Popes Chappel. 3. The Chappel of *Sisto* is that in which the Pope holds *Capella* upon certain days, and where all the Cardinals intervene. In the end of this Chappel upon the wall is Painted the last Judgment by *Michael Angelo*, a Piece Famous over all the World. The green Garments of St. *Katherine*, and the Head of St. *Biagio*, are of the Painting of *Daniel* of *Volterra*, who was presently set a work to make those Garments, when the Pope had given express order, that this rare Picture should be defac'd, because of some nakedness in it. Upon great days this Chappel is hung with a rare suit of Hangings of the design of *Rapheal Urbin*, wrought with Gold and Silk, containing the Acts of St. *Peter*, and St. *Paul*.

The Popes Sacristy. 4. Behind this Chappel stands the Popes Sacristy; a place scarce known to Strangers, and therefore seldom seen by them, tho' very well worth the seeing. It's kept always by a Prelate, who is always an *Augustin* Fryar, and a Bishop, and called *Monsignor Sacrista*. In Authors of high times we find mention of this Officer, under the names of *Cimiliartha*, or chief *Sacristan*. Here I saw rare Church-Ornaments for the Popes use. These in particular I cannot

let

let pass without mentioning. The Cope of St. *Silvester* Pope, thirteen hundred years ago. The neat Chasuble of Cloth of Tissue, with the Pictures of the ministring the Seven Sacraments, all embroider'd in it in Silk and Gold so rarely, that the late Lord Marshal of *England*, Tho. Earl of *Arundel*, got leave to have it painted out, and so much the more willingly, because it had been given to the Pope by King *Henry* the VIIIth, a little before his Schisme. Then the incomparable Suits of Ornaments for Priest, Deacon, and Sub-Deacon, to be us'd in high *Mass*, which were given by King *Sebastian* of *Portugal*, and set all over with Pearl, and these Pearls were the first that came out of the *Indies*, and were in all eight Hundred pounds weight of Pearl. The other rare things here, were the Head of St. *Laurence*, which I saw near at hand, through a Chrystal: a piece of the Spunge, in which the *Jews* gave our Saviour gall to drink: the *Camisia* of St. *Prisca* a Primitive Saint Martyr'd in it 1400. years ago, the Crucifix in which is set under a Chrystal, a piece of the Holy Cross carved with the passion of our Saviour in it: a Thorn of our Saviour's Crown of Thorns, which belonged to *Pius Quintus*, a Cross set with Diamonds and Pearls, which the Pope wears at his breast in great Functions, a great Ring which he also weareth in such Functions; it's set with a fair Saphyr, and four great Pearls: a fair Crucifix enamel'd and beset with store of Pearl and Jewels: the Popes *Pallium* which he wears in great Functions: the Fistula or Pipe of Gold, wherewith the Pope receives the consecrated Blood of our Saviour in the Chalice upon great days: the rare Chalices of

St. Laurence his Head.

E e   Gold

Gold set with Pearl, and yet more precious for their Workmanship than for their matter; the great Chalice of Gold, into which the Cardinals put their written Votes in chusing the Pope by Scrutiny; the five Triple Crowns called *Regni*, four whereof are set thick with precious stones and Pearls of great value, and therefore ordinarily kept in the Castle *Angelo*: two Mitres of the same Richness; the chrystal Pixe in which the Blessed Sacrament is kept in the Sepulcher upon *Manday Thursday*: In fine, the Book of the Gospel's painted in *Minature* by the Famous *Giulio Glorio*, for whose first Picture here (of the last Judgment) *Paulus Terrius* sent him fifteen hundred Pistols, as *Monsignor Sacrista* assured me.

5. Passing from hence through the *Sala* again, I was led into the great Room hard by, where the Pope washeth the Feet of thirteen Pilgrims upon *Manday Thursday*; and then giveth every one of them a great Meddal of Gold with Four Pistols, and another of Silver.

The Gallery painted by Raphael. 6. Thence I was led into the open Gallery which looketh upon the Court; I mean the second Lodg (for there are three such open Galleries) where the Histories of the Bible are painted most curiously in the roof of it by prime Masters. That of *Adam* and the Creation: that where *Adam* sows: that where the Sheep drink? that where *Jacob* saw the Ladder: that of the last Supper of Christ with his Apostles: that where *Moses* shews the Laws, are all of the hand of *Raphael Urbin*. That of the Deluge, and of the adoration of the golden Calf, are of the hand of *Raphael dal Borgo*. That where *Josue* commands the Sun to stop: that of *Bersabe* and the like,

Part II. *A Voyage through* Italy.

like, are of the hand of *Pierino del Vago*. That of the Chariot and some others are of the hand *Caravagio*. That of *Moses* striking the Rock; that of the Judgment of *Solomon*, and some others, are of the hand of *Julio Romano*. That of the Baptism of Christ, with other such like, are of the hand of *Pellegrino da Modena*. Yet because in all these Pictures *Raphael Urbin* gave either the design, or some touches, this Gallery is called *Raphael's* Gallery: Indeed nothing but the Divine History it self can be finer than this Painting of Divine *Raphael*. And it belongs only to *Rome* to have the Bible set out thus in its own colours: and if Pictures be the best Books for ignorant People, who can say that the Bible is kept from the People here, seeing it's painted and Printed here in the most vulgar Tongue, and known Language, Pictures? In a word, *Raphael's* Colours seemed to me to illustrate the Text very much, and to be an excellent Comment upon the Holy Scripture.

7. From this Gallery I was led into the great Chamber, where *Constantine's* Victory over *Maxentius* is so rarely painted upon the walls by *Raphael's* own hand; that this Painting serves this Chamber not only for a rich Tapestry, but also for an Internal Trophee to that Emperor. The several postures here of Men and Horses all in Confusion, yet all in such due proportion, make this Picture (in the Judgment of *Monsieur Poussin* a famous Painter) the rarest thing in the World for design. In the other following Rooms there are divers other rare pieces of the same hand; as that of *Attila* and Pope *Leo*: that of St. *Peter* in Prison, a Piece much admired for the perspective

Constantine's Battel with Maxentius.

The best designed Picture in the World.

of it: That of the B. Sacrament: that of the burning of the *Borgo*: that of *Æneas* carrying his Father *Anchises* out of the Flames, are of *Raphael's* hand. The History of *Heliodorus* over the Chimney, is of the hand of *Julio Romano*, *Raphael*'s Scholar.

8. Going up from hence into the highest open Gallery, you'l find it painted with Geographical Maps of the Hand of *Antonio da Varese*. The roof of it is also well Painted by *Pomerancio*, *Paris Romano*, and *Bronzini*, excellent Painters all.

Sala Clementina. 9. Then coming down, I saw the *Sala Clamentina*, a Noble Room. The rare perspectives in the Roof, and in one of the Corners, both of them expressing the Arms of *Clement* the VIII. are worth your attentive consideration.

10. Then the divers Chambers of his Holiness, hung all with Damask Hangings in Summer, and Velvet Hangings in Winter, are very neat. In the Popes Bed-chamber, I saw the grave Picture of our Lady with her Son in her Arms, called *S. Mary Major*, is painted curiously upon a white Transparent Stone, three fingers thick, and yet, shewing the Picture on both sides; if held before the Sun.

11. The great Room gilt over head, where the Pope treats at Dinner great Princes, when they come to *Rome*.

12. The old Appartment of *Pius Quintus*; with the great wooden Bed, or rather the little wooden Chamber of *Paulus Quintus*.

A rare Piece of Perspective. 13. The rare piece of Perspective, over the door of the long Room leading to the Gallery of Maps. At the first looking upon it, you see nothing but certain Types or Figures of the Blessed

Part II. **A Voyage through** Italy.

sed Sacrament out of the Old Testament; but being placed directly under it, and looking upwards, you see all the foresaid Types contracted into the form of a Calice, and an Host over it, to shew, that those old Types and Shadows, prefigured only the Body and Blood of our Saviour, in the holy Sacrifice of the Altar.

14. The Long Gallery of the Maps of *Italy* painted upon the Walls on both sides, by *Paulus Brillus* a *Flemming* and others; and that so distinctly, that you see plainly every State, Province, City, River, Village, Castle, High-way of *Italy*, and where any Famous Battel was Fought, either in the *Romans* time or since: A Gallery which I wish I had spent as many hours in, as I spend days in going up to *Rome*. Divers other Galleries there are in this House, which I pass over in silence. *The rare Gallery of Maps.*

14. But I cannot pass over so, the long Gallery leading to the *Belvedere*, in which is kept the Conclave of all Popes: In this one great Room, Fifty or Threescore Cardinals lodge, and have, every one two Chambers, one for himself, and the other for his Conclavist; *Ex ungue Leonem*, you may judge by this what the whole House is; or else by this what they assure you, when they tell you, that there are five Thousand Chambers in that Palace. *The Gallery of the Conclave.*

15. From the middle of the foresaid Gallery, you enter into the *Vatican* Library, Famous all the learned world over, for having in it, besides the Registers of the *Roman* Church, the choisest Manuscripts of the World in holy Languages. This *Baronius* found, who drew from hence notable succor, for the maintaining this Ecclesiasti- *The Vatican Library.*

cal History, and as the **Centuriators** of *Magdebourg*, who wanting these assured aims, and being otherwise wrongly biassed, made faults in their History as many as their Centuries, and as great as their Volumes. The description of this Library hath been made by learned *Angelus Rocca* in *Latin*, and by *Mutius Pansa* in *Italian:* Yet for the satisfaction of my curious Countrymen, I shall say something of it. First the Room is a vast long Room, spreading it self in the further end, into two wings of building, which are full of Presses, where the Manuscripts are kept carefully from Mice and Rats, and moist weather. At the entrance into this Library, you are let into a fair Chamber full of Desks for a dozen of Writers, who have good stipends to copy out Books in all Languages; and they are bound to be writing so many hours in a morning. Round about this room hang the Pictures of all the Cardinals that have been *Bibliothecarii* since *Sixtus Quintus* his time. Then entring into the Library it self, I saw the vast wide Room supported (like a Church) by great square Pillars, about which are as many Cupboards where the Manuscripts are conserved. On the wall on the right hand, are painted in *Fresco* the General Councils of the Church, with the Bible in the midst, laying open upon a stately Throne, and with the order and place of precedency observed in them: As also some notable Accidents in Ecclesiastical History. On the left hand are painted all the famous Libraries anciently mentioned by Authors: And upon the great Pillars are painted the first Inventors and Promoters of Learning. This long room spreads it self at last

The Library it self.

into

Part II. *A Voyage through* Italy.

nto two wings on each hand; both which are full of curious Books, both Manuscripts and Printed Books; divers of which were shewn me with great civility, by *Monsignor Holstonius* then Keeper of this Library, whom I had formerly known. The chief of these Books were these.

A vast Hebrew Bible, too heavy for any man to lift up.

An Ancient Copy of the *Septuagints* Translation in Greek, after which the Bible hath been Printed both in *Rome* and *London*. *Some rare Books here.*

The Acts of the Apostles in Greek, curiously written in Golden Letters.

The Gospel written by St. *Chrysostom*'s own hand.

An Hebrew Bible written in sheets of Parchment pasted to one another, and rowled up; hence the word *Volumen* for a Book.

A little Book written in Bark of Trees: hence the word *Folium* for a Leaf in a Book.

Certain old *Roman* Table-books.

A *China* Table-book of Wood, in which they wrote with a pointed Steel.

A curious *China* Book all in Hieroglyphics, and folded up in many folds: Our *Purchas* in his curious Navigations hath both Printed and deciphered it.

Polidore Virgil's History of *England*, written with his own hand.

An old Book of Sermons in Latin, in whose Margin St. *Thomas* of *Aquin* hath made notes with his own hand.

An old *Virgil*, with the Pictures of the History in old Painting.

A **Voyage through** Italy. Part II.

An Old *Terrence* written Twelve Hundred years ago, and the ancientest that ever *Politan* saw, as he testifieth under his own hand, in the inside of the cover of this Book.

Baronius his Annals in his own hand Writing.

The rare quotations out of the ancient Fathers, painfully and faithfully Collected out of the best Copies, by Learned Cardinal *Sirleto*, in the time of the Council of *Trent*, and sent by him weekly, by the Post from *Rome*, to the Fathers in the Council, who proceeded to their Definitions, by the Ancient Tradition of the Church, found so plainly and unanimously in those Fathers. Those Quotations make six Volums in Folio: And this was it, which our Adversaries call, the sending down of the Holy Ghost to *Trent*, in a Cloak-bag; when it was only the sending down of these faithful Testimonies of the Tradition of the Church, gathered out of the most Ancient and Authentic Copies.

K. Henry the VIII. his Letters to Ann Bolen.

The Letters of *Henry* the VIII. of *England* to *Ann Bolen* his Mistriss then, in his own hand Writing, some in *English*, some in *French*, but all Amatory. It is easie to imagine them written by him, if you compare the Hand-writing of these Letters, with those two Verses written by the Kings own hand, in the Frontispiece of the following Book; to wit,

K. Henry the VIII. his Book against Luther.

The Book which the said *H.* wrote against *Martin Luther*, and Dedicated it by a couple of *Latin Verses*, written with his own Hand, in the Frontispiece of it, to Pope *Leo* the X*th*. Which Book purchased to K. *Hen.* the Honourable Title of *Defender of the Faith.*

Then

Part II. *A Voyage through* Italy. 41

Then I was shewn the Library of the Duke of *Urbin*, who dying without Heirs Male, bequeathed his Library to the *Vatican* Library here. In this, I saw many rare Manuscripts written in Parchment, and painted in *minature*: Especially that Book, in whose Margins are Painted by a rare hand, and wonderful diligence, all the Insects in Nature, in their lively Colours and true Resemblance. *The Library of the Duke of Urbin.*

Over against this Library, they shewed me in the same Room, the Library of *Heidelberg*, sent to *Rome* by the Duke of *Bavaria*, after he had dispossessed the Elector *Frederick*, Prince *Palatin* of *Rhene*, of his Country, as well as of the Kingdom of *Bohemia* which he had seiz'd on, at the instigation of *Bethelem Gabor* and others. See the *Mercure François*. They shewed me here, among divers other Books, the Book of designs of the said Prince *Elector Palatin*, which he had designed being young. Happy Prince, if he had not designed to himself another Mans Crown. *The Library of Heidelberg.*

In the great room of this Library, there is an Iron door, which letteth you into a more secret Room, where the Registers of the Church of *Rome* are kept: The Keeper of which Registers was anciently called *Chartularius*; an Office much like to that in the Greek Church; called *Chartophylax*. *The place of Registers.*

In fine, I was shewn here divers Letters of great Persons and Princes, written with their own hands, as of S. *Charles Boromeus*, to Cardinal *Sirleto*, who had a hand in his Education; of Queen *Mary* of *England*; King *Philip* the Second of *Spain* her Husband, stiling himself King of *Spain*, *England*, and *France*; of *Francis* the first *Some Letters of great Persons.*

first of *France*; of *Margeret* of *Parma* that Governed *Flanders* when it revolted; of President *Vargas* a Spaniard, and a great Statesman in *Flanders*, but no great Latinist, as it appeared by his Answer to the Doctors of *Lovain* (petitioning him in Latin for their priviledges) when he said; *Non curamus vostros privilegios. Mali fexerunt templa; boni nihil fexerunt contra: Ergo debent omnes patibulari:* The terms of the expostulation, being as harsh as the conclusion of it; and some old polite Orators had rather have been hang'd indeed, than threatned in such bad Latin.

Harsh Latin.

A little before I went out of this Library, I saw near the door, the Statue of *Hyppolitus* Bishop of *Portua* (who lived 1400 years ago) sitting in a Chair of stone, upon which is cut in Greek Letters, the ancient Canon *Paschalis*, upon which *Schaliger* and others have written. It's a curious piece of Learned Antiquity, and worthy to be taken notice of.

Canon Paschalis.

16. Having seen the Library, we were led on by the long Gallery, mentioned before, unto the Belvedere, where we descended into the Popes private Garden, full of Orange-trees, fine Walks, and Fountains. Here are three or four unavoidable wetting places to those that are not acquainted with them. Hence you go down to see the rare Fountain of the Iron Ship. In this Garden I saw the Pine-apple of Brass gilt, which is as great as three men can fathom about, and twice as high as the tallest men can reach. Here also stand by it the two great Peacocks of Brass gilt, which stood anciently upon *Scipio Affricanus* his Tomb, and are some three or four yards long.

The Belvedere.

The great Pine-apple.

The two Peacocks.

17. From

Part II.   *A Voyage through Italy.*   43

17. From hence we were led hard by, to see *The Belvedere of the Maschere.* the *Belvedere* of the *Maschere*, which *Michael Angelo* called his Study. It's a square Court set with Orange-trees, in whose walls are great Niches, with leaves to them of wood, where the choice Statues of the World are conserved under Lock and Key, and free from ill weather. The chiefest Statues are these: That of the River *Nilus*, and that of *Tyber*, both in cumbent postures: That of *Antinus*, minion of the Emperor *Adrian*, it's of pure Oriental Marble, and rarely cut: That of *Cleopatra*: That of *Venus* coming out of a Bath: That of *Commodus* the Emperor: That of *Laocoon* and his Sons, involved about with Serpents. This Statue of *Laocoon* is the Master-piece of Sculpture. That in the middle of the Court, of *Hercules*, without Arms, Legs, or Head, is so rare a trunk, that *Michael Angelo* profess'd, he had learn'd more skill out of that broken Statue, than out of all the whole ones he had ever seen. Hence you see always a world of Sculptures designing it out: A piece of Lyons skin, yet appearing, made me not doubt but it was the Statue of *Hercules*. *Rare Statues.*

Michael Angelo's Study.

18. From hence we stept into the great Garden of the *Belvedere*, full of Exotick Trees, curious Fountains, shady Walks, and great variety of Grots and wetting sports. *The great Garden of Belvedere.*

19. Lastly, in your return again through the *Vatican* Palace, we saw the Armory full of Arms for Thirty Thousand Men, Horse and Foot, and well kept. *The Armory.*

Having thus seen the *Vatican* Palace, I went on with the rest of the Curiosities of the Town, and took them in order as they lay. Hence going from S. *Peters*, and leaving the Palace of the

Santa

A Voyage through Italy.   Part II.

The Santo Officio. *The Hospital of St.* Spirito.

Santo Officio, on my right hand, I came presently to the Hospital of S. *Spirito*, which is hard by. The situation of this Hospital near to S. *Peters* Church, was not done casually; but without doubt, upon design, and for this end, that Men might learn by the very situation of Hospitals, near unto great Churches (as I observed in many other places, both in *Italy* and *France*) that Christians, after they have performed their duties to God, ought to pay in the next place their duties to their Neighbour; and let that Faith, which they came from exercising in the Church towards God, be made appear by good works, exercised presently in Hospitals toward Men. Now this Hospital of S. *Spirito*, is one of the fairest in *Europe* both for bigness and revenues. It hath a thousand Beds in it for the sick: A Prelate to govern it; store of Priests, Physicians, and under Officers to attend on them, and a revenue of Seventy Thousand Crowns a year. There is also a Monastry of Women in it, in a place separated from the rest, capable of 500 young girls. In the Appartments above stairs there is handsome accommodation for poor Gentlemen, founded by the Gentleman-like Charity of Pope *Urban* the VIII, to this end, that those whom Fortune had priviledged by better Birth, might not be involv'd in common miseries. There is also a grate towards the street, where little Infants are put into a square hole of a Turn, and so turned in by Night by their unlawful Mothers, who not daring to own them, would otherwise dare to destroy them. *Constantine* the great founded such Hospitals for exposed Children. The person that brings the Child in the Night rings a little Bell, whose

Lewis Guyon *in diver. lec. l. 2. c. 16.*

Part II. *A Voyage through* Italy.

whose Rope hangs at the outside of that grate, and an Officer within comes presently and receiveth it; and having first ask'd whether it be baptiz'd or no, carrieth it presently away, and recommends it to a Nurse, of which there are always store in readiness entertain'd there at the Cost of the Hospital on the Womans side of the House. When the Children are grown fit for Instruction, they are set to Trades, the Girls are carefully brought up by Religious Women there, till they be fit for Marriage, or a Nunnery, according to their Vocation.

From hence I went to *Onofrios* Church upon the hill, where I saw the Tomb and Picture over it, of rare *Torquato Tasso*; whose warlike Muse is able to inspire mettle into his Reader's Breast, and dispose him to the engagement of a new *Croisade* against the *Turks*. This I can say of him, if *Virgil* hinder'd him from being the first of Poets, he hinder'd *Virgil* from being the only Poet. *S. Onofrios Church. The Tomb of Torquato Tasso.*

Returning down again, and going along the *Longara*, I saw the stately Palace of the Duke of *Salviati* on the right hand, and the *Villa* of *Chisi* (now called the Garden of *Farnesi*) on the Left hand. In this *Villa* I saw rare painting attributed to *Raphael Urbin*. *Longara. Villa Chisi.*

Over against this Garden, lives now the Queen of *Suede*, in whose Palace, besides the rare hangings of Cloth of Gold, and of Arras, hangings of Silk and Gold, I saw a curious Collection of Pictures, Originals all, and of the prime Masters of the World: That of Sir *Thomas Moor* is without doubt of *Hans Holbains* hand, and a rare Piece. *Queen Christinas Palace.*

Passing

Passing on the *Longara* still, I came to the *Porta Septimiana*, so called from *Septimius Severus*, who built here his *Thermæ*; and so up the hill to Saint *Pancratius* his Gate, and to the Church of that Saint, possessed now by discalced Carmelites. Under this Church is the *Cæmeterium Calepodii*, where many Martyrs Bodies were buried. Here was buried *Crescentius* the Tyrant, who seizing upon the Castle *Angelo*, sway'd all in *Rome* for a while.

St. Pancratius his Church. Cæmeterium Calepodis.

From hence I went to the *Villa Pamfilla*, which is hard by. It's a new *Villa*, but its seated very high, and from the tarrass upon the top of the House you have a fine Prospect. There are divers good Pictures and Statues in the House, and fine Water-works, and a *Grotta* in the Garden. The best Pictures here are the Crucifixion of St. *Peter*, and the Conversion of St. *Paul*, of *Michael Angelo's* hand. The entry of the Animals into the Ark of *Noah* is a rare piece: the best Statues are the wrestling of *Jacob* with the Angel in white Marble: *Seneca's* Statue, and the *Busto* of Innocent the X. of Porphiry: and his Head in Brass.

Villa Pamfilis.

Returning again into the Town the same way we came. I saw the brave Fountain made by *Paulus Quintus*, who caused the water to be brought thither from the Lake of *Bracciana*, above thirty Miles off, by a stately Aqueduct; and from hence it is dispers'd into the City, and there makes new Fountains.

The Fountain of Paulus V.

Hard by stands the Convent of *Franciscans*, upon a Hill, called St. *Pietro Montorio*, where St. *Peter* was Crucified with his Head downward, in that very place of the Court where there's now

San. Pietro Montorio.

Part II. A Voyage through Italy.   47

a round Chappel. Entring into the Church, I was much taken with the Picture, for the high Altar representing our Saviour's Transfiguration. It was the last and best piece of *Raphael Urbin*'s making, and then I may say it is the best in the World. I guess it to be the best of *Raphael*'s pieces ; because dying he commanded that this Picture of all his Pictures should be set up at his Feet after his Death. In this Church lies buried the Earl of *Tyrone*, who fled from *Ireland* hither in Queen *Elizabeth*'s time. Here are two fine Statues in Marble of St. *Peter* and St. *Paul*, of the hand of *Michael Angelo*.

Going out of this Church you have a fair sight of *Rome* under you from this Hill. This Hill was anciently called *Janiculus*; and upon it was buried *Statius* the Poet, and at the Foot of it *Numa Pompilius*. *Mons Janiculus.*

Near the Foot of this Hill stands the Church and Convent of the *Scala*, belonging to the Discalced *Carmelits*. The high Altar is very neat, and the good Fathers shewed us in a little Chappel within the Convent the Foot of St. *Therasa*, which is plainly seen through a Chrystal, in which it's kept. *La Scala.*

Not far from hence stands *Santa Maria Transtevere*, the first Church built in *Rome* (saith *Baronius*) and built there where anciently stood the *Tabernæ Meritoriæ*; where the maimed Souldiers received their Pittance daily. The gilt Roof, and the two rows of Marble Pillars, do much beautify this Church. Under the high Altar is yet seen the place where Oil issued out, as from a Fountain, a little before our Saviour's Birth, as denouncing his Birth to be at hand, who was *Santa Maris Transtevere.* *Tabernæ Meritoriæ.*

to

to be called *Christus*, that is anointed. In this Church lie buried Cardinal *Hosius*, a most learned Trent Father, and Cardinal *Campegius* the Popes Legat in *England*, in *Henry* the VIII. time. You see here the Stone that was ty'd about the Neck of St. *Calixtus* Pope, when he was thrown into a Well.

Here also you see great round stones which were hung at the Feet of the Martyrs to torment them.

S. Francesco in Pipa Grande. The Convent of *Franciscan* Fryars, called S. *Francesco in ripa grande*, is hard by, where I saw the Chamber where great St. *Francis* lodged when he lived in *Rome*. It's now turned into a Chappel. In the Church there is an excellent Picture of Piety, made by *Caraccio*. Here in the Church is the Tomb of *Beata Ludovica Matbei* of the third order of St. *Francis*.

Ripa Grande. I took the *Ripa Grande* in my way, and saw there the Boats of Merchandise which come to *Rome* from *Ligorn*, *Civita Vechia*, *Naples*, and other places, and disembark their goods here.

S. Cicilies Church. From the *Ripa* I went to St. *Cicilies* Church, built where her House was, and where she was put to death for the Christian Religion. Under *St. Cicilies Tomb.* the high Altar of this Church is the Tomb of this primitive Saint, with her Statue in a couchant Posture, and just as her Body was found in *Clement* the VIIIths time, wrapt up in vails stain'd with Blood; and cover'd with a Robe of Gold. The neat Decoration before the high Altar, with the Silver Lamps burning before the Tomb of this Saint, was the Foundation of Cardinal *Sfondrati*. At the end of this Church, as you come in, are seen yet the Stoves in which St. *Sitily* was shut up

Part II.   **A Voyage through** Italy.   49

up in her own house to be stifled, but that failing she was Beheaded. The stoves are yet entire, and shewing the manner of the ancient stoves. In the Church Porch I found the Tomb of one *Adam* an *English* Bishop of *London*, and Cardinal of this Title; who died in *Rome*, An. 1397. It hath these Verses upon it.

Cardinal Adams Tomb.

Artibus iste pater famosus in omnibus Adam
Theologus summus, Cardinalisque erat
　Anglia cui patriam, titulum dedit ista Beatæ
Ædes Cæciliæ, morsque suprema Polum.

For Fuit.

Not far from this Church, stands St. *Chysogonius* his Church, a neat Church, repair'd some years ago by Cardinal *Burghesi*. The four Pillars of the high Altar look as if they were of Sand and Chrystal petrified together. On the Left hand of the Wall near the great door lies buried *Robert* Arch-Bishop of *York*, and titular of this Church; this was all I could learn out of the Tombstone.

St. Chrysogonus.

Cardinal Robert Archbishop of York.

Having thus wandred over the *Trastevere*, I made towards the Ile of St. *Bartholomew*, in which stands a good Hospital, and a Convent of *Franciscans*, in whose Church reposeth under the high Altar in a fair Porphyry Tomb, the Body of St. *Bartholomew* Apostle. This Ile was anciently called *Insula Tiberina*, and it was first made by the Corn of *Tarquinius Superbus*, which being (after his ejection out of the City) pluck'd up by the roots, and thrown into the River, by reason of the quantity of Earth that stuck to the roots, stopped here where the water was low; and this stoppage once begun, all the Mud of the River came

St. Bartholomews Tomb.

D d　　　　afterwards

A Voyage through Italy.   Part II.

afterwards to stop here too; and so in time to form a little Ile in the midst of the River.

Ponte quarto Capi. Going out of the Ile by the Bridge of four Heads, anciently called *Pons Fabricius*, which joyns this Ile with the City, I looked down the River on my Right Hand, to see the *Pons Sublicius*,

Pons sublicius. which *Cocles* alone defended against an Army, till the Bridge was cut down behind him: Which he perceiving leapt into the River armed, and swam safe to his fellow Citizens, who were as glad to see him come off safe, as to find themselves safe. It was called *Pons Sublicius*, from the word *Sublica* in Latin, which signifies great Beams of Wood, of which it was made: It was afterwards built of Stone by *Æmilius*. From this Bridge the wicked Emperor *Heliogabalus* was thrown into the River and drowned, with a great stone about his neck.

The Jewry. No sooner was I over this Bridge, but I saw on my left hand, the great back door of the Jewry; for here the *Jews* live altogether in a Corner of the Town, and are locked up every night. I entred into their Synagogues here (which they call their Schools) where they meet upon Saturdays, and sing and pray.

I wondred at first, that they had learned no more manners in these their Schools, than to enter into them to pray, without either putting off Hats, lifting up Eyes, or bending of Knees to the great *Jehova*, whom they rather fear than love. *Moses* going to him, put off his Shooes, and I expected, that these Men should at least, have put off their Hats at the entrance into their Synagogues: But they are Arch Clowns, and their fowl Towels, at the entrance into their Synagogues,

Part II. *A Voyage through Italy.* 51

gogues, told me as much. I once saw a Circumcision, but it was so painful to the Child, that it was able to make a Man heartily thank God that he is a Christian. And really, if the little Child could speak and wish, I believe he would wish himself the greatest curse in the World, and to be a Woman rather than a Man upon such terms. I saw also a Marriage here performed with many Ceremonies.

Returning out of the Jewry by the same Gate I entred, I saw on my left hand, the Palace of Prince *Savelli*: It's built upon the ruins of the Theater of *Marcellus*, built by *Augustus*, in honour of his Nephew *Marcellus*: It was capable of Fourscore Thousand Men. *Theatrum Marcelli.*

Passing on, I came to an Ancient Church called *Santa Maria in Cosmedin*, or in *Schola Græca*, where St. *Austin*, before his Conversion, taught Rhetorick. In the Porch of this Church stands a great round stone, cut into the face of a Man, with a great wide mouth, commonly called, *La Bocca della verita*, the mouth of truth; but this not being affirmed by the mouth of truth, I dare not believe it: I rather believe it served in some old Building for a Gutter spout: I know truth may speak loud and have a wide Mouth; but he that takes every wide mouth for the mouth of truth, is much mistaken. *Santa Maria in Cosmedin.* *Bocca della Verita.*

The next Church I came to was *Santa Maria Egyptiaca*. It was the Temple of the *Sun* and *Jupiter*. This Church is neatly adorned with curious chanelled Pillars. It belongs to the *Armenians*, who have an Hospital also here, belonging to the Catholick Pilgrims of that Country: And the Pope allows them to celebrate Mass here after their own *Armenian* rite. *St. Maria Egyptiaca.*

D d 2   On

On the other side of the great *Piazza* stands the Church of St. *Steven*. Its rounded with chanelled Pillars also. It was anciently the Temple of *Juno Matutina* Morning *Juno*, or *Alba Dea*, the break-of-Day Goddess: A Goddess, which our Ladies that never rise till noon, would never have been devout to.

The Cloaca Maxima. Close by this Church (which stands by the River side) the great sink of *Rome*, called *Cloaca Maxima*, emptied it self into *Tyber*. And tho this were but a sink, yet it deserves to be mentioned among the rare Magnificencies of ancient *Rome*. For it was nobly built by *Tarquinus Priscus*, of Free-stone, Arched over head, with a world of Springs running into it: And it was so great, that a Cart might have gone in it. This sink was one of the evident tokens of the greatness and magnificence of *Rome* anciently; and indeed a far greater evidence than that of *Heliogabalus*; who caused all the Spiders Webs of *Rome* to be gathered together and weighed, that by so many pound weight of Spiders Webs, the greatness of *Rome* might the better be conjectured.

Marks of Rome's greatness anciently.

Going on from hence by the River side, I came to the foot of the Mount *Aventin*, and left on my left hand, a Chappel belonging to the Knights of *Malta*. Our Antiquaries tell us, that near to this place stood the Temple of the *Bona Dea*, into which no Man was to enter: And that *Cacus* his Den was also in the side of this Hill, into which he drag'd *Hercules* his Oxen by the tails, that no man should find out his theft by the Footsteps. Upon the side of this hill stood also the *Scalæ Gemoniæ*, down which Criminal Persons were tumbled into *Tyber*.

The Temple of Bona Dea. Cacus his Den.

Scala Gemoniæ.

Going

Part II. **A Voyage through** Italy.   53

Going up this Hill I went to St. *Alexius* his *St. Alexi-*
Church, where I saw the wooden Stairs, under *us his*
which this Saint lodged for seventeen years in *Church.*
his own Fathers House (after fifteen years ab-
sence) without being known to any Body, till
after his death. The body of this Saint lies under
the high Altar, together with that of St. *Boni-
facius* the Martyr.

Hard by upon the same Hill, stands St. *Sabi-* *St. Sabinas*
na's Church, whither the Pope comes upon *Ash-* *Church.*
wednesday in a Solemn *Cavalcata*, accompanied
with the Cardinals.

Here also upon this hill, stood anciently the *The Armi-*
Temple of Liberty, and the *Romans Armilustrium*. *lustrium.*

Descending from hence, I made towards St.
Paul's Gate; and in the way I saw on my right
Hand the hill called *Mons Testacius*, which was *Mons Te-*
made of the broken Pots thrown there in the *stacius.*
Romans time by the *Potters*. Its half a Mile a-
bout, and 160 foot high.

A little nearer the Gate of St. *Paul*, I saw the
Tomb of *Caius Cestius*, built like a *Piramid* of *The Tomb*
Ægypt, and all of pure white Marble. This is *of C. Ce-*
the most entire work of all the ancient *Roman* *stius.*
works. This *Cestius* (as the words upon his Tomb
import) was *septemvir Epulonum*, that is, one of
those seven Men called *Epulones* anciently, be- *Epulones.*
cause they had the devouring of those Banquets,
which were set before the Gods in their *Lectister-
nia*, in the Temple of *Jupiter Capitolinus*.

Passing thence through the Gate of St. *Paul*, *The Gate of*
anciently called *Porta Tergemina*; and *Porta Osti-* *St. Paul.*
ensis; I went to St. *Paul's* Church, a little Mile
from the Town. In the way I took notice of a
little Chappel on the Left hand, where St. *Peter*

Dd 3   and

and St. *Paul* took leave of one another, before they were led to *Martyrdom*.

St. Paul's Church. Soon after I came to S. *Paul*'s Church, here S. *Paul* was buried by *Lucina* a *Roman Lady*, and therefore *Constantin* the Great built this Church in the honour of S. *Paul*, as he had done that of S. *Peter* mentioned above. It's built cross-wise, and the body of it is 477 foot long, and 258 broad; with a hundred pillars in all, set in four ranks; all of them ancient round marble pillars, taken *In proœmio.* out of the *Baths* of *Attonius*, saith *Vassari*. Yet in all this vast body of the Church there are no Chappels, nor any decoration, except at the very end of it, near the great door, where there is an *Altar* with these words in stone over it, *Hic inventum est caput S. Pauli*. The most remarkable things which I saw here, were these.

1. The high *Altar*, with a Canopy of stone like a *Tabernacle*, born up by four Porphyry pillars, and adorned with statues. Under the *Altar* reposeth half of the bodies of S. *Peter* and S. *Paul*, (as I observed before in S. *Peter*'s Church) and as the Inscription upon the side of the Altar here affirms in these words: *Sub hoc altari requiescunt gloriosa corpora Apostolorum Petri & Pauli pro medietate*. Behind this *Altar* stands the Confession of S. *Paul*, like that of S. *Peter* described above. Under the little low doors which let the Priest into the steps of the *Altar*, are written these words in golden Letters, *Limina Apostolorum*, *Limina Apostolorum.* which makes me bold to hold against some Modern Writers, that this was the precise place, and not the door of the Church, which was called *Limina Apostolorum*.

2. In

Part II. A voyage through Italy. 55

2. In the old Arch in the top of the roof, is yet seen a piece of Mosaic Work representing our Saviour in the midst of the four and twenty Elders of the *Apoclaypse*. This piece was made there twelve hundred years ago in the time of S. *Leo the great*; and at the cost of *Placidia Galla* (Daughter of *Theodosius*, and Sister of *Honorius*) as the two Verses in that Arch testifie thus:

Placidiæ pia mens operis decus omne reportat,
Gaudet Pontificis studio splendere Leonis.

3. The famous Miraculous Crucifix (standing in a Chappel on the Epistle side of the High *Altar*) which spoke to S. *Bridgit*. This Crucifix favours the opinion of those who affirm that there were two nails in our Saviour's feet.

The miraculous Crucifix. Baron.

4. The neat Chappel and *Tabernacle* of the B. *Sacrament*; with the rare pictures relating thereunto, made by *Cavalier Lanfranco*.

5. The picture of the *Altar* of S. *Steven*, made by a Lady of *Bologna*, called *Lavinia Fontana*.

6. The chief Relics kept here, are the Head of the *Samaritan* Woman Converted by our Saviour: The Arm of S. *Anne* Mother of our blessed LADY, and the Chain of Saint *Paul*.

Baron. ed Matirol. Rom. 20. Martii.

From S. *Paul*'s Church I went to the *Tre Fontane* above a mile and a half off, and in the way, I passed over the place where S. *Zeno*, and ten thousand *Christians* were martyred at once by the command of *Dioclesian* the Butcher. Their blood made this way holy all along.

Dd 4 Arriving

Tre Fontaine.

The Church of St. Vincent and Anastase.

Baronius An. 627.

Baron. An. 627. and An. 713.

The round Church.

Tre Fontane.

Arriving at the *Tre Fontane* I saw there three Churches standing within a place anciently called, *ad Aquas Salvias*. The first of these three Churches is that of S. *Vincent* and *Anastase*, because of their Relics sent hither. For about the year 627. the Emperor *Heraclius* sent the Head of S. *Anastasius* with the Picture of the same Saint unto Pope *Honorius* the First. A courteous Father, of S. *Bernard*'s Order here, did me the favour to shew me near the high *Altar*, this Head, and this Picture. These two are most authentical things, for the attestation of them is in the very Acts of the second Council of *Nice*, held an. 789. where to prove the lawfulness of sacred Images against the *Iconoclasts*, the sacred Council cites a Miracle wrought by this very Picture of S. *Anastasius*: and *Baronius* quotes divers others wrought by the same Picture.

In the second Church here, to wit the little round Church on the right hand, there is a famous Picture of *S. Bernard's Extasis*. Under this Church I was led into a Vault where many of the Bodies of the foresaid ten thousand Christians, who were martyred with S. *Zeno*, are buried. This Vault goes a mile under ground.

In the third place stands the little Church of the *Tre Fontane*, so called, because S. *Paul* was here beheaded, and where his head jumpt thrice three Fountains gushed out. Upon an *Altar* on the left hand, is an excellent picture of *S. Peter's Crucifixion*, of the hand of *Guido Rheni*. On the other side is seen a little block (within an iron grate) upon which they say *S. Paul's* head was cut off.

Going

Part II. A Voyage through Italy. 57

Going from hence, I went over the Fields to *The An-*
the Church of the *Annunciata*, one of the Nine *nunciata.*
Churches of *Rome*, visited by Pilgrims; and
from thence to S. *Sebastians*.

St. *Sebastian*'s Church is one of the Seven *S. Sebasti-*
Churches, and of great Devotion by reason of *an's*
the *Catacombes* which are under it. Here I saw the *Church.*
Tomb of St. *Sebastian* under an Altar on the left
hand: many relics kept over an altar on the right
hand, and the Vault underneath where Pope *Steven* was beheaded in his own Seat of Stone, and
where St. *Peter*'s and St. *Paul*'s Bodies were hidden many years.

Thence I was led into the *Catacombes*, which *The Cata-*
are under this Church, and which from thence *combes.*
running many Miles under ground, made anciently a Christian *Rome* under the Heathen. There
were divers of these *Catacombes* in the primitive
times, and they were called diversly: *Arenaria,
Cryptæ, Areæ, Concilia Martyrum, Poliandria*;
but most frequently *Cæmeteria*, that is, *Dorme-
toria*, because here reposed the Bodies of the holy Martyrs and Saints, *qui obdormiverunt in Do-
mino*. But the greatest of all these *Cæmeteria* was
this of *Calixtus*. In these *Catacombes* during the *Cæmeteri-*
Persecutions raised against the Christians by ten *um Calixti.*
Heathen Emperors, the faithful Believers, toge-
ther with their Popes and Pastors, used privately to meet to exercise their Religion, and steal
their Devotions; that is, to hear Mass in little
round Chappels painted over head poorly; Minister the Sacraments; bury the dead Martyrs
and Confessors in the Walls of the long Alleys,
Preach, hold Conferences; and even celebrate
Councils too sometimes. I descended several
times

A *Voyage through* Italy. Part II.

times into several parts of these *Catacombes* with a good experienced guide (which you must be sure of) and with wax Lights (Torches being too stifling) and wandered in them up and down with extraordinary Satisfaction of Mind. The Streets under ground are cut out with Mens hands and Mattocks. They are as high as a Man for the most part, and no broader than for two Men to meet. All the way along, the sides of these Alleys are full of holes as long as a Man, and sometimes there are three rows one over another, in which they had buried their Martyrs and Confessors, and that Posterity might afterwards know which were Martyrs, which Confessors, they engraved upon the Stone which mur'd them up, or upon one of the Bricks, a Palm Branch, in sign of a Martyr; and a *Pro Christo* in Cyphers for a Confessor; it's recorded, that during the foresaid Persecutions, a hundred and seventy four Thousand Martyrs were buried here in this *Cæmetary* of *Calixtus*: among whom were nineteen Popes Martyrs. Hence these *Catacombes* have always been esteem'd as a place of great Devotion, and much frequented by devout persons: The words over the door, as you descend into them from the Church of St. *Sebastian*, tell you, how St. *Hirome* confesseth, that he used every Sunday and Holyday, during his stay in *Rome*, to go to these *Catacombes*, and a Picture hung over the same door, sheweth how St. *Philip Neri* used to frequent these holy places in the Night; and from whence I believe he sucked that true Spirit of the primitive Church, which reigned in him, and still reigneth in the breasts of his most vertuous Children, the pious *Priests* of the Oratory of *Rome*,

St. Hierom *in* Ezechiel. C. 40.

Rome, whom I must always praise wheresoever I find them, because I always find them either writing holy things, or living them; that is, either writing Books fit to be lived, or living lives fit to be written. Indeed it's incredible how much the presence of these holy Martyrs bodies hath sanctified this place: in so much that no man enters into the *Catacombes* but he comes better out, than he went in. *Catholics* come out far more willing to die for that faith, for which so many of their Ancestors have died before them. The Adversaries of the *Roman* Church come out more staggered in their faith, and more mild towards the Catholic Religion, to see what piety there is even in the bowels of *Rome*; *Atheists* come out with that belief, that surely there is a God, seeing so many thousands of Martyrs have testified it with their blood.

From S. *Sebastians* I went to the place hard by, called *Capo di Bove*, standing upon the *Via Appia*. It is a great Building faced about with marble stones. It was the Sepulcher of *Metella* wife of rich *Crassus*. It's now called *Capo di Bove* because of the Ox heads cut in marble which compose the Cornice that runs about the top of the *Moles*. Entering into it you will wonder at the thickness of the walls, which are above eight ells thick. It was begun to be pulled down, especially the great marble stones on the outside of it, to make up the *Fontana di Trevi*; but Cardinal *Barberino* would not suffer it to be so defaced.

Capo di Bove.

Close by stand the ruins of the *Pretorium*, the Quarters of the *Pretorian* Bands, which the Emperors lodged here, a little out of the throng of the Town, that they might not occasion so easily tumults;

The Pretorium.

tumults; and that they might exercise themselves often in the *Circo* of *Caracalla* which was hard by.

Circus Caracalla. This *Circus* was made by the Emperor *Caracalla*, and is the most entire of all the *Circos* that were in *Rome*. You see where the *Carceres*, or starting place was, where the *Meta*; where the *Guglia* were. You see how long it was, and the walls yet show you what compass it carried. In the midst of it stood that *Guglia* which now stands in the midst of *Piazza Navona*. I saw it lye here broken in three pieces, and neglected quite, till the Earl of *Arundel* our late Lord *Marshal*, offering to buy it, and having already deposited threescore Crowns in earnest for it, made the *Romans* begin to think that it was some fine thing, and stop the transporting of it into *England*. At last it light upon a good stone-setter, who joyned it so well together, that it now stands streight upon a rare *basis*, and adorns the very heart of *Rome*: Thanks to that ingenious Architect *Cavalier Bernini*, who set it up there in the *anno sancto*, and whom it set up too again in the Pope's favour *Innocent* the X. which he had lost, by a crack in the roof of the Porch of S. *Peter's* Church, caused by the heavy steeple which he had placed upon it.

The Temple of Vertue and Honour. Near the end of the *Circus* of *Caracalla*, stands an old round Temple, with another little Ante-Temple, close joyned to it; and out of which you go into the other. What if this were the Temple of Honour? into which there was no passage, but through the Temple of Vertue, which was joyned close to it, as this is: to manifest, that Vertue is the way to Honour. Now it's certain that these two Temples stood not far from the

Porta

Part II. **A Voyage through** Italy.

Porta Carpena (now called S. *Sebaſtian*'s Gate) as theſe two do. But I declare that this is but gueſſing.

Hard by the foreſaid old Temple there is an *Eccho* which heretofore (as they ſay) would repeat after you a whole Verſe of *Virgil*; but if ſo, it was my fortune to find her when ſhe had catched a cold ; for I could get nothing from her but the two laſt words of a Sentence. Indeed *Auſonius* calls the *Eccho* the tail of Words ; and *Sympoſius* ſaith, that the *Eccho* is like a modeſt *Virgin*, which ſpeaks nothing but when ſhe is asked. *The Eccho.*

Returning from S. *Sebaſtians* towards the town again, I paſſed by a little Chappel called, *Domine quo vadis ?* and anciently called, *Sancta Maria ad paſſus*, It's called *Domine quo vadis*, becauſe our Saviour appearing here to St. *Peter*, flying out of the Priſon of *Rome*, was asked by *Peter*, *Domine quo vadis ?* Lord whither go you? And he anſwered, *Vado Romam ut ibi iterum crucifigar*, I am going to *Rome*, there to be Crucified again ; which words *Peter* underſtanding rightly, of *Chriſt*'s ſuffering in his Members the faithful Believers, returned again to *Rome*, and was ſoon after Crucified. In the middle of this Chappel are ſeen the Prints of our Saviour's feet in a white marble ſtone, with an iron grate over them. *Domine quo vadis?*

Entring into the Town by S. *Sebaſtian*'s gate, I went on ſtreight to the Church of S. *Nereus* and *Achilleus*, of which Church *Baronius* was Cardinal. The bodies of theſe Saints are under the High Altar. Cardinal *Baronius* cauſed this Church to be painted with the Hiſtories of Saints and Martyrs, to excite others to devotion by their Examples. *S. Nereus and Achilleus.*

Almoſt

S.n Sisto.

Almoſt over againſt this Church, ſtands the Church of S. *Siſto* with its Monaſtery made famous by S. *Dominic*, who made it his habitation, and by whom God wrought many Miracles here. It ſtands in a moſt unwholeſom place called anciently the *Piſcina Publica*, becauſe the People uſe to waſh themſelves here. Here are buried S. *Sixtus*, *Lucius*, *Lucianus*, *Sotberus*, and *Zepherinus*, Popes and Martyrs.

Here's a fine Picture of St. *Vincentius Ferrerius*.

St. John Ante Porsam Latinam.

From thence I went towards the *Porta Latina*, and there ſaw the Church, where St. *John* Evangeliſt was put into a Caldron of boyling Oyl.

St. John Lateran's Church. The Pope's Cathedral

Then following the walls of the Town for a good while, I came at laſt to S. *John Lateran's* Church, the Mother Church of all Churches in the World, and the Pope's Cathedral. In ſaying this I have ſaid enough; and I ſay this after the words which are written in the *architrave* over the Porch of this Church, and after the Bull of *Gregory* the XI. who declared this Church to be the Popes chief ſeat, and to have the preheminency over the other Churches, *Orbis & Urbis*; even over S. *Peter's* Church too by name. It was built by *Conſtantine* the Great upon mount *Cælius*, and dedicated to our Saviour himſelf, for whoſe ſake it deſerveth the headſhip over all the other Churches in the world, as he, to whom it is dedicated, is the head of all the Elect. Yet it is called diverſly by Eccleſiaſtical Authors. Sometimes *Baſilica Conſtantiniana*, becauſe *Conſtantin* built it; ſometimes *Baſilica Salvatoris*, becauſe it was dedicated to our Saviour. Sometimes *Baſilica* St. *Joannis*, becauſe it was near to the two Chappels dedicated

dedicated to the two St. *Johns*, in the Baptistery of *Constantine*: sometimes it was called *Basilica* St. *Joannis* in *Laterano*, or St. *John Lateran*'s Church, because it was built upon the place, where *Plautius Lateranus*, the design'd Consul, had a fair House and a Garden, which *Nero* the Tyrant made bold withal, having first made bold with their Master by killing him. Now this and the other great Churches of *Rome* are called *Basilicæ*, either because they are built after a Royal and stately manner, or else because they are built to the King of Kings.

Tacitus and Juvenal, Sat. 10.

As for this Church of S. *John Lateran*, It is here that the Pope taketh possession of his Papal charge, after he hath been chosen and consecrated Bishop (if he were none before) in S. *Peter*'s Church. For this reason all the chief *Episcopal* functions of the particular *Diocese* of *Rome*, are performed here; as the consecrating of Bishops and Priests, the conferring of the Sacrament of Confirmation; the Baptizing of converted *Jews* and Infidels. For this reason it's looked upon by the Popes with great respect, and hath been not only beautified by them with costly decorations, such as those that *Clement* the VIII. and *Innocent* the X. made; but also favoured by them with great Prerogatives; one declaring by his Papal Decree, that this is the Mother Church of all Churches; another fixing her very Altar it self (of wood) on which St. *Peter* and the primitive Popes had offered Sacrifice; another allowing the Clergy of this Church the Precedency over the Clergy of all other Churches in publick processions, and to carry before them two Crucifixes; another fixing here the Heads of St. *Peter* and St. *Paul*.

A3

As for the things most to be taken notice of here, they are these.

1. The *Soffeta* or roof of this Church most richly gilt.

2. The Body of the Church all made new almost by Pope *Innocent* the Xth, as to the inside of it.

3. The rare painting that runs cross the *Church* from the stately Organs to the Altar of the B. Sacrament, containing the chief actions of *Constantine* the Great, and other Histories. That of the Ascension of our Saviour, with the Apostles looking up after him, is of the hand of *Cavalier Gioseppe*. The Histories and Figures about the Chariot of *Constantin*, are of the hand of *Bellardino*. That of the apparition of our Saviour, that of Mount *Soralte*, that over against *Constantin*'s Baptism, are all of the hand of *Paris Romano*. That of the Baptism of *Constantin*, is of the hand of Cavalier *Ricelli*. In the Quire of the Canons the picture of S. *John* is of the hand of Cavalier *Gioseppe*. In fine, the picture of our Saviour in the very *Tribuno*, or *Abside*, was the first picture that appeared publickly in *Rome*, and which was miraculously conserved in the burning of this Church. There are divers other pictures in that vaulted *Tribune* in *Mosaic* work; and some symbolical figures relating to our Saviour's Life and Passion, which were much used anciently in Churches, as you may see in many other Churches, and in the rare Book called *Roma Sotteranea*.

4. The High Altar here, within which is shut up the wooden Altar, which S. *Peter* and the primitive Popes made use of in saying Mass upon it,

Part II.   *A Voyage through* Italy.   65

it, during the Persecutions, and before they had any setled Churches, S. *Silvester* in the dedication of this Church, fixed it here, and none can say Mass at this Altar, but the Pope, or during the Popes indisposition, some Cardinal, with a particular dispensation, or *Apostolical* Brief which must be fastned to one of the four Pillars of the Altar, during the Cardinal's saying Mass there. Over this Altar stands a great Tabernacle of Marble born up by four Pillars, not only serving for a Canopy to the Altar, but also for an Arca to the Heads of S. *Peter* and St. *Paul*, which are kept within it, and shown there to the People upon great days through an iron grate which environs them. *The Heads of St. Peter and St. Paul.*

5. The Altar of the B. Sacrament adorned by the cost of *Clement* the VIII, with a curious and precious Tabernacle of rich polished stones, and with four pillars of Brass gilt, about fifteen foot high. Over this Altar is the Table it self upon which our Saviour eat the *Paschal Lamb* before his passion, and then presently instituted the Holy Sacrament, of which the *Paschal Lamb* was but a figure.

6. The Brazen Tomb of *Martin* the V. of the House of *Colonna*, who was chosen Pope in the Council of *Constance*.

7. The Tomb of *Alexander* the III, of the House of *Bandinelli* in *Siena*, neatly adorned by Pope *Alexander* the VII, who took his name of *Alexander* from him.

8. The Tomb of *Laurentius Valla*, a learned Roman, and Canon of this Church; of whom, as the restorer of pure *Latine* language after *Gotick* Barbarousness, *Latonius* sung thus:

E e   *Romulus*

Apud Jo- *Romulus est Urbis, Valla est idiomatis author:*
vinu in E.
log. da&or
viror. *Hic reparat primus, primus ut ille struit.*

9. In old *Gotick* Letters upon the *Architrave* of the porch of this Church you read these *Leonine* Verses,

Dogmate Papali datur ac simul Imperiali,
Quod sim Cunctarum Mater & Caput Ecclesiarum.

10. In the *Cloister* of this Church, I saw the Chair of *Porphyry*, which useth to be placed near to the great door of the Church, on that day the Pope taketh possession of his Charge in this Church; in which chair the Pope is placed a while, and at his rising from it again, the *Quire* sings this verse of the 112 Psalm, *Suscitat de pulvere egenum & de stercore erigit pauperem:* and this Ceremony and pierced Chair are only to put the Pope in mind of his human infirmities, amidst His glorious exaltations, and the peoples applauses. For *Caremiale* so also the Greek Emperors on the day of their *Romanum.* Coronation, had a great many marble stones, of *L 1. Sect.* several colours, presented to them, to chuse *2. C. 3.* which of them they would make their Tomb *Zenar and* of. This was to put them in mind of their mor- *Cedren.* tality amidst those great honours.

But it's strange to see how the Enemies of the Popes, give out maliciously, that this Chair (whose use we see so plainly in the very Ceremonial of *Rome*) was only intended *ad explorandum sexum,* and to hinder the inconveniency of another Pope *Joanne.* For this reason I think it not
amiss

Part II. A Voyage Through Italy. 67

amiſs to examine a little this Fable of a ſhe Pope, or of a Pope *Joanne*.

I am not afraid at all to call this a Fable, both for the unlikelineſs of it in general; as alſo for the ſuſpected authority of its firſt broachers; the contrarieties in the ſtory; and the little credit given unto it by the learnedeſt Adverſaries of the *Roman* Church. Firſt, what can be more unlikely than that a Woman ſhould ſurprize ſuch a wiſe nation as the *Italians* are, and ſo groſſy? what more unlikely, than that a woman ſhould paſs her youth in thoſe ſevere ſtudies, which are required in Popes, without being known to have wronged, or diſcovered her Sex; and that ſhe muſt juſt do it, when ſhe was in a declining age, at which age Popes ordinarily are choſen? What more unlikely, than that a woman finding herſelf great with child, ſhould venture to go ſo far a foot in a proceſſion? What more unlikely, than that, if there had been ſuch a ſhe Pope, the Greek Church (which then was at odds with the *Roman* Church) ſhould have paſſed it over in ſilence, and not have upbraided her with ſuch a diſgraceful Paſtor, eſpecially ſeeing the *Roman* Church had upbraided the Greek Church with having an *Eunuch* for her chief *Patriarch*? What in fine more unlikely than that there ſhould have been ſuch a ſhe Pope ſo publickly convinced to have been a woman, and that *Anaſtaſius Bibliothecarius* who wrote the lives of the Popes ſome thirty years after that pretended time, and who muſt have lived in her time, ſpeaks nothing of any ſuch woman, or any ſuch ſtrange accident?

The Fable of Pope Joanne.

Unlikelineſs of this Fable.

Secondly, the firſt broachers of this ſtory make it very much ſuſpected, ſeeing *Martinus Polonus* and

Enemies charge no Proof.

E e 2

68   A Voyage through Italy.   Part II.

and some others of the Emperors faction, (then at variance with the Popes) are the first that mentioned this Fable: and *Platina*, who quotes no higher authors for it, grounds a story of this consequence upon no better authority than a weak, *si dice*, it's said.

Hearsay no conviction.

Thirdly, the apparent contradictions in the Tale, convince it of falsity: as that this *Jone* was an English Woman born in *Mentz*, which all men know to be a Rhenish Town in *Germany*: and that she had studied at *Athens* in *Greece*, which long before this time had been destroyed.

Contradiction in the Tale, a sign of Falsity.

Fourthly, the little credit given to it by the learnedest Adversaries of the Roman Church, to wit, four prime Ministers of *France* (who take this history for a meer fable) proves sufficiently that it's worse than an old wives tale. For Mr. *Blondel* a French Minister, whom I knew in *Paris* above twenty years ago, and a man of that account there, that he was chosen to answer the learned Book of Cardinal *Peron*: this *Blondel*, I say, made a Book in French (Printed at *Amsterdam* by *Bleau*, Anno 1647 in Octavo) on purpose to shew that this story of a she Pope called *Joanne* was a meer fable. And that we may not think that *Blondel* alone of all Protestant Ministers, held this for a fable, Monsieur *Seravius* a great Calvinist and Counsellor of the Parliament of *Paris*, in a Letter of his to *Salmasius*, having mentioned to him this Book of *Blondel*, addeth these words: *Noli autem credere primum aut solum è nostris Blondellum ita sensisse; quamvis fortassis nemo unquam fortius & pressius istud solum calcaverit. Fuere enim in eadem sententia non incelebres inter Reformatos Theologi; & adhuc vigent in hac Urbe insignis fide & pietate viri,*

Adversaries confess it to be a Fable.

Epist. Seravii.

qui

Part II. **A Voyage through** Italy. 69

qui audierunt ex ore Camerii, se istam historiam, vulgò creditam, fabulosis deputare. Vidi nuper scriptas literas docti & vegeti senis, tibique & mihi amicissimi, Petri Molinæi, quibus idem semper sibi esse visum affirmabat.   Chamier.

Penes me sunt literæ *Samuelis Bochartí*, quibus testatur sibi esse pro comperto vanum & fictitium, quicquid hactenus de eâ sit proditum. Thus *Monsieur Seravia* in a private Letter (though his Son after his death printed his Letters) to a friend of the same Religion: And thus you see, how this Fable, maintained highly a long time by the Adversaries of the Roman Church, expired at last (as all lyes do) and was carried to it's Grave upon the shoulders of four *French* Ministers; *Blondel, Chamier, du Moulin,* and *Bochart.* If I have been a little too long in this digression you will pardon me. We are all debtors to Truth; and all Men ought to be glad to see themselves disabused.   Du Moulin. Bochart.

Going out of the little Back-door of this Church, I went to see the Baptistery of *Constantine* the Great, our most noble Country-man, and the first Emperor, that publickly professed Christianity. This Baptistery is built round, and in the center of it in a descent of four steps, stands the very Font, in which the said Emperor was baptiz'd by Pope *Sylvester.* It's environed with low rails of Marble, and adorned with ten or twelve great Pillars of Porphiry (the fairest in *Rome*) which bear up the painted Vault over the Font: So that People standing about these Rails, may see conveniently the Baptizing of Jews and Infidels in the Pit below. Upon the walls of the round Chappel are painted in *Fresco* the most memorable a-   The Baptistery of Constantine.

E e 3   ctions

ctions of *Constantine* the Great: as his vision of the Cross in the Air, with these words above it, *In hoc signo vinces*: his overcoming the Tyrant *Maxentius*: his Baptism here by S. *Silvester*, his burning the Libels against Catholick Bishops, preferred to him by the *Arrians*: his kissing the wounds of those good Bishops in the Council of *Nice*, who had either their fingers cut off, or one Eye put out by the Tyrants.

The Scala Santa. On the other side of St. *John Laterans* Church stands the *Scala Santa*, and the *Sancta Sanctorum*. The *Scala Santa* is called from the Stairs twenty eight in all, up which our Saviour was led in his Passion to *Pilate*'s House. Upon some of them you see the places where the precious Blood of our Saviour had fallen, and for that reason they are covered with little grates of Brass, which let in Eyes, but keep off Knees: I say Knees: for none go up these holy Stairs otherwise than Kneeling, and this out of Reverence to him who often fell upon his Knees as he was drag'd up and down these Stairs. It's painful enough to go up these Stairs upon your knees; yet I saw it done hourly in the Jubile-year, by continual flocks of devout People, both Men and Women; of great Condition as well as of great Devotion. These holy Stairs were sent from *Hierusalem* to *Constantine* the Great, by his Mother Queen *Helen*, together with many other Relics kept in St. *John Lateran*'s Church. They are of white Marble, and above six Foot long.

The Sancta Sanctorum. At the head of these Stairs stands the Chappel called *Sancta Sanctorum*, because of the holy things kept in it. Hence over the Altar in this Chappel, are written these words.

Non

Non est in toto Sanctior Orbe Locus.

Upon the Altar is kept the miraculous Picture of our Saviour, it represents him about thirteen years old, and only his half Body. It's about a Foot and a half long, and its said to have been begun by S. *Luke*, but ended miraculously by an Angel; others says that St. *Luke* having only prepared the ground, and before he had drawn one stroke, fell to his Prayers to beg of God that he might draw his Son right, and rising up again he found his Picture already finished. Hence *Domenico Magri* (a learned *Antiquary*) is of opinion, that this Picture of our Saviour is that very Picture which *Anastasius Bibliothecarius* in the life of *Stephen* the II, calls *Achyropœta*, that is, made without hands. Round about this Picture goes a set of great Jewels, enriching the frame of it. Under the Altar reposeth the Body of St. *Anastasius*, of whose head and Picture I spoke above in the Description of the Church of this Saint at the *Tre Fontane*. Here are also kept the Heads of St. *Agnes*, and St. *Praxedes*, with many other precious Relicks. Anciently, (as the Records here mention) the Holy Prepuce, or fore-skin of our Saviour was kept here too: but being taken away in the Sack of *Rome* by one of *Bourbon's* Soldiers, it was left in a Country Town called *Calcata*, some fifteen Miles distant from *Rome*, by the same Soldier, who could not rest day nor night, as long as he had that Relick about him. I once passed by that Town *Calcata* by chance, and by the civilities of the Lord of the Town, Count of *Anguillara*, at whose House we were nobly entertain'd

See Panchirola.

Lib Della Nomia de Vocaboli Ecclesiastici in verbo Achyropœta.

Calcata: Menochio Centuria 1. & 10.

entertain'd all night, had the happiness the next Morning, to see this precious Relic through the Chryſtal Caſe, this Count keeps one Key of it, and the Pariſh Prieſt the other, without both which it cannot be ſeen.

Triclinium Leonis. Near to the *Scala Santa* is ſeen a famous piece of Antiquity of Chriſtian *Rome*, called *Triclinium Leonis*: where is ſeen a Moſaic Picture of our Saviour reſuſciated, and holding out a Book to his Diſciples, in which are written theſe words, *Pax vobis*, Peace be to you; which Picture *Leo* cauſed to be made eight hundred years ago, as an Emblem of his peaceable return again to his Seat, after he had been chaſed out by his Enemies. Upon a Pillar on the Right-hand is painted our Saviour ſitting upon a Throne, and giving with one hand the Keys of the Church to St. *Peter*, and with the other, the Imperial Standard to *Conſtantine* the great. Upon the other Pillar on the left hand, is repreſented in Moſaïc work alſo, St. *Peter* ſitting in a Chair, and with one hand giving unto Pope *Leo* the III, the Papal ſtole; and with the other the imperial ſtandard unto *Charlemagne*, who had reſtored this Pope *Leo* to his Seat again.

From hence paſſing again by St. *John Lateran*'s Church, I ſaw firſt the Palace of the Pope here, built by the *Sextus quintus*: then the great *Guglia* (with *Egyptian Hirogliphes* figur'd upon it) which had ſtood anciently in the *Circus Maximus*: it's above a hundred foot high, and was brought from *Alexandria* to *Rome*, by *Conſtantine* the great. Laſtly in a low Room joyning to the Church, I ſaw the Statue in *Bronze* of *Henry* the IV. of *France*, ſet up here by the Canons of St. *John Laterans*, for having cauſed ten thouſand Crowns

Part II. A voyage through Italy. 73

a year to be restor'd to this Church, which was
due to it in *France*.

I looked also into the fair Hospital which stands *The Hospi-*
hard by the foresaid Church, and so well serv'd *tal of St.*
and tended, that many persons of quality in their *terans.*
sickness desire to be transferred hither, that they
may be better looked to, than they can be at
home. Taking the Wall of the old *Aquiduct* of
Claudius along with me. I went to *San Stefano* *St. Stefa-*
Rotondo, standing upon the Mount *Cælius* too. This *no Roton-*
Church now belongs to the *Seminarists* of the *Ger-* *do.*
man College. Upon the round Walls are painted
curiously the Martyrdoms of ancient Martyrs;
with the divers Instruments of the Heathens,
wherewith they tormented the poor Christians.

Over against this Church stands the Church of *St. Maria*
Santa Maria della Navicella, so called from a lit- *in Navi-*
tle stone Ship which stands before it, being a vow *cella.*
of certain Boatmen. This Church in ancient Authors is called *in Dominica*, or *in Ciriaca*, because
of a Holy Woman called *Ciriaca*, in whose
house here St. *Lawrence* distributed all the Church
goods, he, as Deacon, had in his hands, unto the
Poor.

Hard by stands the *Villa* of the Duke *Matthei*, *Villa Mat-*
where I saw the *Neat-house* full of curious Statues, *thei.*
and crusted on the outside with rare *anticaglie*.
Among the rest I took particular notice of the
heads of *Brutus* and *Porcia*, Man and Wife in
one Stone: the Statues of *Cleopatra*: of *Hercu-*
les: of three little Boys sleeping and hugging one
another: the Head of *Cicero* rarely well cut: the
Statue of *Marcus Aurelius*, a rare table of precious Stones. In another House here (looking towards *San Sisto*) I saw the incomparable Satue of
Andromeda,

Andromeda, exposed to the Sea-Monster, it's of pure white Marble, and of the Hand of *Oliviero*; that other there of *Apollo* fleaing *Marsias*, is an excellent piece too, and in white Marble: so is also that of the Satyr plucking a Thorn out of his Foot. The curious Alley, Water-works, Grots, Walks, Wetting-places, and the intricate Labyrinth, are all very delightsom.

The Amphitheater. Descending from hence I went to the old Amphitheater, called now the *Coliseo*, because of a Colossean statue that stood in it. This is one of the rarest pieces of antiquity in *Rome*; and though *Rome* be grown again, by her new Palaces, one of the finest Cities of *Europe*, yet her very ruins are finer than her new buildings. And though I am not ignorant how *Rome*, since her Ladyship govern'd the World, and was at her greatness, hath been six several times ruined, and sacked, by the envy and avarice of Barbarous Nations, *Rome sacked six times.* (*Visegoths, Wandals, Erules, Ostrogoths, Totila* who set fire on *Rome* 18 days together, and the *Germans* under *Bourbon*) whose malice was so *Vasari in præfa.* great against *Rome*, that of thirty six Triumphal Arches once in *Rome*, there remain but four now visibly appearing; that of ten *Therma* anciently, but two remain any way visible; that of seven *Circus*, but one now appears: yet as of fair Ladies, there remain even in their old age, fair rests of comliness: so the very ruines of *Rome*, which malice could not reach to, nor avarice carry away, are yet so comely, that they ravish still the beholders eye with their Beauties, and make good the saying of an ancient Author, that *Roma* *Pliny.* *jacens quoque miraculo est: Rome is a miracle even in its ruines.* But to return to the *Coliseo*; it's another wonder

Part II. A Voyage through Italy. 75

wonder of the world: and I wonder indeed, how such prodigious stones could either be laid together in a building, or being laid together, could fall. *Vespasian* began it, but *Domitian* finished it; and *Martial* flattered it as a wonder which outstript all the wonders of *Egypt* and its *Pyramids*.

Omnis Cæsareo cedet Labor Amphitheatro, unum præcunctis famaloquatur opus.

It was of a prodigious height, as that part of it yet standing sheweth. The form of it was round without, and oval within, and the outside of it was adorned with the three orders, of pillars, great arches below, open galleries above, both to walk in, and to let People into the *Amphitheater*, and out again without crowding, so that two hundred thousand people could go in or out in half an hours time, without crowding. Within, it went up from below by steps of stone unto the top, and afforded room enough to all that world of people to sit conveniently, and see the combats and sports that were exhibited in the *Arena*. Anciently the top of it was set round with statues, and in time of great heats or rains, it was all overspread with great sails. From its roundish form it got the name of *Amphitheater*, from seeing on all sides. Underneath were the Caves for the wild beasts, out of which they turned them loose to fight, sometimes against condemned men, sometimes against innocent Christians. *Nero* made the Christians be clad in the skins of Beasts; and so to be exposed to Lyons and Bears. Sometimes also Gladiators fought against Gladiators; and one Gladiator against twenty others: Nay, the very noble *Romans* themselves would now and then fight here publickly, either to shew sport or valour. And all this was done by the politick *Romans*, to teach Men not to be afraid of bloodshed and death in time of wars,

wars, with which they had been so acquainted in time of peace.

Meta Sudans. The old round rubbage of Brick, which is here near the *Amphitheater*, was anciently a fine Fountain called *Meta Sudans*, serving for the use of those that came to the sports here. It was all faced with Marble, and had a Statue of *Jupiter* of brass upon it.

The Triumphal Arch of Constantine the Great. Hard by stands the Triumphal Arch of *Constantine* the great. It's all of Marble, with a world of curious Statues anciently, but now headless, and with histories in *bassi rilievi*. It was erected to him in memory of his Victory over the Tyrant *Maxentius*, as to the freer of the City, and Founder of publick quiet. As the words here import, *Liberatori Urbis, Fundatori Quietis.*

St. Gregories Church. From hence I went to the Church of St. *John* and *Paul*; and thence to St. *Gregories* Church, which anciently had been his house. They shew us yet the Place and the Table where this Holy Man, In recompence of his charitable hospitality to the poor, deserved to have an Angel, and the Lord of Angels for his Guests, he treated daily here twelve poor Men in honour of the twelve Apostles. In one of the Chappels, you see a fine Statue of white Marble, of S. *Gregory* in his Pontifical Robes; it was erected to his honour by Cardinal *Baronius*, who was a devout admirer of him.

In the Garden belonging to the Monastery of St. *Gregory*, there is to be seen a Cave in which I saw upon the wall some old painting of the highest times of *Pagan Rome*: Pitiful stuff, yet considerable for its ancientness.

From

Part II. **A voyage through** Italy.

From hence I went to the *Baths* or *Thermæ*, of Antonius the Emperor *Antonius*, looking more like a Town, his Baths. than a bathing-place. Indeed *Ammianus Marcellinus* out-throws me, and calls these, and the other *Thermæ* in *Rome*, *Lavacra in modum Provinciarum exstructa*: Bathing-places built like Provinces. And judge whether of us hath more reason, by that which we read in the *Exceptis Olympiodori*, where it's said, that these baths of *Antonius* had a thousand six hundred seats of polished marble; for as many persons to sit and bathe in a-part: nay, some of those bathing-places were paved with silver, and were adorned so curiously with silver pipes for the water, with Statues, Pictures, and precious Stones, that *Seneca* cries out; *Eo deliciarum venimus, ut nisi gemmas calcare nolumus*; We are come to that delicacy that we scorn to tread upon any thing but Jewels: Now these Baths serve only for the *Roman* Seminarists to recreate in.

Returning from hence between the Mount *Aventin*, and the Mount *Palatin*, I saw the place where the *Circus Maximus* stood. This was the *Circus* greatest of all the *Circus* in *Rome*, as its name Maximus. shews. It was begun by *Tarquinius Priscus*, but afterwards much augmented by *Julius Cæsar* and *Augustus*. It was three stades long, and four acres wide (the *Roman* stade was 625 foot, or 125 paces) at last it was adorned with statues and pillars by *Trajan* and *Heliogabalus*. A hundred and fifty thousand men could sit conveniently in the three open Galleries; one of which was for the Senators, the second for the Gentlemen, and the third for the common People. The two great *Obelicks*, to wit, that before *Porta del Populo*, and that before S. *John*

John Laterans stood in it. Under this building were many vaulted Caves, called in Latin *Fornices*, where lewd women prostituted themselves for mony, and so from these *Fornices* came the word *Fornication*.

The Emperors Palace. Going from hence to S. *Georges* Church, I saw on my right hand, the goodly ruins of the Emperors Palace, called *Palazzo Maggiore*. It possessed almost all the *Palatin* hill, as the ruins shew. Stately ruins I confess: but ruins, and imperial ruins. And here I could not but wonder to see the Palace of the persecuting Emperors ruined quite, and the Church of the poor Fisherman standing still, more glorious than ever.

Templum Fani. Before I came to S. *Georges* Church, I stept into S. *Anastasius* Church, which was anciently the Temple of *Neptune*; and from thence to the old square Temple, commonly held to be the Temple of *Janus Quadriforis*: and with some reason, because it hath four doors in it, and twelve Niches upon every side of the square out-side. The four doors represented the four Seasons of the year; the twelve niches, the twelve months of the year; yet others will have it to have been only an Arch, or Portic, or a Lodge; and while they dispute it, I'll go on to S. *Georges* Church; hard by to which Church is joyned an old Arch curiously carved in marble, which was erected here, by the Merchants or Goldsmiths, to the Emperors *Severus*, and *M. Aurelius*.

St. Georges Church.

The Velabrum. Near unto this Church of S. *George* came anciently the Water of *Tyber*; and this water or creek of the River was called *Velabrum*; because men passed over the River here by Boat, and sometime with a little sail, when the wind stood fair.

From

From hence I went to the round Church of *S. Theodoro*, standing in the *Foro Boario*. This was anciently the Temple of *Romulus* and *Remus*, because it was here that those two Brothers were exposed, and nourished by a she-wolf, which found them here.

Forum Boarium.

Not far from hence I stept into the Hospital of our Lady of Consolation. This was once the Temple of *Vesta*. And here it was that the Vestal Virgins (instituted by *Numa*) kept the Eternal fire; the extinguishing of which was held by the superstitious heathens, fatal to the state; and therefore they committed the keeping of this fire to Virgins of great repute and honour. These Virgins were to be 10 years in learning their profession, 10 years more in exercising it, and other 10 years more in teaching it to others. And for this reason they had great Priviledges given them. For if in going up and down the City, they met by chance, a criminal man going to be executed, they had power to free him. If any of these Vestals, forgetting her self had wronged her virginity, they would not, out of reverence to her Profession, lay violent hands on her by the common Executioner, but they buried her alive in a low vault made for that purpose.

The Temple of Vesta.

The Vestal Virgins.

See Plutarch in Numa.

From hence I entred into the *Campo Vaccino*, and presently fell upon three Pillars of admirable structure; they belonged to the Temple of *Jupiter Stator* built by *Romulus*; the occasion was this, *Romulus* in a battel against the *Sabins*, seeing his men give back, made a vow presently to *Jupiter*, that if he would stop their flight and make them stand to it, he would build him a Temple; *Siste fœdam fugam*, said he to *Jupiter*; the Men stood, and the Temple was built to *Jupiter Stator*,

The Campo Vaccino.

The Temple of Jupiter Stator.

who

A Voyage through Italy. Part II.

who made Men stand. But this *Jupiter-Stator* could not make his own Temple stand; for it's now so ruin'd, that Antiquaries are scarce sure where it stood.

Close to these three Pillars stands the Church of *Santa Maria Liberatrice* at the foot of the *Palatin* Hill. Why this Church is so called, both a long writing in the Church, and *Baronius* in his Annals, tell at length.

Ad an. 324 Lacus Curtii. ‘ Near to this Church stood the *Lacus Curtii*, a stinking puddle which annoy'd the *Romans* much, and which the Oracle assured was not to be stopt up but by casting into it the most precious thing in *Rome*. Hereupon the Ladies threw in their best Jewels; and the Noblemen every one what he had the most precious, but all in vain. At last *Curtius*, a brave young Nobleman, thinking that there was nothing more pleasant than a gallant Man; mounting on Horse-back in a brave Equipage, in sight of all the People, jump'd into this Lake alive, as a Victim devoted to his Countries Service, and the hole hereupon closed. I confess a brave Cavalier is a precious Jewel indeed: and I remember that a *Roman* Lady having shewed her Jewels to *Cornelia* the Mother of the *Gracchi*, and having desired her to shew also her Jewels, she called for her two young Sons (brave youths) and said, here Madam are my Jewels: and in my opinion, *Curtius* was somewhat Vainglorious, to think himself to be the bravest Man in the City. If the Votes and Judgment of all the People had declar'd him to be so (as they did afterwards declare *Scipio Nasica* to be the best Man of all the *Romans*; and the Matrons declared *Sulpitia* to be the chastest Matron of her time) then he might have devoted himself more freely for his Countries safety.

See Tit. Livius, and others.

The finest jewels.

Going

Part II.   *A Voyage through Italy.*   81

Going on from hence on the Right-hand still, I came to the door of *Farneses* Garden. This *Farnese Garden* stands upon the Mount *Palatin,* where anciently the Emperors had their Palace, which took up all the upper part of this Hill, but not all the Skirts of it; for I find that the Goddess *Feaver,* and the Goddess *Viriplaca* had their Temples here, and *Catalin* and *Cicero* their houses. Entring into this Garden I found some pretty Water-works and grotts at the Entrance, and fine high Walks above, overlooking the place where the *Circus-Maximus* stood anciently. The Scholars of the *English* College in *Rome* have a piece of this hill for their *Vinea* and recreation place, to breath on upon days of *Vacancy.*

The English Vineyard.

Following still my right hand, I came to the Arch of *Titus*: a Triumphal Arch, erected to him upon his victory over the *Jews.* Hence you see here engraven in *Mezzo rilievo* the said Emperor in a Triumphal Chariot, and on the other the Holy Candlestick of the Temple of *Hierusalem,* the Ark of the Alliance, and the Tables of the Law, which this Emperor brought with him after his taking of *Hierusalem,* to grace his Triumph: This is the most ancient Triumphal Arch in *Rome,* and it stood in the *Via Sacra* which went under it.

The Arch of Titus.

Wheeling about the *Campo Vaccino,* still on my right hand, I came to the Church of *Sancta Francesca Romana,* otherwise called *Santa Maria nuova.* Here I saw the neat Tomb of that Saint in Brass gilt, made at the cost of Pope *Innocent* the X. Here's also cut in white Marble, and standing upon an Altar the History of the Pope's returning again to *Rome* from *Avignon.* I saw

The Church of St. Francesca Romana.

F f   also

A Voyage through Italy. Part II.

also here a rare Suit of Hangings belonging to this Church, and given by the Sister of Pope Innocent the X.

The Temple of Peace. Hard by stands the Temple of Peace, that is, some remnants of that Temple. It was once the most noble of all the Temples (as the pillar before St. *Mary Majors* great Door, which belonged to this Temple, sheweth) it was 200 Foot large, and 300 long: but now little signs of its Beauty remain: Wars and time defacing the monuments of Peace. It was built by *Vespasian* who plac'd in it the spoils of the Temple of *Hierusalem*, brought to *Rome* by *Titus*.

Behind this Temple stands a neat Garden, belonging once to Cardinal *Pio*, where I saw neat Water-works. It's now sold to another Master.

The Church of St. Cosmo and Damiano. Going on still in the *Campo Vaccino* on the right hand, I came to the Round Church of St. *Cosmo*, and St. *Damiano*, anciently the Temple of *Castor* and *Pollux*: because the *Romans* having seen two Men upon sweating Horses, that told them news of a Battel won by their Consul, and so vanish'd, they imagin'd them to be *Castor* and *Pollux*, and thereupon decreed them this Temple. The Mosaick work in the roof of the *Tribune* deserves your particular attention, for the Symbolical Figures sake.

St. Lorenzo in Miranda.
Messa in vita M. Aurelii, & Sabellic. lib.4.c.11.
Going on still, I came to the Church of St. *Lorenzo* in *Miranda*. It was once a Temple dedicated to *Faustina* the Empress, by her Husband *Antonius*. Poor Man! he could not make her an honest Woman in her Life-time, and yet he would needs make her a Goddess after her Death. The Porch of this Church is stately still, by reason of its great marble Pillars.

A

Part II. *A Voyage through* Italy. 83

A little further stands the Church of St. *Andriano*, anciently dedicated to *Saturn*, who first taught the *Italians* to make Money, and therefore the *Romans* plac'd their *Ærarium Publicum*, the publick Treasury in this Temple, and had their *Mint* hard by it. *St. Andriano.*

St. *Martinas* Church follows the next; and in a low Chappel neatly adorned, I saw her Tomb; here stood anciently the Temple of *Mars* the Revenger.

Before this Church stands the Triumphal Arch of *Septimius Severus* rarely cut with figures in marble in *mezzo relievo*. Half of it is buried under ground, the other half is sore battered with the air. Who would think the Air and the Earth to be devouring Elements, as well as the Fire and the Water? But why do I accuse the Air, when it's only time (which taketh a pride to triumph our Triumphs) that hath battered this Triumphal Arch, and mouldered even marble? *The Triumphal Arch of Severus.*

A little higher on the Hill-side stands the little Church of St. *Joseph*, where I saw in the low Grot underneath, the Prison called anciently *Tullianum*, into which Prison St. *Peter* and St. *Paul* were shut up. I descended into the low Dungeon where St. *Peter* baptiz'd *Processus* and *Martinianus*, his two Keepers, with divers others. The Fountain of Water that sprung up miraculously for that holy function is still seen there in the bottom of that Dungeon. *St. Joseph. The Tullianum.*

Many other brave buildings stood anciently in this *Foro Romano*, worth remembring, as the *Comitium*, or publick place of Assembly; so called a *Coeundo*, it being the great Hall of Justice, in which was erected a large Tribunal, where the *The Comitium.*

Ff 2 Prætor

Prætor (our Lord Chief Justice) sat in an Ivory Chair, called *Cella Curulia*, and ministred Justice to the People. In this *Comitium* stood the Statue of *Horatius Cocles*; and in the Corners of it, those of *Pythagoras* and *Alcibiades*. In this *Foro* also stood the *Rostra* (a great Pulpit made of the *Rostra* or brazen snouts of the Ships won from the *Antiates*) where Orators used to Plead, and where *Tully* Thunder'd. Behind the *Rostra* stood *Romulus* his Tomb, and before the *Rostra* the Tomb of *Faustus*, the *Foster* Father of *Romulus*.

Mounting up from hence to the Capitol by the Coach-way, I saw upon the side of the Hill, the Pillars that belong'd once to the Temple of *Concord* built by *Camillus*, and not far from hence, three other pillars of neat Fabrick which belonged to the Temple of *Jupiter Tonans*, Thundering *Jupiter*, built there by *Augustus Cæsar*, after he had escaped a Thunder-clap which kill'd his Litter-man close by him.

The Capitol. Arriving at the Capitol, I was glad to see that place so famous in the *Roman* Story. Its name of Capitol came from the Head of a Man (*Caput* in *Latin*) found under ground when they first laid the Foundation here of the Temple of *Jupiter Capitolinus*. *Justus Lypsius*, as if he had been the Godfather of that Man whose Head was found here, saith, that his name was *Tolus*, and that from *Caput Toli* came *Capitolium*. This Head found here portended, that *Rome* should one day be the head of the World. And this title is so universally known to belong to *Rome*, that all Authors affirm it, and every petty Artisan in *Rome* will tell you so: though in false *Latin*, as one did me, when hearing me praise *Rome*, and

Part II. *A Voyage through Italy.* 85

and thinking that I did it not enough, cried out to me half in *Italian*, and half in *Latin*, *Caspitra, Signore, Roma est caput mundi*; which saying made me both smile and say to my self, that such a Head as this Fellows, found now under ground, would portend the ruin of the *Latin* Tongue.

I went first to the highest part of that Hill, called anciently *Rupes Tarpeia*, it looks down upon the Theater of *Marcellus*, and is nothing so high a Hill as I conceiv'd when I first read *Livy*. For I expected to have found here a Hill at least like that in *India* called *Dorin*, which *Curtius* describes, *Munster* paints out, and *Hercules* could not take; but coming to it, I found it to be a Hill of that easie ascent, that I had ridden up higher in *Savoy* and *Swisserland*. *Rupes Tarpeia*.

2. Then returning the same way again to the *Piazza* of the Capitol, I saw there the Famous *Equestris Statua* of *Marcus Aurelius*, once gilt over, but now appearing to be plain Brass. This is the Noblest Statue in the World; and I was going to say, the noblest Statue Living; for it seems almost to Live and Breath by the Workman's Art: It is noble also, because it represents a Man so Noble as *Marcus Aurelius*, who was a double Emperor, being both a great Emperor, and a great Philosopher. *The Equestris Statua of Marcus Aurelius.*

Hard by this *Equestris* Statue are seen two *Colossean* Statues, pouring out two Rivers, the one representing *Nilus*, the other *Tygris*. Over them stands a Statue of *Rome* something like *Pallas*, her Face is of white Marble, her Garments of Porphyry.

3. I saw the Trophies of *Marius* cut anciently in Stone in honour of that great General, who *The Trophies of Marius.*

Ff 3 from

from a common Souldier, came by his Warlike Vertue, to be seven times Consul.

4. I viewed the two great Statues of *Constantine* the Great in white Marble, with the Horses.

The Milliarum.
5. I saw the *Milliarum;* that is, a little pillar of Stone, with a great round Brazen Ball upon it. This Pillar stood anciently in the *Foro Romano* before St. *Adrian's* Church, and it was erected by *Augustus Cæsar*. It was called *Milliarum*, because from it the *Romans* counted the Miles that were from *Rome* to every great City of *Italy*, or of the Empire, and the first Mile distant from this Pillar, was called *primus ab orbe Lapis*; and so of the rest.

The Conservatorio.
6. Then entring into the *Conservatorio*; that is the Palace of the *Conservatori*, or *Senators*, I saw there the Statues of *Julius Cæsar* and *Augustus Cæsar*. Then in the little Court I saw marked up upon the out-wall in a Marble Stone, the *Roman* Measures, as their *Canna, Palmo,* &c. (as we have all measur'd by the Ell, and Yard,) that all Merchants may know where to find whether his Measure be Lawful and Just, or no. Then the Foot, Hand, Thighs and Head, in Marble scattered here and there in this Court, yet all looking as if they had belonged to the great *Colossus* of *Apollo,* made by the command of *Lucullus*. Then the rare Statue of a Lyon tearing a Horse. The Tomb of *Mamea* and *Alexander Severus* her Son, with the Rape of the *Sabines* upon it in a *Basso Relievo*. The little *Egyptian* Idol set high up over this Tomb. The head of the Emperor *Commodus* in Brass, with a hand of the same.

Colonna Rostrata.
7. Hard by the Stair-foot as you mount up to the Chambers, stands the *Colonna Rostrata*, a marble

marble Pillar some twelve foot high, decked with *Stems* of Ships cut in Marble, and sticking out of the Pillar, with an Inscription in the *Basis* below in scurvy old *Latin*. I found it spoke of a Sea-Victory won over the *Carthaginians*, and of *Duillius*; and I car'd for no more, because *Livy* in better *Latin* tells me the rest: to wit, that it was *Dulius* that of all the *Romans* got the first Naval Victory; and then I easily concluded, that this Pillar was erected to him for that Service. It's almost as hard a thing to construe this old *Latin*, as to have won that Victory; and therefore I'le leave the words to *Petrus Cioconius* a flegmatick *Spaniard* to comment upon. Yet I learnt out of this Left-handed *Latin*, this observation, that the brave *Romans* of the highest times, cared more to do well, than to speak well; and that the *Roman* Common-wealth was turned towards her decline, when fine Language was in vogue.

8. Hard by this Pillar stand mounted two little quarter Cannons: a poor *Arsenal* for the *Roman Senators* now a-days.

9. Then mounting up some ten Steps, I came into a little Court, whose Walls are all encrusted over with four excellent pieces of *Marcus Aurelius* his Triumph cut in Marble. In one of them he triumpheth in his open Chariot: in another he Sacrificeth: in another he giveth Largesses to the People: in the fourth he receiveth the Presents of the *Romans*. They are all so well cut, that you doubt whether it be the Emperor or the Sculptors that triumphs here. Indeed the Emperor's Chariot hath got new Wheels of late, and his Horses new Shoos and Feet, else all is old.

M. Aurelius *his Triumph*

10. Then

10. Then going up the Stairs higher, I saw an old Plate of Brass nailed up, in which the *Roman* Laws of the ten Tables were written; good Laws, but few. And I was glad to see them yet kept; if that be to keep Laws, to keep them nailed fast to the Wall.

Leges Decem Tabularum.

11. Then entring into the Chambers and great Hall, I saw the Statues of *Alexander Farnese* Duke of *Parma*, of *M. Antonius Colonna*, the Pope's General in the Battel of *Lepanto*: and of *Don John* of *Austria Generalissimo*. I saw upon the walls painted in *Fresco*, the rape of the *Sabins*, the duel of the *Tergemini Fratres*, three Brothers against three Brothers, *Horatii* against *Curiatii*: *Scevola* holding his hand over the burning Coals: *Cocles* defending the Bridge alone against an Army of Men: *Scipio*, and *Hannibal* with their several Armies, so rarely painted by *Pietro Perugino*, that the *Romans* now are in love with *Hannibal*. Then the Picture of the first *Consul Brutus* commanding the Death of his own Son: that of the *Tarquinii*: that of the conquering of the *Sabines*, &c. All pieces as bold as the very actions they represent. Here also in the other Chambers, I saw some fine Statues, as that of *Caius Marius*; that of *Hercules* in Brass being but yet a Lad; that of *Junius Brutus* in Brass; the heads in Marble of *Diogenes*, *Plato*, *Socrates*: the Statues of *Cicero*, *Virgil*, and *Plato*; the Brazen Statue of the Wolf that gave Suck to *Romulus* and *Remus*. But the best Statue here is that of the young Man picking a Thorn out of his Foot. It's only of Brass, but worth its weight in Gold. The Story of it is this. A young Foot-post bringing Letters of singular Importance unto the Senate, and prick-
ing

ing his Foot as he ran, would not stay to pick out the Thorn; but haftning to *Rome* with all speed, delivered his Letters in full Senate prodigiously soon, as it appeared by their Dates. But then clapping himself down upon the ground before them all, he began to pick out the Thorn, in the posture you see him here. The Senate seeing the haste he had made, and the pain he had endured, decreed prefently, that his Statue in that posture, should be erected in the Capitol.

Thus the old *Romans* not having then recompences enough for well deserving men, or else not willing to recompence them otherwife, perfwaded men, that no recompence was like to that of a statue in the Capitol, or to walk up and down the streets with a Crown of *Laurel*, or *Oaken* Leaves upon their heads. Poor Fools! Was a Crown of leaves such an honour, when even Bawdy-houses and Privies, faith *Tertullian*, were crowned too? Or was it such a solid honour to have a statue in the Capitol, when Geefe and Wolfs were honoured so too? But *quod rarum, charum est*. And as *Alexander* the Great hearing that the *Corinthians* would make him a *Citizen* of their Town, scorned it at first: but after he had been assured that they never offered that honour to any man but to *Hercules* and him, he was well pleased with that offer: so the rarity of having a Statue in the Capitol being an honour granted to few, and those well deserving men, made men think it the highest of recompences. Among those few, were *Scipio*, for having overcome *Antiochus*: *Æmilius Lepidus* for having, while he was but yet a Boy, freed

Tertul. *de Corna Milit.*

Senecal. 1. *de Benefic.*

a *Roman* Citizen in a battel: *Metellus* for saving the *Palladium* out of the burning Temple of *Vesta*: *Cornelia* for having furnished Corn to the People in a dearth, out of her own moneys; and some few others.

Ara Cœli. Having thus seen the Capitol, I went into the Noble Church of *Ara Cœli*, which is joyning to the Capitol upon the same hill, and built in the same place where anciently stood the Temple of *Jupiter Capitolinus*, or *Jupiter Feretrius*. Here it was the *Sybille* shewed unto *Augustus Cæsar*, at the birth of our Saviour, that a greater Lord than he was born; whereupon *Augustus* forbad, that any man should call him Lord from that time forward. In this Church is the Tomb of S. *Helen*, Mother of *Constantin* the Great.

The Jesuits Church. Descending from hence by the marble stairs, which are a hundred in all, and all so large, that twelve men in a breast may go up at once; I came to the *Jesuits* Church and House called the *Casa Professa*. The Church is neat and capacious, the Chappels well painted, and the Ornaments in the Vestry very rich. Under the Altar where S. *Ignatius* his Picture is, lyes the body of that Saint, Founder of the Order of the *Jesuits*. Near the high Altar on the Gospel side is the Tomb of Cardinal *Bellarmin*. In the House of these Fathers I saw the Chamber of St. *Ignatius*, now turned into a Chappel, and a fair Library.

S. Marks Palace. Passing from hence, I stept into a Palace of S. *Mark*, belonging to the State of *Venice*, and the lodging place always of the *Venetian Ambassadors* residing in the Court of *Rome*. This Palace, as also that of the *Cancellaria*, and that of

Farnese,

Farnese, are said to have been built of the stones that were taken from the great *Amphitheater*; and yet a great part of it remains still; and I believe, as much as would make three more such Palaces.

From St. *Marks* Palace I went towards the Mount *Quirinal*, now called *Monte Cavello*, and as I went, passed through that part of the Town, which anciently was called *Forum Trajani*, and there saw that which *Trajan* himself never saw, to wit, the wonderful Pillar of white Marble erected there to *Trajan*, and therefore called *Colonna Trajana*, but never seen by him: For he died in foreign expeditions, returning from *Persia* without ever seeing it. This Pillar is made of four and twenty great stones of Marble, in which are carved the exploits of *Trajan*, especially in his Wars against the *Dacians*. It's a hundred twenty eight foot high, without its *basis*, which is twelve foot high. Within it there are a hundred fourscore and five stairs, which deliver you up to the top of it, and there are forty little Windows, which let in light enough for you to go up. On the top of all this Pillar were anciently buried the ashes of *Trajan* the Emperor: But *Sixtus Quintus* caused, in place of them, the Statue in Brass gilt of St. *Peter* to be set up here. Heretofore all the basis of it was buried under ground in the ruins, but now they have digged about it and cleared it; yet by this we may see how much the streets of *Rome* are higher than they were; *Rome* now being built upon the ruines of *Rome*.

Colonna Trajana.

From hence going up the hill, I came to the Palace and Garden of *Aldobrandini*. The House is

The Palace of Aldobrandini.

is but little, yet neatly furnished with Statues and Pictures. Some whereof are these: An old Picture made in the time of the *Pagans*, representing a Marriage after the old *Romans* fashion. I take this to be the ancientest Picture in *Rome*, and the rarity of it is so great, that *Cavalier Pozzo* (a brave Gentleman, and a great *Virtuoso*) got leave to copy it out, and this copy is to be seen in the house of his Brother, among other rare curiosities, near St. *Andrea della Valle*. Next after this I was shown in the foresaid Palace, the true Picture of *Martin Luther*: A rare St. *Sebastian* in the Chappel, of *Raphael*'s hand: Upon the Stairs a Statue of a Man hanging by the hands, with great stones at his feet, weighing him down: A torment much used by the Heathens, and practised by them upon Christians: With a world of other Pictures and Statues in the Chambers.

The Palace of Mazzarini. From hence I went to Cardinal *Mazzarini*'s Palace, and there saw in the Garden the famous Picture of the *Aurora*, made by *Guido Rheni*, famous over all *Rome*. In the Court of this Palace, I saw the best riding Masters of *Rome* teach young Gentlemen to ride the great Horse: But I found them here far short of the Masters in *France*, both for good Horses, and good Scholars, and graceful riding. In the same Court, in the Sommer Evenings, they play at *Ballon*, a manly exercise much used in *Italy*, and far more gentile than our rude Foot-ball Sport.

The Pope's Stables. Near to this Palace stand the Pope's Stables, where I saw all the Genets that had been presented to the Pope, since his creation, by the King of *Spain* for the Kingdom of *Naples*; every year one, with a Purse of Gold. The other Horses

Horses here were only Coach-Horses; for when the Pope goes any whither abroad upon publick Ceremony, the Cardinals and Prelates upon Mules, and the Noble-Men of *Rome* upon their own Horses, wait upon him: and when he goes out of Town, his own Horse-guards attend him.

From hence I was presently in the *Piazza* of *Montecavallo*, where I saw the two Famous Horses in Marble, with each one a Man holding him; they were sent to *Nero* for a Present by *Tiridates* King of *Armenia*. In the Pedestal of these statues, are written, under the one of them, *Opus Phidiæ*: under the other, *Opus Praxitelis*. It's said that these two Horses and Men were made by these two ancient Sculptors of *Greece*, to represent *Bucephalus*, and *Alexander* the Great. However these Horses give name to this Hill; and whereas it was formerly called *Mons Quirinalis*, it's now called *Montecavallo*. Upon this Hill stood anciently the *Thermæ Constantiniauæ*, or Baths of *Constantin* the great, of which there are seen some remnants in the garden of *Colonne*, which lies behind the wall of this *Piazza*.

Montecavallo.

Over against the foresaid Horses stands the Pope's Palace where he ordinarily lives in Summer. The house is a noble structure, and the rooms stately: but I saw nothing rare in them but themselves. The Garden of this House is curious for fine Walks, store of Fountains, and the cool *Grotta* under great shady Trees, where there are fine Water-works, and an Organ playing without any fingers to touch it. Over against the back-door of this Garden stands the Noviciate of the Jesuits, with the neat new Church, and fine Gardens.

The Pope's Summer Palace.

Returning

S. Sylvester's Church.

Returning from hence, I ſtept into the Church of St. *Sylveſter*, over againſt the Palace of *Mazarina* belonging to the *Theatins* ; and there ſaw the Tomb of Cardinal *Bentivoglio*, the modern *Livy* of *Italy*. The Garden here ſtanding in a fair Proſpect, is very pleaſant and delightſome.

St. Agatha's Church.

Deſcending from hence, by a private Street, I went to St. *Agatha*'s Church in the *Saburra* near the foot of the *Quirinal* hill. The Body of St. *Agatha* lies under the Altar. Before the door of this Church are ſome ancient Statues of ſome little Boys, in the habit of a *Prætexta*, a habit belonging to Noblemens Children.

St. Peter's ad vinculam.

From hence, paſſing by the Church of *Madonna del monte* (a Church of great Devotion) I went up the Hill to St. *Peters ad vincula*; where I ſaw the famous Statue of *Moſes* ſitting. It's of white Marble, and adorning the Tomb of *Julius Secundus*. It's enough to tell you that it was made by *Michael Angelo*, and admir'd by all Sculptors. Here's near unto the door of the Church, an Altar with the Statue of St. *Sebaſtian*, at the erecting of which, the Plague ceaſed in *Rome*, ſaith *Baronius*. In the Sacriſty of this Church I ſaw the Chains in which St. *Peter* was fetter'd in Priſon ; and which make this Church to be called St. *Peter ad vincula*.

Baron. An. 680.

St. Martino in Monte.

St. *Martino in monte* follows next, and is a neat Church now. In a Cave below there were two Councils held by St. *Silveſter* in the primitive times of Perſecution, as the words upon the wall as you deſcend into the Cave, and *Baronius* teſtifie. It's ſaid that in this place was exerciſed the firſt publick Profeſſion of Chriſtian Religion.

Then

Part II. A Voyage through Italy. 95

Then to the Church of St. *Praxedes*, where *St. Prax-*
I saw the Pillar at which our Saviour was *edes.*
whipp'd. It's a low round Pillar of speckled *The Pillar*
Marble. It stands within a little grate of Iron. *at which*
The old writing over the door of that Chappel, *our Savi-*
tells you, that it was brought to *Rome* from *Hieru-* *our was*
salem four Hundred years ago, by Cardinal *Co-* *whipp'd.*
lonna. In the midst of the Church is a Well
(now covered) where St. *Praxedes* hid the Relics
and Bodies of Martyrs. In another Chappel I saw
the Picture of the descent of our Saviour from the
Cross, made by *Guido*. In the Balconies above
in the Pillars, I saw, by special favour, many
curious Relics.

From hence I went to St. *Mary Majors* Church, *Santa Ma-*
so called, because it is the greatest of all the *ria Mag-*
Churches of our Lady in *Rome*. It's built upon *giore.*
the *Monte Esquilino*, and upon the place which
was covered, miraculously with Snow upon the
fifth of *August*. The History of it is known by
the Solemn Feast in the Kalender, called *Sancta
Maria ad Nives*, and it is expressed in the old Mosaick Pictures, which are set here in the Wall
over the Pillars that bear up the roof. The most
remarkable things I saw here were these.

1. The Tomb of the Founder of this Church,
Patritius, whose Body lies in a Tomb of Porphyry near the great door.

2. The noble gilt Roof, or *Soffita*, which
was gilt with the first Gold that came out of
the *Indies* in *Alexander* the VIths time, whose
Arms are set up in this Roof.

3. The Mosaick Pictures which run along this
Church, containing the History of the old and new
Testament,

Testament, and the History of the building of this Church.

4. The high Altar under which reposeth the Body of St. *Mathias* the Apostle, whose Head is exposed upon the Altar in a Chrystal upon his day.

5. The Tomb of an Embassador of *Congo* to *Paulus* V. It's over against the Statue in Brass, of *Paulus* V. near the Sacristy.

6. The little back Court there, with the Eccho in the Well, which answers you indeed, but like a sharp Scold, too quick and short.

The Chappel of Sixtus V.
7. The rare Chappel of *Sixtus* V. made by *Dominico Fontana*, which cost Seven Hundred Thousand Crowns. The most famous Actions of *Sixtus Quintus*, and of *Pius Quintus*, who made *Sixtus* Cardinal, are carved in white Marble round about the Chappel. St. *Hierom's* ashes

St. Hierom's Tomb.
are buried here in a side Altar on the left hand: and where should we look for St. *Hierome*, but

The Holy Crib of our Saviour.
near our Saviour's Crib? which is here enchased in Chrystal in a low Chappel, under the high Altar of this Chappel. It's shewn publickly upon *Christmas* day. The Tabernacle of Brass, held up by four Angels of Brass with one hand, and holding each one a Torch in the other hand, is most Stately.

The Chappel of Paulus V.
8. Over against this Chappel stands the Chappel of *Paulus* V. much like the other in all things, except that the chief Altar stands not in the middle, but at the end of it. This Altar is a very neat contrivance, and of as rich materials. Four great Pillars of Jasper pollish'd, adorned with Capitels and Bases of Brass gilt, hold up the back of this Altar, which is all of *Lapis Lazuli*,

or

Part II. ⟨...⟩ Italy.   97

or Oriental blue Azure Stone; in the midst of which is a little *Nichio* in the Wall, where the Picture of our Blessed Lady, with our Saviour in her Arms, made by St. *Luke*, is conserv'd and seen. This *Nichio* is surrounded with a row of rich precious Stones of great value, set thick about it; and shut up with two little half-doors, of two whole Agates, each of them two foot long, and a Foot large. *Theodorus Lector* an ancient Author makes mention of this Picture, and saith, *Pulcheriæ, Eudocia Imaginem matris Christi, quam Lucas Apostolus pinxerat, Hierosolymis misit*; That is, *Eudocia* sent unto *Pulcheria* from *Hierusalem* the Picture of the Mother of Christ which *Luke* the Apostle had painted. The Picture it self is so old, and plac'd so high, that it's hard to perceive the lineaments of the Face, unless you see it with a wax Taper at the end of a long Pole, as I did. In fine, this was the Picture which St. *Gregory* the Great, a Thousand years ago, carried in Procession upon *Easter* day, when he saw over the *Moles Adriani*, an Angel sheathing his Sword in sign of the ceasing of the Plague. The roof of little *Cupola* of this Chappel is painted by the hand of *Guido Rheni* of *Bologna*. The side Walls of this Chappel are of white Marble cut in *Mezzo relievo*, and containing the chief actions of *Clement* VIII. and *Pius* V. whose statues are also here in white Marble.

A Picture of our B. Lady, made by St. Luke.

Theodor. Lector in initio collectaneorum.

9. Without the Church stand two great Pillars at each end of it: the one an *Egyptian Guglia* cut with Hieroglyphics; the other a *Roman* Pillar taken out of the Ruins of the Temple of Peace, which is of a prodigious height, with the Statue

G g

of our Saviour and our Lady upon it, in Brass gilt.

SS. Vito & Modesto. The Arch of Galienus.

From St. *Mary Majors* I went to the Church of St. *Vito* and *Modesto*. It's built near the ruins of the Triumphal-arch of *Galienus* the Emperor. The great Keys that are nailed to the top of that foresaid Arch, were the Keys of the City *Tusculum* (now called *Frescate*) and hung up here in memory of a Victory won over that Town, under *Honorius* the V. almost five hundred years ago.

S. Eusebio.

From hence I went to the Church of St. *Eusebio*, built upon the ruins of the *Thermæ* of the Emperor *Gordiano*, and his Palace, whose Court had Fifty Pillars on every side. Near unto this Church were found the Trophies of *Marius*, which I spoke of above in the Capitol.

Santa Croce in Hierusalem.

Continuing on my way, I came at last to *Santa Croce* in *Jerusalem*. It's one of the seven Churches of *Rome*, and built by the Emperor. *Constantine* the great. It stands near the Walls of the Town in the end of the Mount *Cælius*. Hard by it appear some Prints of the Temple of *Venus* and *Cupid*, which the said Emperor ruined, to build a Church in the place of them, in honour of the Holy Cross, and so repair the injury which the Infidels had done to the Holy Cross in *Hierusalem*, by placing the Statue of *Venus* upon Mount *Calvary*, and striving to blot out the name of *Mont Calvarie*, and bring in that of *Mons Venerie*. This Church is called *Santa Croce* in *Hierusalem*, because of the Earth of *Mount Calvarie*, which was brought from *Hierusalem*, and laid here. The things I observed here, were these.

See Baronius in his Anna's.

1. The Painting in the Tribune, or roof of the Choir, containing the history of the Exaltation of the

the Holy Cross. It looks like the Painting of *Pietro Perugino*, or some of his Scholars; and it was thought fine work, before *Raphael* raised Painting to a greater height.

2. The Chappel below, where the Holy Earth sent by St. *Helen* from *Hierusalem*, to her Son *Constantin* the Emperor, was put.

3. The Relics in the Sacristy above, to wit, three pieces of the Holy Cross, one of the Nails of the Cross of our Saviour; two Thorns of the Holy Crown of Thorns; a great piece of the Title of the Holy Cross; a finger of St. *Thomas* the Apostle; and one of the thirty pieces of Money for which our Saviour was sold.

Not far from hence stands the Church of *Santa Bibiana*. This Church stands in the place called anciently *Ursa Pileata*, because of the Statue of a Bear with a Hat on, which stood there. This place is also famous for the Church-yards sake, or *Cæmeterium*, called *inter duas lauros*. Here is some good Painting in this Church of *Campelli* and *Pietro Cortonese*. The Statue of the Saint is of *Bernini*'s hand.

From hence I found a way that led me to the Gate of St. *Laurence*, through which I went to the Church of that Saint called *San Laurenzo furori delle mura*, by reason of divers others built in honour of that Saint within the Walls. This Church was built by *Constantine* 100, and enriched by him, with many Presents and Ornaments. It was built upon the *Cæmeterium Sanctæ Ciriacæ*, where that Holy Woman used to bury the Bodies of the Holy Martyrs. It stands in the *Via Tiburtina*, and is one of the seven Churches of *Rome*; and one of the five *Patriarchal Churches*,

A Voyage through Italy. Part II.

and therefore is not titular of any Cardinal. The things that I saw here, were these.

1. The Tomb of St. *Laurence,* under the high Altar.

2. Behind the high Altar, the Stone upon which the Gridiron stood, upon which St. *Laurence* was broiled. It's covered with a great glass through which you see it.

3. In the roof of this Church I found these words cut in great Letters of wood, *Quam clarificata est Hierosolyma Stephano, tam illustris facta est Roma Laurentio,* taken out of S. *Leo* in his Sermon upon the Feast of S. *Laurence.*

4. The Catacombes under this Church, where many Saints Bodies were buried anciently.

S. Antonio Returning again into the Town, I stept into St. *Antonies* Church and Hospital, near to St. *Mary Majors*; before which Church stands a Pillar with a Cross upon it, erected here upon the conversion of *Henry* the IV. of *France.*

S. Pudentiana. Passing behind St. *Mary Majors,* I went to Santa *Pudentianas* Church, standing in the ancient street called *Vicus Patricius.* This Church was built upon the place where the house of *Pudens* a Senator and Father of St. *Pudentiana* lived. And here it was that St. *Peter,* at his first coming to *Rome* lodged, having Converted this *Pudens* and his two Daughters, *Pudentiana* and *Praxedes.*

Baronius *ad an. 44.* Here I saw these things.

1. The dry Well into which St. *Pudentiana* put many Relics of Martyrs to conserve them. I looked into it with a lighted Taper let down in a string; and saw many curious Relics desked up in the side of the wall.

2. The

Part II. *A voyage through* Italy.

2. The wooden Altar upon which St. *Peter* said Mass at his being here.

3. The two Marble Statues of our Saviour and St. *Peter*. They are both excellently well cut, and perchance by rare *Olivieri*.

4. The neat Chappel of the *Caetani*, with the back of the Altar in white Marble, curiously cut by *Olivieri* in a *basso rilievo*, representing the adoration of the *Magi*.

Near the high Altar, is the Picture of the forementioned Senator *Pudens*, in his Senators Robes.

From hence I went to St. *Lorenzo* in *Panisper-na*. Here it was that St. *Laurence* was broiled upon a Gridiron, by the command of the Emperor *Decius*, whose Palace stood where this Church now stands. Upon the wall of this Church is painted the Martyrdom of St. *Laurence* in *Fresco*. Here lie buried the Bodies of St. *Bridget* a Holy Virgin of *Scotland*; and of the Cardinal *Sirletus*. *St. Laurenzo in Panisperna.*

Going from hence by a little unfrequented street, running under the foot of *Montecavallo*, I came to the Church of St. *Vitalis*, which stands joined to the Garden of the Jesuits *Novitiat*. It's said, that the Temple of *Quirinus* or *Romulus* stood here, and that it was here that *Proculus* swore he saw *Romulus* after his death, who bid him go tell the *Romans*, that he would be adored by them under the name of *Quirinus*: When indeed it was thought that the Senators had torn him in pieces in the Senate-House, and carried away under their Gowns, every one a piece of him; and finding the People to mutter much at his not appearing, had got this *Proculus* to depose *S. Vitalis. See Plutarch.*

Gg3

as above; and so quieted the People, who are as easily pacified again with a vain tale, as stirred up with a fond rumour.

Quatro Fontane. From hence I went to the *Quatro Fontane*, which stand at the head of four streets which meet here. These Fountains issue out from four Statues which lie here in cumbent postures; and they were made here by *Lepidus*.

Santa Maria della Vittoria. Then following that fair street, I went to *Santa Maria della Vittoria*, so called from the Victory won at the Battel of *Prague*. The Flags and Cornets taken in this Battel, are set round about the Church. In one of the Flags over the door, I found Cross Keys, Cardinals Caps, Miters and Priests corner'd Caps, all turned topsy turvy, with this single motto, *Extirpentur*. Here are very neat Chappels, especially that on the left hand, where is seen the representation of S. *Teresa* wounded by a *Seraphin*. It's an admirable piece of *Bernini*. In the Convent you see painted in a *Sala*, the Battel of *Prague*, and in the Sacristy, a Sepulcher of our Saviour all of Ivory, extraordinarily well wrought.

Before the door of the aforesaid Church, stands the great Fountain, called *Fontana felice,* where the Aqueduct of *Sixtus Quintus* (who before his assumption to Ecclesiastical Dignities, was called in his Monastery *Fra Felice*) disburdeneth it self into a great stone Basin, and from thence is carried into divers parts of the Town.

The Garden of Montalto. From hence I went to the garden of *Montalto*, which is hard by. This is one of the best gardens in *Rome*, and therefore deserves well to be seen.

At your entrance into it, you see a round table of a blewish stone, upon which the Arms of the House

House of *Montalto* are engraven, at which, while you gaze curiously and near at hand, the Gardiner, by pressing his foot upon a low Iron Pump, under the Table, presseth out water on all sides of that round Table, and welcometh the strangers that come to see his Garden.

Then mounting into the little Palace near the door, I saw divers good Pictures and Statues, of the House of *Montalto*, and others. There also I saw a wooden Organ, Pipes and all, and yet of no ungrateful sound.

There also I saw the Picture of *David* killing *Goliath*: It turns upon a frame, and shews you both the fore-side of those combatants, and their backsides too, which other Pictures do not. Here are curious Urns; the true *Busto* of *Sixtus V.* a Tabernacle of rich stones. There is a Picture in stones of several colours, which held one way, represents nothing but a bunch of Herbs; but held up another way, it represents a Mans head and face. In fine, here is in this little Palace, a neat Library in a cool room, over the door of which, on the inside, are written these words *Medicina animi*; as if Libraries were nothing but Physick-gardens for the mind.

Descending again into the Garden, I saw store of wetting-sports, and water-works, most curiously contrived, and most stately walks. From hence we went to the *Carthusians* Church, which is hard by. This Church and Monastery are built upon the Ruins of the Baths of *Diocletian*. For this cruel Emperor with his associate *Maximian*, condemned Forty Thousand Christians to work in this Building, for the space of fifteen years together, and afterwards condemned many Thousands

The Baths of Diocletian.

Thousands of them to death for their Religion, Thus Men work for Tyrants. But such is the wonderful providence of God, Churches of Christians now stand where Christians were condemned to death and torments. The Blood of these Martyrs was but the seed of Christians, and when *Diocletian* condemned Christians to work here, methinks he did but bid them go lay the foundation of a Monastery for *Carthusians*, and of a Church for the worship of that God he so much persecuted.

The Pope's Granaries. Having seen this Church and Monastery, I went to see the Pope's Granaries, vast buildings, two stories high, and always full of Wheat for the present use of the whole City. A world of Officers and Overseers belong to these *Granaries*, and are always turning over, and keeping the vast heaps of Wheat from spoiling and corrupting. By sticking up Canes in the heaps of Wheat, they can tell, smelling at the end of these Canes, whether the Wheat begin to moisten and corrupt, or no, and accordingly give order either to turn it and air it, or presently to give it out to the Bakers: These *Granaries* were also built upon the ruins of *Diocletians* Baths.

The Church of St. Agnes. From these *Granaries* I went to the Town Gate not far off, called *Porta Pia*, and from thence streight along for a good mile, to St. *Agneses* Church. Under the high Altar reposeth the body of that tender Virgin, who being as innocent as her name, suffered Martyrdom at thirteen, and triumphed over the World before she could know it.

Close by stands the Church of S. *Constantia*, another holy primitive Virgin. Here I saw the
Famous

Part II. 105

Famous Tomb, commonly called *Bacchus* his Tomb, but falsely, seeing it was the Tomb of S. *Constantia*. It's a vast *area*, or Chest of one Porphyry stone, above half a Foot thick, and six Foot long. It's all cut on the outside with a *basso rilievo* in a most admirable manner.

From hence crossing over the Fields, I went to *Burghesi*: *Villa* and garden, which are a little half mile from the Town. This is the greatest *Villa* that's about *Rome*. For here you have store of walks, both open and close, Fish-ponds, vast Cages for Birds, thickets of Trees, store of Fountains, a Park of Deer, a world of Fruit-trees, Statues of all sizes, Banquetting places, *Grotta*'s, Wetting-sports, and a stately Palace adorned with so many rare Statues and Pictures, that their Names make a Book in *Octavo*, which I refer you to. As for the Palace it self, it's compassed on both sides, by a fair semi-circle of Statues, which stand before the two doors, like old *Penates* and *Lares*. The Wall of the House is overcrusted with a world of *Anticallio*, or old Marble-pieces of Antiquity: As that of *Curtius* spurring into the *Vorago*: That of *Europa* hurried away by *Jupiter*, become a Bull, with a world of such like Fables. Entring into the house, I saw divers Rooms full of Curiolities.

In the great Hall stands the Statue of *Diana* in Oriental Alabaster, which was once a Deity adored by *Augustus Cæsar*. Here also hang two great Pictures, the one representing a *Cavalcata* when the Pope goeth abroad in Ceremony; the other a *Cavalcata*, when the great *Turk* goeth abroad in Pomp.

Bur-ghesi illa.

2. In another Room stands the Statue of one of the famous Gladiators anciently, who fought alone against twenty others, and being wounded to death, seems to threaten with his looks all his Beholders. It's terribly well made.

3. In one of the Chambers above, is the head, in *Profile*, of *Alexander* the great, cut in Marble.

4. In another Room below I saw the Statue of *Seneca* bleeding to death. It's of a black stone like Jeat, than which nothing can be blacker but the crimes of *Nero* the *Magistricide*, who put this rare man, his Master, to death.

5. The Statue also of *Daphne* and *Apollo* in Alabaster; *Apollo* running after *Daphne*; and she stiffening into a Tree, being overtaken, her Fingers shooting into Branches, and her Toes into Roots, are admirably well done. It must be *Bernini's* work.

6. The Statue also of *Æneas* carrying his old Father *Anchises* upon his Back, out of burning *Troy*. The young Man is brawny and strong; the old man is made lean and weak: As also the young man shews a great deal of tender affection towards his Father, and the Father as much fear in his looks.

7. The Statue also of *David* slinging at *Goliah*. He frowns so terribly as he slings, that you would swear he intends to fright him with his looks, and then kill him with his sling. These two last Statues are also of the hand of *Cavalier Bernini*.

8. In another Chamber above, I saw the great Chair which locketh fast any Man that sitteth down in it. It's said to be a Chair of Revenge, or a Trap-chair for an Enemy: But methinks it would

Part II. A Voyage through Italy.

would be a fine Chair for a restless Student; or a Gossiping Wife.

I saw here also some toys for young men; as the Clock, which being wound up, playeth a tuneable Dance, and little Men and Women of Iron painted handsomely, dance in a-ring to that tune, by vertue of the Wheels. The Fools Paradise representing first a fine green Garden of Flowers, then a Palace, and lastly a neat Library, is made also to recreate Children.

Returning from this *Villa* by the back door which leadeth to the *Porta del Populo*, I stept into the Church of *Madonna del Populo*. This Church hath been much beautified of late by Pope *Alexander* the VII. because of some of his Ancestors buried here. Here I saw the famous statue of *Jonas*, made by the command of *Raphael Urbin*, who shewed the Sculptors of his time how perfectly he possessed the Theory of Sculpture, if he would but have dirtied his Fingers with that dirty Art. In a Chappel near the Gospel side of the high Altar, I saw a good Picture of the hand of *Guido Rheni*. Where now the high Altar stands, stood anciently the Tomb of *Nero*. *Madonna del Populo.*

Going on from hence on the left hand, towards the *Piazza di Spagna*, I first passed by the great *Guglia*, or *Egyptian Pyramid*, carved all over with Hieroglyphs. It's looked upon by three streets, and seen afar off. Then passing a little further, I came to the *Greek* Church and College, where upon certain days, I saw their Ceremonies, and heard the Mass sung in Greek, after the Greek manner. These *Grecians* are in union with the *Roman Church*; and have a Seminary of young Students *The Greek College.*

108 A **Voyage through** Italy. Part II.

Students of their Country, maintained by the Pope to return to their Country in Miſſion.

Mounting from hence on the left hand to the top of the Hill, by the Coach way, I went into the *Villa* of the great Duke, where I ſaw the neat Gardens with Fountains, two or three huge Veſſels of Marble, and ſtore of Statues, both in the Palace, and in the long Gallery. That of the two Gladiators wreſtling: That of the Clown whetting his Sithe, and hearing the Conſpirators of *Cataline* ſpeaking of their Conſpiracy, which he diſcovered, is one of the beſt pieces of Sculpture in *Rome*. That of *Cupid* and *Venus* are admirable. From the Chamber-window of this Palace, you have a perfect ſight of *Rome* under you. In the Garden there is a little *Guglia*, with many other Curioſities.

The Villa of the great Duke.

Going out from this Garden, by the back door, I croſſed over the Street, and was preſently at the back door alſo of the *Villa Ludoviſia*, belonging to the Prince *Ludoviſio*. This *Villa* ſtands in an excellent air, being ſeated high. There are two Houſes in this Garden, and both furniſhed with exquiſite Rarities. That which ſtands near this back door, afforded me theſe curioſities. A rare Picture of the Bleſſed Virgin. *Mary*, made by *Guido Rheni*. It's the beſt Picture of her that ever I ſaw. A Rich Cabinet, with the Picture of Pope *Gregory* XV. in a *Cameo*, and other rich Stones adorning it. A neat little Cloſet full of divers rarities; as a true *Hydra*'s skin with ſeven necks, a petrified *fungus*: The true Picture of *Francis* the firſt of *France*, with that alſo of his Phyſician, both made by *Laurenzo Vinci*, and eſteemed rare pieces, with many other little curioſities.

Villa Ludoviſia.

The firſt Houſe.

riofities. In another Room, the heads in white marble, of *Gregory* the XV. and his Nephew Cardinal *Ludovifio*. A Chamber full of curious Glaſſes. Upon the Stairs a little *Cupid* loaden with a Quiver of Arrows, that another little *Cupid* is forced to hold them up behind him. But that which is the moſt rare thing in this *Villa*, or perchance in any in *Rome*, is the incomparable bedſtead which is ſeen in one of the Chambers of this Palace. It's all of precious ſtones, and valued at an Hundred Thouſand Crowns. The four Bed-poſts are all of Oriental poliſhed *Jaſper*. The reſt of it is of other rich Stones; but the head of it exceeds far the reſt, for Riches and Art, eſpecially the midſt of it, where the Arms of the Family of *Ludoviſio*, are curiouſly ſet in rich Stones of ſeveral colours, according to the colours of the Coat of Arms. Here you have bunches of Grapes, ſome red, ſome white, but all of rich Stones. Here are vaſt *Amethyſts*, one ſquare, another round in pyramidal form. Here *Phaeton* in his Chariot in a *Cameo*, with the Wheels of his Chariot of precious Stones; and a world of ſuch rich work, which makes his Bedſtead the *nonplus* of art and magnificence. I do not know for all that, why Beds ſhould be made of Stones, though precious ones? If it be for the Princeſs of this houſe to be brought to Bed in, it portends unto her a hard labour; if to lodge in it the everlaſting fame of the greatneſs of this Family, it is a vain labour; ſeeing precious ſtones will moulter away in time, as other ſtones do.

Onuria

head and the other parts lie jumbled up together in the Box. If you ask me why they do not put this Body into some Tomb to bury it, I answer you, that it needs no other Tomb than this crust of Stone. Indeed I never saw a body so neatly intombed as this: You would swear that this Tomb is a pure *Justaucorps* rather than a Tomb: It sits as close as if a Taylor had made it. And that you may not think it an impossible thing that men should be thus petrified, I must mind you what *Ortelius* saith, that upon the Mountains situated in the Western parts of *Tartary* are seen figures of Men, Camels, Sheep and other Beasts, which by an admirable Metamorphosis, were changed into Stones, about three hundred years ago. And *Aristotle* himself speaks of men petrified in the hollow caves of a Mountain near *Pergamus*. In another Chamber stands a great Clock of brass, gilt, as tall as a man, and it stands indeed; for I think it hath not gone since it went out of *Germany* to *Rome*. They tell us pretty things that this Clock did, when it was young; but now it cannot so much as stir itself: and: Thus time cashiers at last its own *Heralds*; and breaketh the Clocks by which we know her. In another Chamber of this house I saw a new Statue in pure white Marble, of the rape of *Proserpina*: it is of the hand of *Bernini*. In another Room I saw the rare Statue of *Cestius Marius*, killing himself with his dagger, upon sight of his dead Daughter, who had killed her self for fear of falling into the hands of a lustful Emperor. Descending from hence into a long low Gallery of Statues, I found here some very good ones as that of *Junius Brutus*, of *Nero*, of *Domitian*, &c.

But

Ortelius in Tab. Geograph. Russiæ.

Aristot. lib. de an. c. 50.

But the best thing I saw there was the head of *Olympias* (Mother of *Alexander* the Great) in a *basso rilievo*, and in a frame.

The Capucins.

Going out of this *Villa* by the great door behind the *Capucins*, I stept into the Church of the said *Capucins*, and saw there in the second Chappel on the left hand the Tomb of *Santo Felice*, a Lay-brother of this Order, famous all *Rome* over for his known Sanctity. Here lies also buried Cardinal *Antonio Barberino*, brother to Pope *Urban* the VIII. otherwise called Cardinal *Sant' Onofrio*, who having been long a *Capucin*, was made Cardinal by his Brothers express command; and being Cardinal, lived still a *Capucin* in the esteem of all that knew him. His humility would not so much as let his name be set up on his Tomb-stone; but instead of it, and his other Titles, I found only these words, *hic jacet, umbra, cinis, nihil*. This Cardinal, and Cardinal *Mazat*, made by *Clement* the VIII. are all the Cardinals that the *Capucins* order hath had.

Palazzo Barberino.

Over against the *Capucins* stands the Palace of the Family of *Barberini* possessed now by the Prince of *Palestrina* of that Family, this is one of the noblest Palaces in *Rome*, for its stately situation upon an hills side; for the two neat stair cases; the noble Painting in the roof of the great Hall by *Pietro di Cartona*; the world of Statues and Pictures in the Gallery; the rare sequens of Chambers, one going into another; the double appartiment; each capable to lodge any King in, and each rarely furnished; in fine, for the rare Library of Cardinal *Francesco Barberino*.

Descending from hence towards the *Minims* of *Trinita di Monte*, I stept into a little Church

Part II. Italy.   113

of *Spanish Augustins*, called *Santo Ildefonso*, which   *S. Ildefonso*
I cannot pass by without taking notice of; be-
cause I think no body else doth; it is so little; yet
having described the greatest Church of *Rome*   *The least*
(St. *Peter's*) so exactly; I cannot but say some-   *Church in*
thing of the least Church in *Rome*: Dwarfs are   *Rome.*
Men as well as Gyants, and though this Church
may seem rather to be a map or model of a
Church, than a true Church; yet seeing it hath
not only all the lineaments, features, and meen
of a Church, but also all the noble parts of a
Church, as High Altars, Side Chappels, Cupola,
Quire, &c. I fear not to call it a Church, tho'
for bigness, it would not make the little finger of
St. *Peters*.

From hence I went streight on to the *Minims*   *The Church*
of *Trinita di Monte*, belonging to *France*, and St.   *of Trinita*
Francis of *Paula's* Order. This Convent is the   *di Monte.*
best seated of any in *Rome*, and one of the noblest,
being founded by King *Lewis* the XI. of *France*,
overlooking all *Rome*, and looked upon recipro-
cally by the best places in *Rome*. In the Church
I saw divers good pieces, as the Assumption of
our Lady by *Zuccary*, the Picture of the taking
down of our Saviour from the Cross by *Raphael*;
the Picture of our Saviour's appearing to St. *Ma-*
ry Magdalen, by *Julio Romano Raphael's* Scholar,
and imitating very much in this Picture *Raphael's*
colours. See in the dormitory of this Convent the
curious perspective of S. *Francis* of *Paula*, and a
rare Sun Dial ingeniously contrived.

Descending from hence into the *Piazza di Spag-*   *Piazzo di*
na I saw the Fountain of the Ship, which in sum-   *Spagna,*
mer nights they let overflow, to cool the *Piazza*
and the neighbouring streets. In this *Piazza* stands

H h   the

the Palace of the *Spanish Embassador*, belonging always to him that is *Embassador* here. In the end of the *Piazza* stands the College *de propaganda Fide*, of propagating the Faith, founded by *Urban* the VIII. to maintain divers Students of the Eastern Countries, and even of *India* and *Ethiopia* too, who having finished their studies in this College, are sent back again to their several Countries, with great profit and advantage to those poor Infidels, who would sit still in the darkness of infidelity, were it not for the Pope's care and charity.

Collegio de propaganda fide.

From hence I steered to the *Piazza* of the *Fontana de Trevi*, and in my way, saw divers stately Palaces, inhabited by Cardinals, because they stand near the Foot of *Montecavallo*, where the Pope resides. This Fountain of *Treve* is not yet finished, as to the structure that was intended; but only the water is brought hither, and in that quantity, that it seems to make three little Rivers, at the three mouths, out of which it gusheth.

Fontana de Trevi.

From hence I went nearer unto the foot of the hill *Montecavallo*, and stept into the College of the *Maronites*, in whose Church I heard them singing Mass in their own language, and after their own rites, as the Christians of Mount *Libanus* have immemorably used to do. Their language is *Arabic*, and they have always kept themselves free from *Heresies*; and in Union with the *Roman* Church, these five Hundred years.

The Maronites College.

From hence I went to the Church of the SS. *Apostoli*, built in honour of the Twelve Apostles, by *Constantine* the Great, who in honour of those

SS. Apostoli.

Holy

Part II. *A Voyage through* Italy.

Holy Apostles, carried out of the Foundation, twelve Baskets of Earth, upon his own Shoulders. In this Church lies buried, St. *Philip* and *Jacob*, two Apostles. In the *Piazza* before this Church, stand four fine Palaces; that of the Prince *Colonna*, that of Cardinal *Gbisi*, that of Cardinal *Sforza*, and that of the *Signori Muti*.

Crossing from hence into the *Corso*, I took an exact observation of this Street, which is the fairest in *Rome*. It's called the *Corso*, because here it is that they make Horses run against Horses, Jews against Jews, Boys against Boys, and the like, in *Carneval* time. Here also it is that the *Mascarades* march in *Carneval* time, and make themselves and others merry: And all this is allowed the *Italians*, that they may give a little vent to their Spirits, which have been stifled in for a whole year, and are ready else to choak with gravity and melancholy; most men here living alone in their Houses and Chambers. If our Statesmen in *England* had gone on in the course their wise Ancestors had shewed, and had suffered, as they did, some honest recreations to the People, as Bowling, Shooting, Racing, &c. to give vent to their active Spirits, we had all been happier: But while both the Tribunals, and the Pulpits thundred out against moderate Recreations and Assemblies, out of Fear and Faction, they made the humour of the English then grow so sowr and Bitter, that nothing would please them, but flat Rebellion, and Fanatick Heresies. Now here in *Rome*, once a year, in *Carneval* time, every one vents his humour according to his fancy, and (as it seems) according to his need. One plays the Doctor of the

The Corso.

Hh 2 Law,

A Voyage through Italy.   Part II.

Law, and goes up and down the streets with his Book in his Hand, disputing with every man he meets, and uttering pure rallery: And if by chance two such Doctors meet, they make sport enough for half an hour, by their abusing one another. Four of these pretended Doctors, with their Gowns and Caps on, and their Books of the *Codex* before them, got an Ass into their Coach, who had also another Book before him; and thus they went along the streets, studying and turning over their Books. Another takes himself to be a grand *Cyrus*, and goes a Horse-back, with a rich *Persian* Habit, and Plumes highly mounted. One went a Foot gravely, with a Cloak on, and cried a *Secret against Mice*, and opening his Cloak, shewed a *Cat* that he had under his Arm; another went up and down the street, combing his Hair like a *Spaniard*, saluting the Ladies, and twirling up his Mustaches with a stayed gravity. Some go in Coaches and there play on Instruments: Others go on great Carts, with little stages of boards thrown upon them, and there act little Plays as they go along, and abuse Tradesmen. One rides like a Physician upon a Mule, with a world of Urinals hung round about him. Others ride gravely through the streets, with great Cloak-bags behind them, as if they came from *Polonia*. Some Princes here make glorious *Carro*'s, with four Horses on a breast, drawing them, and with rare Pageants upon them, and a great train of Horsemen and Trumpeters clad exotically, accompanying the *Carro* in a most glorious manner. Some Noblemen of highest Quality, as Dukes and Princes, I have seen going a Foot, pelting, with sugar-plumbs,

Part II. *A Voyage through* Italy.

plumbs, those that were in Coaches and Windows, and angering them with their sugar affronts. But never did any *Mascarade* please like that speculative *Italian*, who mocked both the *French* and the *Spaniards* at once, by walking up and down the street, clad half like a *Don*, and half like a *Monsieur*. One side of his hair hung down in a long curled lock, powdered white: The other side was black and sweaty. Half of his beard was turned downwards: The other half was turned up with Irons, and twirled in like the hilt of an old Dagger. One eye was bare, and the other had a Glass or half Spectacle before it, held on by a small wire from under his Hat. Half his Hat was a narrow three fingered-brim'd Hat, with a little half Feather upon the Brim: The other half of it was a broad Brim, without so much as a Hat-band. One half of his Band about his neck, was of a broad bone Lace, starched white, the other half was made of course Lawn, starched blew, and standing out upon a pickydilly of wire. Half of his Face looked white with Meal and Powder, the other half looked black and tawny. Half of his Doublet was white Satin with an open Sleeve, and a world of shirt huffing about his wrist, and half on his wast; the other half was of black Freeze, with a black Taffety sleeve close and strait to the arm, and a hanging sleeve of Freeze. One half of his Breeches was of Scarlet, and vastly wide at the knee, with a confusion of Ribbonds, of six colours; the other half was of black Taffety, close at the knee. Upon one leg he had a Linnen Stocking, with a great laced Canon turn'd down to his half leg; on the other he had a black silk

Stocking

Stocking drawn up close. In fine, on one Foot he had a white Spanish Leather Shoe, with a stiff knot of six coloured Ribbond, a quarter of an Ell long; on the other a little black flat soled Shoe, tied with a short narrow Ribbond. Thus this moral *Hermaphrodite*, and walking Emblem of peace, between the two Nations, walked up and down the *Corso* gravely; yet laughing within himself, to see how he carried about him two such *Antipathetical* Nations in one Suit of Cloaths. By this you may guess at their other fooleries in *Carneval* time, and see how innocently they divert themselves: For you must know, that none are suffered to carry Swords or Arms, while they go masked thus; nor to enter into any house, nor to be abroad masked after it grows dark; nor to do or speak any thing scandalously, that may shock civility or publick view: for which reason here are always Guards set, and Sergeants riding up and down the Street of the *Corso*, to keep all in order, and to make even Mirth observe Decency.

Some Palaces in the Corso.

In this Street also of the *Corso* it is that Noblemen and Ladies take the Air every fair Evening in their Coaches. For this reason there are many fine Palaces built in this Street; as the Palace of *Signor Vitelleschi*, where I saw ten Chambers on a floor, and all of them filled with a rare Collection of Pictures and Statues. Among the Statues I was pleased exceedingly with that of *Cincinnatus*, and with that of *Brutus*, defac'd by the command of the Senate, where the very marks of the punches of the Halberts wherewith they defac'd it, are yet seen. Not far from it stands the Palace of *Principe Pamfilio*, in which I saw

more

Part II.   A Voyage through Italy.   119

more Riches and rare Furniture than in any house *The Palace of Pamfilio.*
in *Rome*, or almost in *Italy*. For here they shewed me excellent Plate of Gold and Silver: an Agate Cross fixed upon a foot of the root of *Saphyr-Stone*, and under it a *Basis* beset round about it *Cameos* cut into Pictures: a great Silver Crucifix upon an Ebony Frame, the whole worth 12000 Crowns: a rare Cabinet with the Picture of our blessed Lady in it, the whole valued at 6000 Crowns: a Sword whose Hilt is of three great Turky-Stones of great value: a Basin of gold set thick with Turkey-Stones: three or four great *Bezoar* Stones, as big as Pearmaens, which had been presented to *Clement* the VIII from all Parts, because he stood in need of them: a rich Mitre, set with precious Stones of great value, and a world of curious Originals of the best Painters hands: curious Saddles, Harness, Liveries of show Embroidered with Gold and Silver, with many other rich Curiosities. The other Palaces in the *Corso* are these; that of *Principe Carboniano*; that of Cardinal *Franciotti*; that of *Don Augustino Chisi*, that of *Principe Ludivisio*, that of the Duke *Caetano*.

There are also in this Street some Churches worth taking notice of; as that of St. *Maria* in *Santa Maria in Via Lata.*
Via Lata, which stands near the Palace of the Prince *Pamfilio*. It's an ancient Church, and Cardinals Title. *Baronius* saith, that it's built there where St. *Paul* lodged at his first coming to *Rome*. It's said also that in the Oratory here St. *Luke* wrote the Acts of the Apostles.

There is also in the *Corso* the Church of St. *Marcello*, a title of a Cardinal. It was built in *S. Marcello.*
the place where anciently stood the Temple of the
H h 4   Infamous

infamous *Egyptian* Goddess *Isis*, which *Tiberius* himself caused to be pulled down, the Idol thrown into *Tyber*, and all the Priests of it to be crucified, for having favoured a great crime committed by a *Roman* Lady. Behind this Church stands the Oratory of St. *Marcello*, called the Oratory of the Holy Crucifix, where there is a famous *Confraternity* in which many noble Men of *Rome* are enrolled. Every *Friday* in *Lent* there is excellent Music, and one of the best Preachers in *Rome*. From hence also in the Holy year I saw march a Procession of 15000 Men, all in black Buckram Coats to the Heels, with a white Torch in their hands; and they went from hence on the Night of *Monday Thursday* unto St. *Peters* Church.

St. Carlo in Corso. Then the Church of St. *Carlo* in *Corso*, where I saw the Heart of St. *Charles Barromeo* in a Chrystal case. This Church belongs to the *Milanese*.

St. Jacomo de gl' Incurabili. Then the Church of St. *Jacomo de gl' Incurabili*, a neat round Church belonging to the Hospital here, where they that are afflicted with incurable diseases, are entertain'd and well tended.

The Convent of the repented Whores. Lastly, the Church of the Penitent Whores with their Convent; where all those poor Souls that repent themselves of their bad life, are receiv'd and kept all their Life-time, at the cost of this Convent. And here I found a great difference between this Convent and the house in *Amsterdam*, where Whores are clap'd up. For here these poor Souls are lock'd up with their own consent and desire: there they are lock'd up by force and violence. Here the poor Women do great acts of Austerities and Penance; as the bloody Walls of their *Cells*, laid open by a Conflagration,

Part II: *A Voyage through Italy.*

on, shewed unto all the City: there the young Women laugh, and are merry. Here no Man is permitted to speak alone with them, except their Confessor and Physician; there many Men go to prattle and pass their time with those wanton Girls, at a separation of rails. Here a Vail hides these poor Womens faces: there I saw divers with black Patches on their Faces. Here all signs of true Repentance are seen, there none. Here the love of Virtue and Penance locks up these: there the vice of Love locks in those, and not true Repentance; for really all the Repentance I saw there was, that it repented me, that I had suffered mine Host (who would needs shew me all the Rarities of *Amsterdam*) to lead me thither.

O but said an *Hollander* to me, the Pope allows Whores in *Rome*. *Objection.*

To whom I answered, no more Sir, than your States do Drunkenness, which is a greater Sin of the two, because it rides double, and carrieth Luxury behind it. Do not drink Wine in which is Luxury, *Ephes.* 5. *Answer.*

But saith an *English* Writer, I am told that the Pope both permits, and takes Money of them too for that permission. *Object.*

You have been told many other false tales by those who think it lawful to tell untruths, so they speak but against the Pope: in the mean time I that have been five times in *Rome*, can tell you the contrary; if, by permitting, you mean allowing and approving of them in that course. There's a great difference between allowing and permitting a thing. *Moses* allowed not, but yet permitted the Libel of divorce to the *Jews*; for the hardness of their Hearts. So Usury is permitted, *Answ. Fenton in his Treatise of Usury. l. 2. c. 9.*

Mat. 1. 8.

but

A Voyage through Italy. Part II.

but not allowed in divers Countries for Trades sake.

Object. But why takes he Money of them?

Answ. This Money is taken up by you upon credit, not the Pope. For the Pope is so far from receiving any Money of these drabs, that he goes to great cost to hinder their trading. No Man perhaps hath told you this, and therefore I'le tell you: know then that the Pope, to hinder all young Women from being naught, hath founded Hospitals for poor Girls, where they are carefully brought up till they become either married wives, or Nuns. Nay he gives them Dowries also to execute this their choice, distributing yearly, upon the Feast of our Lady day, in Lent, in the Church of the *Dominicans, supra Minervam*, a Purse of Money a piece, to three hundred young Maids who are presented to him by the Overseers of the aforesaid Hospitals. Nor is this all, for he causeth young Girls of tender years to be taken from their poor suspected Mothers, lest Poverty *quæ cogit ad turpia*, should make them sacrifice those tender Virgins to Rich Mens Lusts. In fine, *Perusa* he hath caused a Monastery to be built in *Rome* *S. Romu-* to receive those poor unfortunate Women in, *aldo in his* who would leave that infamous course, if they *Chronolo-* had but means to live on. Nay, he granteth Indulgences to any that will marry any of those *sure.* Women to free them from that lewd Course, and make them mend. All this the Pope doth, and much more; which would be a destroying of his own trade and gain, if it were true, that he countenanceth and alloweth of Whores for his gain. No Miller ever turned the Current of Water from his own Mill.

Object. But why doth not the Pope discountenance and

and punish Whores that are known to be such?

    He doth so. For it is not a discountenancing of *Answ.* them, to forbid them to come to publick Meetings, and Assemblies, where women of Honour meet? as at the *Corso*, in the Evenings; at public Marriages; at their sung *Opera's* and the like? Is it not a discountenancing of them to forbid them to go in Coaches in the day time; or to stir out of doors in the night? Is it not a punishment to them to forbid them to live together, where they might encourage one another, and pass their time more chearfully? But for the most part they live alone, condemned to the melancholy horror of their Crimes, and the Solitude of seven whole weeks in *Lent*; when, upon pain of rigorous Punishments and Imprisonment, they dare not admit of any Customers. The like rigour is used against them also in Advent, that during the space of those holy times, these unholy Women may have time to think of themselves, and admit of Gods holy Inspirations for their amendment. Is it not a *Pu-* *nishment* to them to be oblig'd to enter their names publickly in the List of Whores? For if *Tacitus* Tacit. An-
observes that the old *Romans*, *Satis pœnarum ad-* nal. 2.
versum impudicas in ipsa professione flagitii apud Æ-
diles credebant; thought it Punishment enough, a-
gainst unchast Women, in their very professing them-
selves to be such before the Ædiles. I cannot but think it a great Punishment to Christian Whores (who are at least as sensible as the Heathens, of the horrible Disgrace of having their Name listed) to be thus defam'd for ever, by remaining Whores upon Record. Is it not a punishing of them, to deprive them all their Life-time (as long as they live Whores) of the holy Sacraments; and after their Death, of Christian Burial?

A Voyage through Italy. Part II.

al? Is it not a Punishment, and a deterring of them from Vice, to throw their Bodies when they die into an obscure place, out of the Walls of the Town, as if they deserv'd no other Burial-places than that of Asses? Is it not, in fine, a Punishment to them not to be allow'd to make any Will or Testament, but to leave all their Goods confiscated either to the Hospitals of poor honest Girls, or to the maintaining of those Guards, that are to watch over their deportments? If these Punishments both of Body, Soul, and Honour, be inflicted upon Whores in *Rome*, as they are, do not urge any more, that Whores are not punished in *Rome*, nor discountenanced.

Object. ' But why doth not the Pope punish them home, and root them quite out by banishment?

Answ. This hath been attempted by divers Popes, and namely by *Pius Quintus* of happy memory; (as *Thuanus* in his History writes) but seeing greater Inconveniencies, and greater sins arose upon it, Prudence, which is the Salt that must season all moral Actions, thought it not fit to carry on that rigor; nor yet allow of Fornication neither. So that all the permission of Whores in *Rome*, that can colourably be imagin'd, is only a not Punishing of them in all rigor; and even that too, for a good end; and to hinder greater Evils.

Object. But the Pope being both a Temporal and an Ecclesiastical *Superior*, is bound, in my Mind, to break through all reports, and settle Innocency in the World.

Answ. It's Zealously spoken, and I wish he could do it; but *difficilem rem optas, generis humani innocentiam, he wisheth a hard thing, who wisheth for the Innocency of Mankind,* saith a Wise Man. And if

Seneca.

Princes

Part II. A Voyage through Italy. 125

Princes sometimes do not punish factious Subjects, when they see that the punishing of them would pull the whole State to pieces over their heads, and put the whole Kingdom in danger, as it did in *Henry* the Third's time in *France*, upon his causing of the Duke of *Guise* to be killed in *Blois*: if Generals of Armies take no notice of some treacherous Commander, who is universally belov'd by the Soldiers; lest the punishing of one Man, lose them the affection of the whole Army, as we saw lately in the case of *Lubemirsky* (how truly guilty I know not) and some years ago I remember, in the case of *Walstein*, whose Punishment had almost undone the Emperor: why may not the Pope, without approving the Sin of Whores, prudently wave the punishing of it with all Rigor, when he sees that such rigor would cause greater disorders in that hot Nation, and in that City where all nations seem to club Vices, as Virtues? Hence learned *Abulensis*, a great Divine *in c. 8.* saith; *Licet leges humanæ aliqua mala permittant l. 1. Reg. non puniendo, nullum tamen malum permittunt statuendo.*

But the Pope should not govern according either to humane Policy, or humane Laws and Examples. *Object.*

You pretend Zeal, but you would do well to take her Sister Prudence with her, as our Saviour did, who when he heard his Disciples desiring him to let them call down Fire from Heaven upon the criminal *Samaritans*, answer'd them calmly, *you know not of what Spirit you are.* Nay doth not God himself, who being able to punish all criminal Persons, and root them quite out of the World, *Answ.*

Luke 9.

World, suffer both his Sun to Rise and shine upon Sinners, and Sinners to offend in this Sunshine, and often by it? Hence St. *Thomas* saith much to my purpose: *Humanum regimen derivatur a divino regimine & ipsum debet imitari. Deus autem quamvis sit Omnipotens, ac summe bonus, permittit tamen aliqua mala fieri in universo, quæ prohibere posset; ne iis sublatis, majora bona tollerentur, vel majora mala sequerentur.* Humane Government is deriv'd from Divine Government, and ought to imitate it. Now God although he be Almighty, and highly good, yet he permits Evils to be done in the World, which he could hinder, lest by taking away them, greater Goods should be taken away, or greater Evils should follow. But I wade too far in this puddle: yet remember who thrust me into it, and you'll pardon me.

S. Tho.
2.2.q.10,
art. 11. in
Corpore.

St. Silvestro in Capite.

Behind the Church and Convent of the aforesaid Penitents, stands the Church of *Sgn Silvestro in Capite,* so called from the Picture of our Saviour's Head and Face, which our Saviour himself made by Miracle, and sent to *Abagarus,* King of *Edessa;* as you may read at length in *Baronius,* and in *Bosius* in his rare Book called *Roma Soterranea.* Now this Picture is kept here in this Monastery, and with great Probability, seeing it was here that divers *Greek* Monks, driven out of their Country by *Constantine Capronimus,* for the defence of Sacred Images, were entertained by Pope *Paul* the first; and it's very likely that these good Men brought with them this famous Picture of our Saviour, to save it from the fury of the *Iconoclasts.*

Returning

Part II. A Voyage through Italy.

Returning from hence into the *Corso* again, I went to see there the *Colonna d' Antonino*, the great Pillar of *Antoninus* the Emperor. It's built just like that of *Trajan* describ'd above. It was built by *Marcus Aurelius Antoninus* the Emperor, in honour of his Father *Antonius Pius*. It's all of white Marble, engraven without with a *Basso relievo* from top to bottom, containing the memorable actions of *M. Aurelius*. It's 175 foot high, and hath in it 106 stairs which lead up to the top of it, and 56 little Windows giving light to those Stairs: and yet this high Pillar was made of 28 Stones of Marble. The Carving that is upon it, contains the brave Actions of *Marcus Aurelius* over the *Armenians*, *Parthians*, *Germans*, *Wandals*, and *Sarmats*, or *Polonians*, but age hath so defac'd these *Bassi relievi* that it is hard to decypher them. He that's curious to know them, may buy them in the printed Cuts sold in *Rome*. Upon the top of this Pillar stands mounted the Statue in Brass gilt, of St. *Paul*, set up here by *Sixtus Quintus*. From the top of this Pillar I had a perfect view of *Rome*, and of almost all the seven Hills upon which it is built, and are within the Walls; which are these.

Colonna Antonia.

The seven Hills of Rome.

1. The *Capitolin* Hill, where now *Ara Cœli* stands, and the *Conservatorio*.

Mons Capitolinus.

2. The *Palatin* Hill, I could not see because it stands behind the former. It was so called from the Emperor's Palace that stood upon it.

Palatinus.

3. The *Aventine* Hill so called from *Aventinus*, King of *Alba*, buried here where now St. *Sabinas* is.

Aventinus.

4. The *Cælian* Hill beginning at St. *Gregories*, and running to St. *John Lateran*'s.

Cælius.

5. The

Esquilinus.   5. The *Esquiline* Hill, *Exquilinus quasi extubinus*, because of the nightly Watch and Guard upon it. Here stands St. *Mary Majors*.

Viminalis.   6. The *Viminal* Hill, so called from *Vimina*, that is, *Osiers*: wherewith it was anciently covered. Here stands the *Thermæ Diocletiani*, and the *Villa Montalto*.

Quirinalis.   7. The *Quirinal* Hill, so called from the Temple of *Quirinus*, or *Romulus*, which stood upon it. Here now stands *Montecavallo*. These were the seven ancient Hills of *Rome*, to which were added three more, to wit, the *Janicule* hill, so called,

Janiculm. from *Janus* buried here. Here stands St. *Petro Montorio*.

Vaticanus.   The *Vatican* hill, so called from the *Vaticinations* and Soothsayings made here. St. *Peters* Church stands now upon it.

Pincius, or hortorum. The Pazzorella.   The *Pincian* hill, now called *Montrinita*. Descending from hence, I went to the *Pazzorella*, where they keep Madmen and Fools; and saw there strange variety of humours in Folly: yet I was pleased to see with what Charity and Care those poor Men were tended there.

From hence I stept to consider in the *Piazza di Pietra*, the row of curious Pillars which adorn'd the *Basilica* of the Emperor *Antoninus*, who had his Palace here, and his *Forum*.

The Roman College.   Then turning by little unfrequented Streets, I came to the *Roman* College belonging to the Jesuits.

It's a fair Building, and stands conveniently for Concourse of Scholars from all Parts. Here I

Kerkerius his Gallery. saw the Schools and Gallery of famous *Athanasius Kerkerius*, full of pretty Curiosities and Experiences, both *Mechanical*, *Mathematical*, and *Hydraulical*:

Part II.   *A Voyage through Italy.*   149

Hydraulical: yet in my Opinion, its far short of *Canonico Settala*'s Gallery in *Milan*, or *Monsieur Serviers* in *Lyons*. Here's also a fair Library, having no fault in it but the common fault of most Libraries, to wit, Locks and Keys to it. Good Books should be as common as the Sun, seeing they are the lights of our Minds, and made publick by the Press: and I cannot but pity a Book that is imprisoned and lock'd up in a Library, by saying unto it: *Odisti claves & grata pudica, Paucis ostendi genus, & communia laudas.* In fine, I saw here the Apothecaries Shop, where a Lay-Brother makes excellent *Roman* Treacle, and other odoriferous Distillations of Soveraign Virtue. The Church belonging to this College is design'd to be a noble thing, but it's but half built, for want of a whole Founder.

From hence I went to the Dominican's Convent, called *La Minerva*, because it's built upon the place where anciently stood the Temple of *Minerva.* Hence also the Church is called *Sancta Maria supra Minervam:* In this Church I saw many neat Tombs, as those of *Leo the* X. and *Clement the* VII. both Popes of the House of *Medices:* They stand in the Quire, and are neatly wrought by that great Artist *Baccio Bandinelli.* Then the Tomb of Cardinal *Pimentelli,* a modern Cardinal. The Tomb of great Cardinal *Moronus*, Legate for the Pope in the Council of *Trent;* and a Man who had been thirteen times *Legate a Latere.* Here also lie buried the Ashes of *Egidius Foscaria,* Bishop of *Modena,* buried in the Council of *Trent. Luminare Majus.* The Tomb of a Lady of the Family of the *Capel*, is very neat for the new manner of spreading

L l   Ing

La Miner.

ing (as I may say, and as you would think) of black Marble upon another coloured Marble; and both of them upon a round Pillar. Here on the Gospel side of the high Altar standeth a Statue of our Saviour, made by *Michel Angelo*, of white Marble; a rare piece. At the Entrance of the great door of this Church, lies buried, under a plain flat Stone, *Thomas a Vio Caetanus* St. *Thomas* of *Aquin*'s Second, his Brother in Religion, his Name-sake, his learned Commentator, and only not he. Out of humility he would not be buried within the Church, but out of it. In the Sacrifty of this Church, I saw the Chappel of *Katherine* of *Siena*, and this Chappel was once her very Chamber in *Siena*: Cardinal *Antonio Barberino*, Protector of this Order, caused it to be transferred hither from *Siena*. Her Body lieth under the Altar of the *Rosary* in this Church.

St. Andrea della Valle. From the *Minerva* I went to Saint *Andrea della Valle*, a fine Church belonging to the *Theatins*. It's built upon the place where the Theater of *Pompey* stood, anciently; and where, in latter times, stood the Palace of the Family of the *Picolomini*; and perchance this was the reason why two Popes of that Family, to wit, *Pius Secundus*, and *Pius Tertius* are now buried in this Church. The *Cupola* was painted by *Cavalier Lanfranco*; the three Corners under the *Cupola*, and the Tribune are of the hand of *Domenichini*. The next Chappel of the *Barberini*, made by Pope *Urban* the VIII, while he was but yet Cardinal, is built upon the very place where St. *Sebastian* was beaten and thrown into a Sink after he had been shot. There had been formerly a little Church built upon

Part II. *A Voyage through* Italy. 131

upon this place, and over this Sink, but *Sixtus Quintus* gave leave it should be pulled down, upon condition a Chappel of the new design'd Church should be built in place of it. In fine, take all this Church together, and it is one of the neatest Churches (except the *Basilica*) that are in *Rome*, being of the Architecture of *Maderna*.

In the *Piazza*, or rather the Street which goes before this Church, lived not long ago, *Pietro della Valle*, that ingenious *Roman* Gentleman, who having spent great means in Travelling, hath left us three Volumes in *Quarto* of his curious relations of Voyages. In this house here he had three whole *Mummies* with their Coffins or Cases painted anciently, and adorned with divers *Hieroglyphics*. He spent much Money in buying many other rarities, which he kept also here. *Pietro della Valle.*

Behind this Church lived, when I first was acquainted with *Rome*, another great *Virtuoso*, and Gentleman of *Rome*, I mean the ingenious *Cavalier Pozzo*, with whom I was brought acquainted, and saw all his Rarities, his curious Pictures, Medals, *Bassi relievi*, his excellent Books of the rarest things in the World, which he caused to be Painted, Copied, and design'd out with great Cost. *Cavalier Pozzo.*

From hence I went to the Palace of the Duke *Matthei*, where I saw many good Pictures and Statues, especially that long Picture representing fully the manner of *Clement* the VIII his going from *Rome* to take possession of *Ferrara*. *The Palace of Matthei.*

Thence falling in at St. *Carlo in Catenari*, a neat round Church, I went to the *Cancellaria*. This Palace was built of the Stones of the *Colifeo*, by Cardinal *Riarii*. The chief thing *The Cancellaria.*

I i 2

I saw in it was the Gallery of Pictures of Cardinal *Barberin*, who being *Vice-Chancellor*, liveth always in this Palace, to exercise his Charge the better.

San Lorenzo in Damaso.

This Palace looks into the Church of *San Lorenzo* in *Damaso*, a *Collegiate* Church. Under the high Altar reposeth the Body of St. *Damasus* Pope. The Walls of the Body of the Church are rarely painted with the History of St. *Laurence*.

The Palace of Farnesi.

Not far from hence stands the Palace of *Farnesi* belonging to the Duke of *Parma*. Before it stands a noble *Piazza* with two rare Fountains in it. The Palace it self is one of the best in *Rome*, or elsewhere. It makes an Isle, that is, it hath no houses joyning to it. The form of it is square, and it hath, in the midst of every square, a great door, letting you into the Court. This Court is built upon Pillars and Arches, with a fair open Gallery above, letting you into several appartiments. In this Court I saw the famous Statue of *Hercules*, leaning upon his Club, which was found in the *Therme* of *Antoninus Caracalla*? One of the Legs is modern, the rest old, and made by *Glyco* an *Athenian*, as the Greek words upon it told me.

There is another Statue of *Hercules* opposite to it, and just like it, but not so good, being but a Copy of the former. The other Statues here of the two *Flora*'s, the two *Gladiators* and others, are excellent pieces. Mounting up the great stairs to go into the Chambers and open Gallery, I saw the curious Statue of the Boy and the Dolphin; and at the door of the great Hall, the Statues of two *Parthian* Captive Kings. Entring into

Part II. *A Voyage through* Italy.

into that Hall, I met presently with the rare statue of *Alexander Farnesi*, Duke of *Parma*, trampling upon two prostrate Statues, representing Heresie and Rebellion, while Fame Crowns him. All these four several Persons are of white Marble, and of one entire Stone. Its pity that such a Statue stands not in some more publick place, to teach Men to beware of the Mother and the Daughter, Heresie and Rebellion; and shew them what long hands Kings have. In the same Hall I saw the two excellent statues of Charity and Plenty, in cumbent postures; and they are the Fellows to those two statues which adorn the Tomb of *Paulus Tertius*, the raiser of this Family, in St. *Peter*'s Church. Round about this Room also, stand a world of statues of Gladiators, standing with their Swords in their hands, and in several postures, upon their guard. In the next Chamber I saw rare Pictures, containing some actions of *Paulus Tertius*; and they are of the hand of *Salviati* and *Federico Zuccari*. There is also the Picture of *Luther* disputing with *Cajetan*; and a Picture of the four Latin Doctors of the Church, St. *Hieronie*, St. *Ambrose*, St. *Augustin*, and St. *Gregory*, of the hand of *Perdonini*. In another Chamber, a world of ancient statues of Philosophers and Poets: As *Euripides*, *Plato*, *Possidonius*, *Zeno*, *Seneca*, *Diogenes*, *Pacchys*, *Meleager*, and others: Another Room full of Pictures of choice hands, and a curious Table of *Pietre Commesse*, about twelve Foot long, and five wide. Then the rare Gallery of Statues, with the Roof of it painted most admirably, by the ravishing hand of great *Hunibal Carraccio*, and containing the representation of the

The Statue of Alexander Farnesi.

loves

loves of the Heathen Gods and Goddesses. This Painting may be compared, if not preferred, before all the Galleries of *Rome* or *Europe*; and the very cuts of it in Paper Pictures, sold at the Stationers shop, are most admirable and worth buying. In the same Gallery also stands the incomparable statue of *Apollo* in a flint stone. Here is also a curious Library, in which, besides the curious Books, are many rare pieces of miniature, and rare Pictures of *Raphael* and *Titian*, and divers excellent designs of the same *Raphael*, and of *Michel Angelo*; that especially of his Judgment. Returning again through the same Rooms, I could not but gaze again at the statue of my favourite *Heros*, *Alexander Farnesi*, and began at last to think that I was mistaken, even now when I said, that *Hercules* his statue stood in the Court below; for upon better reflection, I find no statue in the Palace to resemble *Hercules* so much, as this of *Alexander* of *Parma*; of whom I may say, as *Sulla* said of *Cæsar*, *In uno Cæsare, multi sunt Marii*: *In one* Alexander *of* Parma, *there are many* Herculeses.

Then mounting up into an appartment over the former, I saw divers Chambers exquisitely furnished with Pictures and lesser Statues. In the long Gallery there are divers rare pieces, of the hand of *Caraccio*. In the other Rooms many ancient curious things, as an ancient piece of Painting, found in *Adrian's Villa*, and made fifteen hundred years ago; another ancient Picture of *Eugenius* the IV. studying, and St. *Bernard* standing by him. A rare design of *Vassari*, representing a Town in *Flanders*, taken by *Alexander Farnesi*. *Michael Angelo's* true Picture. The *Ve-*
nus

Part II. **A Voyage through Italy.** 135

nus of *Michael Angelo*. The little old Picture of our Lady, and St. *John Baptist* in a small Mosaick work. A Crucifix in Ivory of *Michael Angelo*'s making. The design, or rather the perfect model of the Bridge thrown over the *Sceld*, by which *Alexander Farnese* took *Antwerp*. A great Cabinet of *Medals*, with a world of other rarities, too long to be related, but never enough to be seen.

Then descending into a little back Court, I saw there the famous *Toro*. It is a Statue of a great Bull, to whose Horns, a Rope being tied at one end, and at the other end of it a Womans hair, two lusty Fellows are striving to push this Bull from a promontory, into the Sea below, and the Woman together with him, to make her away. The story is known, and it is of *Amphion* and *Zetus*, who to revenge their Mother *Antiope*, for the wrong done her by *Dirce* (who had got *Licus* King of *Thebes*, to repudiate *Antiope*, for to marry her) took this *Dirce*, and tying her to a Bulls Horns, threw them both, the Bull and the Woman into the Sea. The Bull, the two Brothers, the Woman, a little Boy, and a Dog are all cut out of one Marble stone. The lasling Fellow that keeps this Bull, or rather, whom this Bull keeps, will tell you another story of this Statue through the Nose: But seeing he tells his story as well as tells it, you had better give him a *Julio* betimes, to be rid of him, than hear another long and new Fable.

The famous Bull.

Going from hence into the great *Piazza* again, I stept into the house of the *Signor Pighini*, which stands over against the Palate of *Farnese*; to see two Statues, the one of *Venus*, the other

I i 4   of

of *Adonis*; both ancient ones, and so rarely made, that the Earl of *Arondel*, late Lord Marshal of *England*, offered twelve Thousand Crowns for them, but was refused.

Passing from hence towards the Palace of Cardinal *Spada*, I entered into it, and there saw many exquisite Pictures.

Ponte Sisto *The Hospital of the Holy Trinity.*
Thence I went to *Ponte Sista*, and from thence to the Hospital of the Trinity, which receives all Pilgrims coming to *Rome*, for three days, and treateth them plentifully. I confess, I went often hither, and as often admired the wonderful charity which is done here daily; but especially in the holy week in *Lent*, by the *Confraternity* of this *Hospital*, of which, most are Gentlemen. Here Noblemen, Bishops and Cardinals wash the Pilgrims feet, and then serve them at Supper in the long Refectory, where there are frequently, in the holy week, four hundred Pilgrims at once at Table.

S. Girolamo della Charita.
Returning from thence, I went to St. *Girolamo della Charita*, a Church and House of good Priests, and most of them Gentlemen, living of their own expences, yet all in Community. St. *Philip Neri* instituted them, and lived among them thirty years. In the Church I saw, upon the high Altar, an excellent Picture of St. *Hieronit*.

The English College.
Hard by stands the English College, once an Hospital for the English, and built by the English Merchants in *Rome*, to receive English Pilgrims in; because a poor English Woman had been found worried by Dogs, in the night, for want of Lodging. In the Church of this College

Part II. *A Voyage through* Italy.   137

lege lies buried, Cardinal *Alan*, the last English Cardinal of our Nation.

From hence I went to the *Chiesa Nuova*, be- *The Chiesa*
longing to the good Priests of the Oratory. This *Nuova.*
is one of the neatest Churches in *Rome*, and the
best served. It's all painted in the roof, by the
rare hand of *Pietro di Cartona*, and richly gilt.
Here I saw the neat Chappel of St. *Philip Neri*,
a primitive Saint in all things but time. He was
the Institutor of this holy Company of Priests,
who are Religious Men in all things but in vows,
and name. The Chappel and Altar of this great
Saint, is on the Gospel-side of the high Altar,
his true Picture there, was made by *Guido Rheni*.
Under this Altar, in a lower Chappel, or Vault,
lieth the body of this Saint, in an Iron Chest: If
you desire to know his Merits and Life, ask all
Rome which lately saw them, and daily feels
them. On the other side of the high Altar with-
in the Rails, lies buried *Cæsar Baronius*, once a *Cardinal*
Priest of this house, and forced, after much re- *Cæsar Ba-*
luctancy, to be made Cardinal by *Clement* the *ronius.*
VIII. He deserved this honour in the opinion of all
Men, for having written his incomparable Ecclesiastical History: and if *Hercules*, for helping *Atlas*
to bear up Heaven one day only, was feigned by
Poets to have deserved to be taken up to Heaven; I may justly say, that *Baronius* deserved
well the purple of the Church, for having alone
born up the cause of the Church of God, a-
gainst a whole Troop of Centuriators. For my
part, I reckon it among my felicities, to have lived after *Baronius*, and to have spent a good
part of three years study, in reading his Sacred
Annals, which cost him ten times three years
study

138 A Voyage through Italy. Part II.

study in writing. And here I could enter into a fair field of his Praises; and like the Eagle, in the story, having nothing else to give him, give him a Feather, that is one cast of my Pen; but that I write of Countries now, and not of Men; and that his full Praises may be included in those three short Encomiums; *Ecclesiæ Cocles*; *Cæsar Christianus*; *Orbis Locupletator*.

[margin: The Oratory]

The house of these good Priests deserves also to be seen, for the Libraries sake, which is one of the best in *Rome*, and for the great Oratories sake; where there is every Sunday and Holy-day in *Winter* at Night, the best Musick in the World.

[margin: La Pace.]

From hence I went to the Church *de la Pace*, a neat Church, and adorned with excellent Painting and Statues. Here many famous Painters have signaliz'd their Memories, as *Peruzzi* of *Siene*, *Vasaria*, *Lavinia*, a Lady of *Bolognia*, *Fontana*, *Gentileschi*, *Cavalier Gioseppe*, *Rossi*, and *Raphael Urbin* himself, who painted the Prophets and *Sybils* in the Chappel of *Augustino Chigi*: and some think that he made the little Boys that are so well done. The Statues of St. *Peter* and S. *Paul* are of the Hand of *Michel Angelo*.

Going from hence through the Street of the Stationers, I came to *Piazza di Pasquino*, which is thought to be the very Center of *Rome*. And here I cannot forget *Pasquin* himself, who forgets no man.

[margin: Pasquin.]

This *Pasquin* is an old broken Statue, something like that of *Hercules* in the *Belvedere*, described above, and of some rare Hand. And because it stands near three or four Streets, whereby to escape when they have fixed the *Libels*, jeering Wits set up here, and father upon poor *Messer Pasquino*, their Satyrical Jests, called

from

Part II. A Voyage through Italy.

from him, *Pasquinades*; which *Morforius*, another Statue near the *Capitol*, useth to answer.

From hence passing on to the Church of S. *Pantaleon*, belonging to the Fathers of the *Schole Pie*. I was willing to enter into it, and see it, because four Hundred years ago it was a Collegiate Church, and possessed by *English* Priests, as may appear by the Inscription upon a Bell which was cast then. *St. Pantaleon.*

From hence I stept into *Pizza Navona*, called so by corruption, from *Piazza d'Agona*, because this *Piazza* was anciently a *Circus* for Sports, and it was called *Circus Agonalis*. In the midst of it anciently stood a great *Egyptian* Pillar, with Hieroglyphics upon it; and now of late it hath gotten another such Pillar set up here by Pope *Innocent* the X, with a rare Fountain issuing forth at the Foot of it, and adorned with four great Statues of white Marble, representing the four Parts of the World. In this place also stands the new Church of St. *Agnes*, built upon the place where she was condemned to the Stews. This Church is built at the Cost of *Princeps Pamphilio*, whose Palace joyns upon it. This Palace overlooking the *Piazza Navona*, deserves not only a glance of an Eye, but also an hours Inspection within. The Chambers are many and fair, and the great Hall a most lovely Room, if Paintings and variety of Pictures in Frames can make a House handsome. *Piazza Navona. The Church of Agnes. The Palace of Pamphilio.*

In this *Piazza* I saw the Palace of the Duke of *Braccino*, of the House of *Orsini*, and that of the Family of *Torres*.

The *Spanish* Church here called St. *Jacomos*, is not to be forgotten. Here lies buried in it *Ciaconius*, *St. Jacomo.*

conius, a learned Critic for a *Spaniard*. The Picture here in Oyl of *San Diego* is of *Annibal Caraccio*.

The Sapienza.

Over against the Back-door of this Church stands the *Sapienza*, a fair College, where the publick *Lectures* are read. This College was begun by *Eugenius* the IV, but much beautified of late with handsome Schools, and a new Church, by *Urban* the VIII, and a public Library by *Alexander* the VII. We have had in my time two *Englishmen* that were Readers here; Doctor *Hart*, and Doctor *Gibbs*, a noble *Cesarean* Laureat Poet, and the *Horace* of this Age.

St. Lewis.

From hence passing through the *Piazza Madama*, and before the Palace of the Grand *Duca*, I went to St. *Lewis* his Church, belonging to the *French* Nation. It's an handsome Church, and well served with *French* Priests. There's also an Hospital belonging to that Church and Nation. In the Church I found, upon a Pillar on the left hand, the Picture of great Cardinal *Dossat*, a *French-man*, whom I may justly call Great, because he was both a great States-man, and yet a very good Man; that is, he was a great Servant to his King, and yet a great Servant of God. His rare Letters shew the one, and his Life written by *Du Verdier* shews the other. Here lies also buried, in the middle almost of this Church, an *English* Priest of great Vertue, by name *More*, of the Family of great Sir *Thomas More*; and Heir of that Family, if I mistake not. His younger Brother and he striving whether of them should be Priest, It was his prerogative of Age, which making him to be four and twenty before his Brother, made him enter into Orders before him,

Part II.   *A Voyage through* Italy.   141

him, and become Priest, leaving the Estate to his Brother. It was he that set us out the Life of Sir *Thomas More*, in *English*: at last retiring to *Rome* to be Agent for his Brethren the Clergy, having ended this Business there happily (which was the procuring a Catholic Bishop) he ended his Life so too, and was buried here by his own Choice.

From hence I went to the Palace of *Justiniani*, which is hard by. Here I saw so many Statues of the old heathen Gods, and such Rooms full of old Marble Feet of them, that you would almost swear the Heathen Gods, when they were banished out of the *Pantheon*, had been committed hither as to a Prison: or that some of the Ancestors of this House had been Shoo-makers to the old Gods, and therefore was oblig'd to have their Lasts and Measures. For they had Gods of all sizes, seeing (as *Varro* saith) they had 30000 Gods. A world of these Statues are yet seen in the Gallery above, and in every Room in the House, which they clog, rather than adorn. And yet scarce one of them but is a *Palladium* to this Family; and would portend its sudden ruin if alienated. For as I remember the old Prince *Justiniani* dying without Heirs Male, left this Man his Heir, with this *Proviso*, that he should not so much as alienate one Statue upon pain of forfeiting the whole House and Goods. Judge then whether he had not need to keep the Statues chain'd up, as the *Tyrians* did their Gods, in a Siege; or whether the throwing of one of these Statues out of the Window, would not be properly a throwing the House out of the Windows. Upon which occasion, I cannot omit to tell you how the ancient

The Palace of Justiniani.

ancient Statues of *Rome* were grown at last to be
so many in number, that (as *Cassiodore* saith wittily of them) *posteritas pene parem populum urbi dedit, quam natura procreavit*, Posterity had made almost as many Men, by Art, in the City, as were made by Nature. And these Statues grew to that excess too, that Marble ones were thought too vulgar, and Gold and Silver ones were erected by riotous Men, who scorned to be like others in any thing but in being Mortal. But to return again to this House, I cannot leave it without minding you of some rare Pictures, of *Titian* and other prime Masters, which are shown in the Gallery above; especially the rare Picture of St. *John* the Evangelist, of the hand of *Raphael Urbin*; and that of our Lady and St. *Joseph* in another Room, which is a rare Copy of that famous Picture in the Cloister of the *Annunciata* in *Florence*, of *Andrea del Sarto*.

St. Eustachio. From hence I went to the Church of St. *Eustachio*, having seen in the way the goodly Ruins of the *Tverme* of *Alexander Severus*. In the Porch of this Church I saw an Inscription in a Stone, which told me that *Alexander* of *Parma* was Christened here with his Brother, being Twins. This Church stands in the place where St. *Eustachius* with his Wife *Theopista*, and his Sons *Agapitus* and *Theopistus*, were put into a Brazen Bull, and martyr'd by the brazen Heart of *Trajan*, whom *Eustachius* had served twice as General of his Armies, and gained him as many Victories.

The Rotonda or Pantheon. From hence I went to the *Rotonda*, otherwise called anciently the *Pantheon*, because it was dedicated to all Gods. This is a bolder piece of Architecture

Part II. A Voyage through Italy.

cture than Men think. For whereas other Vaults are strengthened and made good by being shut up close at the top, and in the Center of the Vault, which hinders the Vault from shrinking; here this great massive Vault is left wide open at the top, with a hole above three yards wide in Diameter. Indeed *Sebastianus Serlius*, an experienced Man in Fabrics, thinks this Church to be the Unic example of perfect Architecture; and *Pliny* in his time placed it among the rarest Works that were then extant. It hath no window in it, nor any other light, but what comes in at the wide hole mentioned above. Anciently it was covered with Brazen Tiles, and those gilt too, as *Lipsius* thinks; but now it's covered with great flat Stones. It's an Hundred and forty Foot high, and as many broad: and yet it hath no pillars to bear up that great Roof. Indeed it hath thrust all the Pillars out of doors, and makes them wait in the Porch; where there are thirteen great Pillars all of one piece, each one 53 Foot high, and six in Diameter, all of a granite or speckled Marble. The *Capitelli* of these Pillars are the best in *Rome*, of *Corinthian* order. Here is the Tomb of the incomparable Painter, *Raphael Urbin.*

Ille hic est Raphael, timuit quo sospite vinci,
Rerum magna Parens, & moriente mori.

In this Temple stood anciently the famous *Minerva* made by *Phidias*, of which Histories ring. There also was plac'd the Statue of *Venus*, in whose Ear that incomparable Pearl of *Cleopatra* hung, which upon a riotous Wager with *M. Antony*

tony (whether of them should make the most costly Supper) she was going to throw into a glass of Vinegar, to macerate it (as she had done another before) and drink it up: But *M. Antony* stopping her hand, and confessing himself overcome, the Pearl saith *Pliny*, was put in the Ear of *Venus* in the *Pantheon*. In the round holes over the Altars, were set those Heads of the Gods of the Heathens, which are now seen in the *Belvedere* of the *Maschere*. This Temple and its Porch were so lined anciently with Brass, that there was enough of it to make divers great Cannons, by Pope *Urbans* Command, and the great Canopy with the four Pillars which adorn St. *Peter*'s high Altar. And though the People and *Pasquin*, two equally senseless things, murmured much at the taking away of this Brass, yet seeing the *Pantheon* receiv'd no damage thereby, and seeing it was improv'd to that heighth, that it became *Ecclesiæ Ornamentum & Urbis Munimentum*, the wiser sort of Men thought it well employed, and let the People and Malice talk. I had almost forgot to tell you that this Temple was made by *Agrippa*, who had been thrice *Consul*, as the words in the *Architrave* of the Porch yet shew.

S. Lorenzo in Lucina. From hence I went through the *Campo Marzo*, unto the Church of St. *Lorenzo* in *Lucina*, which is served by *Clerici Regolari Minori*. It's an ancient Church neatly repaired of late, and the greatest Parish Church in *Rome*.

The Palace of Burghesi. From hence I went to see the Palace of *Burghesi*, which is hard by. This is one of the noblest Palaces in *Rome*: It gives you a fair Broadside of Windows, three Stories one over another, and its Length is Prodigious. Mounting up to the

Part II. *A Voyage through* Italy.

the Chambers I found a fair open Gallery built upon Arches and Pillars round about the Court. This Gallery lets you into several Apartments; and on that side which overlooks the *Piazza*, I saw a Row of ten or twelve great Chambers, through which I looked at once. In these Chambers, and the other Rooms I observ'd these things. 1. Rich Hangings, and over them rare Painting, made by a *Capucin* Lay-Brother. The History of the Queen of *Sabaa* coming to visit *Solomon*'s Court, and the rape of the *Sabines*, which make this *Fregio* over the Hangings, are so rarely well done, that *Raphael* and *Michel Angelo* could not have mended them for Colours. 2. A great Cabinet of *Ebony*, set with Histories cast in Gold, and set with rich Precious Stones; it's valued at threescore Thousand Crowns. 3. A rare picture of *Hercules* and *Anteus*. 4. *Raphael*'s own Picture. 5. The last Supper, by *Titian*. 6. The Terrass and Garden, with Box, Knots and Fountains of Water, all at the very top of the House, and overlooking the Street, River, Meadows and St. *Peters*. 7. The little black Gallery of Pictures, where among others I was shewn the Pictures of *Martin Luther*, *Nicolas Macchiavel*, and *Cæsar Borgia*; the two last great Corrupters of Policy and Manners. 8. The low cool Gallery, full of Statues and Pictures, especially of the *Borghesian* Family. That of *Paulus Quintus* in a small Mosaick work is scarce to be discover'd from Painting: as also the assumption of our Lady in the same work. There I saw also *Titian*'s own Picture, and the rare *Crucifix* made by *Michel Angelo*, so to Life, that some Men have fabulously given out that he drew It after a crucified Man.

K k From

Mausoleum Augusti.

From hence I went to the *Mausoleum Augusti,* or the Tomb of *Augustus Cæsar,* standing near St. *Rock's* Church, in a place hard to be found out. It was once one of the neatest Structures in *Rome.* And it was but fitting that the first of the Emperors should have an honourable Tomb; and that he who having found *Rome* built of Brick only, had left it all of Marble, should have a Marble Monument erected to him after his Death. *Urbem Lateritiam inveni, marmoream relinquo:* said *Augustus.* The *Mausoleum* was a round

Sueton.

Building of white Marble, going up with four Stories set round with Pillars, and each Story growing lesser and lesser, with green Trees set about every Story; having at the top of all, the Brazen Statue of *Augustus.* It was two Hundred and Fifty Cubits high. But now it's much defaced, and we see something of the greatness of it, but little of its Beauty.

St. Ant. di Padua.

Going from hence to the Church of St. *Antony* of *Padua* belonging to the *Portughesi,* I saw the Tomb of the great *Canonist* and *Casuist Navarre,* or *Martin Aspeleuita,* with his Statue in Busto over it. This good Man hearing how his great Friend *Caranza* was called to *Rome* to answer for himself in Points of Doctrin, which he was falsly accused of, followed him thither of his own accord, to defend his cause and clear his innocency, and having done it, died here.

St. Augustino.

Near to this Church stands the Church and Convent of the *Austin Friers.* In the Church I saw the Tomb of St. *Monica,* Mother to St. *Augustin.* Here also lies buried *Onufrius Panvinus* a Fryar of this Convent; learned in sacred Antiquities, and in the *Hebrew* Tongue. In the Convent

Part II.   A Voyage through Italy.   147

vent I often saw the neat Library, called *Bibliotheca Angelica*, becauſe *Angelus Rocca*, a Biſhop and Maſter of the Popes *Sacriſty*, gave it at his Death to his Convent; with an Obligation of letting it be open in the Mornings. There among many curious Books, I remember to have ſeen the Prophecies of *Joachim*, where among other things he ſaith, that the *Turks* ſhall be overcome and ruined by three Nations: by the *French*, *propter bonos equos*: by the *Engliſh*, *propter bonos marinarios*: and by the *Venetians*, *propter bonum conſilium*. Theſe are his very words.

Bibliotheca Angelica.

Joachims Prophecy of the Turks.

Near to the aforeſaid Church ſtands the Church of St. *Apollinaris*, and the *German* College. Here the beſt Singers of *Rome* meet conſtantly.

St. Apollinaris
The German College.

Over againſt this Church ſtands the Palace of the Duke of *Altemps*: In which I ſaw the great Hall, and in it the triumph of *Bacchus* in a *Baſſo relievo* cut in Marble, with exquiſite Art. I ſaw alſo here the repreſentation of a Town cut in Wood, an ancient and curious piece. The Picture of our B. Lady, with her Son in her Arms, valued at five Thouſand Piſtols; it is of *Raphael's* Hand. The neat Library full of divers good Manuſcripts and other Books. In fine, the noble Chapel with the Tomb of S. *Anaclet* Pope, under the Altar, with the Head of this Saint in the *Sacriſty*, enchaſed in Silver, and ſet thick with rich Stones. The rich ornaments here for the Church Service, coſt the Duke an Hundred and twenty Thouſand Crowns.

The Pallaze d' Altemps.

From hence in fine, I went to St. *John Florentins*, a neat Church belonging to the *Florentins*, at whoſe coſt it was built. Here is in one of the

St. John Florentins Church.

K k 2   Chap-

Chappels the picture of our Saviour's Resurrection, made by *Lanfranc*, a rare piece. And being lodged near this Church, I found that I had wandered all over *Rome*, and was now come again to the Bridg of St. *Angelo*, where I began my first days Journey thro *Rome*.

But seeing that in such Towns as this, there is always something to be seen after all, I made many irregular excursions up and down *Rome*, to view many things which I had not taken in my direct way before: as some Palaces, some rare Fountains, divers Antiquities, studies of *Virtuosi*, and the like, which I have been forc'd, for Methods sake, to pass over; yet because there are whole Books of all the Palaces, Fountains, Statues and Antiquities, set forth in Cuts and Pictures, I remit my Reader to them, while I ask one question.

Where are now those rare pieces of Antiquity which Histories rather mention, than we find now in *Rome* ? as the *Cymborum Mariis* the *Gregostasis*; the *Curia Hostilia*, the Golden House of *Nero*; *Tertul. Lib.* the Theater of *Pompey*, of which *Tertullian* saith, *de Spectac.* *Pompeius magnus solo suo Theatro minor*; the *c. 10.* *Forum Nervæ*; the Theater of *Statilius Taurus*; the *Septizonium Severi*, the Tower of *Mecænas*; the *Hippodromus*; the House of *Gordianus*; the *Circus Flaminius*; the *Circus Maximus*; the *Atrium Libertatis*; *Scipio*'s House; the Triumphal Arch of *Augustus Cæsar*, of *Domitian* ? And a World of other such rare buildings, whereby the *Romans* thought to have eternized their memories; if you ask for these things in Books, you should find their names only, if you look for them now in *Rome*, you shall find no marks at all of them : which makes me cry out with *Petrarch*,

Crede

Part II.   A Voyage through Italy.   149

Crede mihi alia quam lapideis fundamentis eget gloria, ut fit mansura: Believe me, true permanent glory stands in need of other Foundations than those of Stone. Hence *Janus Vitalis* an ingenious *Italian* Poet, having obferv'd that all the old massive Buildings of *Rome* are mouldered away, and that *Fluid Tyber* only remains still, cries out with this sweet Moral;

Potrare. In Reified. utriusque Part.

> *Disce hinc quid possit fortuna; immota labascunt
> Et quæ perpetuo sunt fluxura, manent.*

But I cannot leave *Rome* without taking notice of the Devotion, Music, Ceremonies, Shows, Government, and the Inhabitants of this place: of each of which I will give a touch, both for my Travellers sake, and my Readers.

And first for the Devotion of *Rome*, I found it to be very great and real in those places where the *Quarante Hore* and Stations are kept. For all the year long the *Quarante Hore* go from one Church to another, through all the Churches of *Rome*; and there you shall always see a world of devout People praying and meditating and hearing the Sermons, and giving of Alms, and all this with that profound respect and silence, with that assiduity and concourse, with that fervor and zeal, that you need not ask where the Station is, but only observe where you see the People flocking so fast in the morning, and where the Poor make the greatest Hedge and Lane. In other Churches of *Rome*, upon their Festival days (which happen almost every day, in one place or other) they have the best Music can be got: and though this seems to draw mens Ears to the

Devotion in Rome.

K k 3   Church,

Church, rather than their hearts; yet when I remember what elevated thoughts it breeds in the mind, and how innocently it detains Men from doing worse, I cannot but place Church-Music among the acts of devotion.

The Music of Rome.

Now, as for this Music, it is the best in the world, and in the best kind, which is Voices. For my part having read in a learned Author, that the hating of Music is a sign of a Soul quite out of tune, and not right strung for predestination; and that the *Scythian* King, who held the neighing of his Horse to be far better Music, than the Pipe of famous *Timotheus*; was held for an Ass himself; I thought it both comely and lawful to love Music: And being in a place where the best Music was, I frequented it often with singular satisfaction. Now the best Music I heard, was the Music of the Popes Chappel, consisting of pure Voices, without any Organ or other Instruments: Every singer here knowing his part so well, that they seem all to be Masters of Music. Then the Music of the *Chiesa Nova*; of S. *Apollinaris*; upon St. *Cecilies* day in the Church of that Saint, the *Patroness* of Singers; of the Oratory of St. *Marcello* every *Friday* in *Lent*; of the *Jesuits*, during the *Quarante Hore* in *Shrovetide*; of every good Church of Nuns upon their Patrons day; especially that of the Nuns of *Campo Marzo*, where I heard often *Fonseca* sing so rarely well, that she seemed to me, to cheer up much the Church in its Combats; and to make the Church *Militant*, either look like the Church *Triumphant*, or long for it. In a word, whosoever loves Music, and hears but once this of *Rome*, thinks he hath made a saving Journey

to

Part II.   A Voyage through Italy.   151

to *Rome*, and is well payed for all his pains of coming so far.

Having given my ears many a break-fast up- *The Cere-*
on the Music, I gave my eyes many a Colla- *monies.*
tion upon the Ceremonies of *Rome*, which were
chiefly these. The Ceremony of the Popes o-
pening of the *Porta Santa* of St. *Peter's* Church,
in the *Jubile year*. The Ceremonies of the Popes
Chappel, when he assists there, especially upon
Candelmas-day, *Palmsunday*, *Maunday-Thursday*,
&c. The Ceremony of the Popes washing of
thirteen Pilgrims Feet; of his singing Mass publickly in St. *Peter's* Church, upon St. *Peter's* day,
and other great days; the Ceremony of Beati-
fying and of Canonizing of Saints; the Ceremony
of his creating new Cardinals, & giving them their
Cap in public Consistory; the Ceremony of the
Mass sung in *Greek* and according to the *Greek*
rites, in the Church of the *Greek Seminary*, upon
the Feast of the *Epiphany*, and St. *Athanasius* his
day; the Ceremony of Baptizing the *Jews*; with
a world of others. One Ceremony I was not unwilling to miss in my five several Voyages, because it always implies the death of a Spiritual
Father, I mean, the Ceremony of a *Sede Vacante*:
And of all the bad Compliments that ever I heard
made, I like none so ill as that of a Noble Man
of *Germany*, who being asked by Pope *Innocent*
the X. whether he had seen all the Ceremonies
of *Rome*, answered, that he had seen all, but a
Sede Vacante, as if he had said; Holy Father, I
have seen all the fine sights of *Rome*, but your
death. A horrible *Tramontane* compliment, which
put even the Pope himself to a smile.

Kk 4   As

The Shews of Rome Sacred.

As for the Shows, I saw divers, both Sacred and Prophane. As the whipping Processions in the Holy Week. The great Procession from St. *Marcello's* Oratory to St. *Peter's* Church, upon *Maunday Thursday*, in the Holy Year. The *Spanish* Procession, in *Piazza Navona*, upon *Easter-day* in the Morning, in the Holy Year. The Procession of the *Zitelle* upon our *Ladies* day in *Lent*. The Procession of the Priests of the Oratory upon *Shrove Tuesday*, to the seven Churches; with five or six Thousand persons following of them, all whom they treat in an open field, giving every one a couple of hard Eggs, and a slice of *salsigia*, with Bread and Wine. The several *Cavalcata's* of the Pope and Cardinals. The *Spanish Cavalcata* upon St. *Peters* Eve, when then *Spanish* Embassador presents the purse of Gold, and the *Gennet*. The *Girandola* and Fireworks upon St. *Peter's* Eve and divers such like sacred Triumphs.

Prophane.

For the prophane Shows, I saw the solemn entries of Embassadors, especially those of Obedience, where each Prince's Embassador strives to out-vye the other, and by excessive expences, make their Masters Greatness appear above that of others. Their *Cavalcata's* to Court upon their public Audience: Their reception in a public Consistory: Their Audience of Leave are all stately. Then the curious *Opera*, or musical *Drammata*, recited with such admirable art, and set forth with such wonderful changes of Scenes, that nothing can be more surprizing. Here I have seen upon their Stages, Rivers swelling, and Boats rowing upon them; Waters overflowing their Banks and Stage; Men flying in the Air, Serpents craw-

Part II.   A Voyage through Italy.   153

crawling upon the Stage, Houses falling on the suddain, Temples and *Boscos* appearing, whole Towns, known Towns, starting up on the suddain with Men walking in the Streets; the Son appearing and chasing away darkness, Sugar Plumbs fall upon the Spectators heads like Hail, Rubans flash in the Ladies faces like lightning, with a Thousand such like representations. In fine, the *Carneval* pomps in the Streets, exhibited by Noble-men, with great cost and glory.

As for the Government of *Rome*, I found it divided into two parts: The Government of the City, and the Government of the Church. That of the City is exactly performed by a Governor (some Prelate of great parts) constituted by the Pope, to watch over the City carefully, and to render him an account weekly, of all that passeth. This Governour liveth always in the heart of the City, and hath besides his own Guards, a *Barigello* or Captain of the *Shirri*, or Sergeants, to keep all in order and awe, both day and night. This *Barigello* hath, *Argus* like, an hundred eyes to spy into the deportments of all that live in *Rome*, and, *Briareus* like, as many hands, to carry to prison those that infringe the Laws. Hence Justice here is as exactly performed, as Orders are descreetly given out. The prizes of all things are printed and affixed in publick Places, and Shops Inns and Taverns are bound to have them set up in their entrance, that strangers may know the rates of all provisions, and blame none but themselves, if they be couzened. So that its as hard a thing to be couzened here, as its hard not to be couzened in other places. And for those that cannot read or

The Government of Rome.

That of the City.

speak

speak the Language well, *Sbirri* will ask of them, what they paid a Meal, how much for a pound of Meat, how much for a Pint of such and such Wine, &c. and if they find him to have been couzened either in the quantity, weight, or price, they'l right the stranger beyond his expectation, and punish the delinquent beyond his desire. The last *Jubile* year I was shewn some of the *Sbirri* in Pilgrims habits, on purpose to mingle themselves with the other Pilgrims, the better to observe how they were used or abused by their Hosts in Inns or Taverns, and accordingly punish them. In fine, Justice is so well administred here, and imprisoning cases so many, that the last Prince of *Conde* being in *Rome*, said he wondred much at one thing there, which was, to see so many Men go out of their Houses in the Morning, and return home again to dinner, without being imprisoned. A Knife in a Man's Pocket, a dark Lanthorn, a Sword worn without leave, &c. will suffice to make a Man be sent to Prison; and a Pocket Pistol found about you, or in your Cloakbag, is enough to make you be set to the Gallies, with *tre tratti di corda*, that is, strappada thrice; yet they mitigate the rigor of these Laws to Strangers, who offend out of ignorance.

That of the Church. As for the Government of the Church that's done partly by the Pope himself, in several Congregations held before him: Partly by his Vicar General, a Cardinal who hath under him a *Vice-Gerent* (a Bishop) to help him. There's scarce a day in the Week, but the Pope holds one Congregation or other, about Church affairs, in which Congregations, not only Cardinals intervene,

Part II. A Voyage through Italy.

vene, but also Bishops and Doctors; and where all businesses are headed as well as handled with great deliberation. Every three weeks the *Pope* holds a *Consistory*, where all the *Cardinals* that are in *Rome*, meet his *Holyness*, as at a Grand Council, to advise with him concerning the necessary affairs of the Church. And its pretty to see, how, like the motions of a well ordered Watch, all businesses here move at once, and yet never interfere or clash with one another.

As for the Inhabitants of *Rome*, they follow the fortune of their City, and as when *Rome* was but yet a new Town, the Inhabitants were but three Thousand in all, saith *Dionysius*, and when it was come to its full growth, it had three or four Millions of People: Insomuch, that in a great Plague, the Bills of Mortality came to ten Thousand Men a day, and this for many days together: So now, *Rome* having been six times sack'd and ruin'd (as I said above) is not the tenth part so populous as heretofore it was; and even those Inhabitants that are now in *Rome*, are, for the most part, originary, from other parts of *Italy* and *Europe*; and have been drawn to take up here, either by preferment or business. The Nobility it self is, for the major part, foreign, and sprung out of such Families of Popes, Princes and Cardinals, as have been Foreign before their promotions and preferments. The true, Ancient and Illustrious *Roman* Families, I found to be these few, *Ursini*, *Colonna*, *Favelli*, *Frangepani*, and some few others.

The Inhabitants of Rome.

Euseb. in Chronico.

Having thus, as Painters do, taken *Rome* in all her postures, I confess it happened to me, as it did to *Apelles*, taking the Picture of *Compaspe*;
that

that is, by looking so often and so attentively upon *Rome*, I began to be so far in love with it, as not only to subscribe to *Cassiodorus* his opinion, who affirms it to be a kind of crime not to live in *Rome*, when you can do it. *Piaculi genus est absentem sibi Romam diutius facere, qui in ea constitutis possit laribus habitare*; but also to subscribe to our old *Britain* Kings, *Cadwallader*, *Cedwalla*, *Coenred*, *Offa*, *Ina* and *Burrhed*, who thought *Rome* also the best place to die in. For if those places be thought by all Men, the best places to live in, where a Man may learn the most experimental knowledg, and how to manage great affairs, where can a Man learn more knowledg than in *Rome*? Where all Languages are spoken, all Sciences are taught, the ablest Men of *Europe* meet, all the best Records are found, all Wits appear as upon their true Theater, all Foreign Embassadors render themselves, all *Nuncio*'s at their return to *Rome*, unload themselves of the observations they have made abroad; and where every Stone almost is a Book; every Statue a Master; every Inscription a Lesson, every Antichamber an Academy? And again, if those places be the best to die in, where all comforts of the soul are best had; what place can be better to die in than *Rome*? The very Center and Bosom it self of Catholick Communion; and where there is so much devotion, and so much vertue practised, and where you have this comfort in your grave; that you lie in a ground which hath been bathed in the blood of so many Thousand Martyrs.

And thus much of *Rome*, in the describing of which, if I have been too *Prolix*, remember that

Part II.   A Voyage through Italy.   157

that great Ladies are long in dressing; if too short, remember that I only relate what I saw there, not all that is to be seen there.

Having thus seen *Rome*, I agreed with the *Pro-* *cacsio*, to carry me to *Naples*. Others take with them a *Vetturino*, that lets them have Horses, and diets them too; I mean, defrays a Man for Meat and Drink and Horse-hire, both going and coming, and your Horse five days at *Naples* (but not your diet there) and lets you have his Horses two days, to go see *Vesuvius* and *Pozzolo*; and all this for fourteen or fifteen Crowns a Man. It's true, a Man is ill lodged, and badly treated in that journey, but it doth a Gentleman good to be acquainted with hardship.   *My Journey from Rome to Naples.*

Parting then from *Rome* by the Gate of St. *John Lateran*, we passed through these places.

Marino, a neat little Town belonging to Cardinal *Colonna*. It looks like a painted Town.   *Marino.*

Veletri, famous for the birth of the Ancestors of *Augustus Cæsar*. Here's a brazen Statue of *Urban* the VIII. and a neat Palace and Garden of Cardinal *Ginetti*. Its an Episcopal Town.   *Veletri.*

The *Tre Taberne* where St. *Paul* was met, at his first coming to *Rome*, by the *Christians* of *Rome*. Act. 28. v. 15.   *Tre Taberne.*

Peperno, where *Camilla* the *Amazon* was born.   *Peperno.*

Fossa Nuova, where St. *Thomas* of *Aquin* going to the Council of *Lyons*, fell sick and died.   *Fossa Nuova.*

Taracina (old *Anxur*) the head Town of the *Volscians*, but now bare and bald; shewing nothing but some old ruins of the Heaven which *Antoninus Pius*, here adorned; and of an old Temple. Its an Episcopal Town.   *Tracina.*

Not

Amycla.   Not far from hence stood anciently, the Town
            Amycla, that *Pythagorical* Town which was ruin-
            ed by Serpents, because none would kill them;
            Pythagoras his Doctrin forbidding Men to kill a-
            ny living Creature. Another time it was ruined
Serv. in lib. by silence; no Man daring to speak of the Ene-
10. Æneid. mies coming; too many false Alarms having
            made the Magistrates forbid, under pain of death,
            that no Man should speak any more of the Ene-
            mies coming; so that when they came indeed,
            no Man durst speak of it. Thus, not only Phi-
Amyclas si- losophy, but even silence it self and obedience,
lentium   two noble Vertues are hurtful to Men, if they
perdidit.
Proverb. a- be not accompanied with discretion.
pud S. Hie-   From *Taricini* we went to *Fundi* to Supper,
ron.   having passed through a Forest of Bay Trees,
            and through an open Gate, called *Portella*, which
            lets Men into the Kingdom of *Naples*.
Fundi.   *Fundi* is so called, because its built in a low
            Flat. Its antient, if you believe your Ears, not
            your Eyes. For it looks younger than the other
            Towns I have passed through before. The rea-
            son is, because this Town was burned some 130
            years ago by *Caradin Barbarozza*, Admiral of
Leo Afer.   the great Turk *Solyman*. It was this *Caradin*,
            who, of a famous Pyrat, became King of *Algiers*,
            having persuaded those of *Algiers* to shake off
            the *Spanish* yoke. This *Caradin* being upon the
            Mediterranean Sea, and hearing, by his Spies, that
            Julia Eonsaga (widow of *Vespasian Colonna*, and
            the handsomest Woman in the World) lived
            here in *Fundi*, landed his Men in the Night, and
            sent them to catch her napping, resolved to make
            a fine present of her to his lewd Master *Solyman*.
            But she leaping out of her Bed, rid away in her
                                                        very

Part II. A Voyage through Italy.

very Linnen, and escaped so narrowly, that had she staid to put on any Cloaths, she had for ever put off all liberty. The Pyrats missing of this fair *Helena*, failed not to make a burning *Troy* of *Fundi*; ransacking it, and carrying away the best of its Inhabitants: Such dangerous things are great Beauties to weak Towns.

From *Fundi* we went to *Mela*, upon the *Via Appia*, so called, because *Appius Claudius*, a Noble *Roman* made it, at his own cost, during his *Consulat*. This Cawsey is one of the greatest Proofs of the *Romans* Greatness and Riches. For it was five days Journey long; beginning at *Rome* and reaching through the Kingdom of *Naples* to *Brundusium*. It was as broad as two Carts might easily meet upon it and pass: It was all of great black Flint Stones, each one as big as two Men can carry, and laid so close together, that they have held together these 1800 years, and seem, as *Procopius* saith ingeniously to be rather *Congeniti*, than *Congesti*, born together, than laid together. The frequent passing of Horses and Mules (for so many Years) upon this Cawsey, have made it both so smooth and shining, that when the Sun shines upon it, you may see it glister two Miles off, like a Silver Highway.

Arriving at *Molo*, called anciently *Formia*, I went to see *Cicero's* Tomb, which stands in a Garden not far off. And I the more willingly believe it to be his Tomb, because 'tis certain, that *Tully* had a *Villa* in *Formiis* (which was this place) and thither he was going in his Litter, when he was overtaken by the executioners of the *Triumviri* and Beheaded. There are no words upon

The Via Appia.

See Plut. *in Graccho.*

Procop. l. 1. de bell. Goth.

Mola Formiae.

Val. Max. l. 1. c. 4.

his

France *gave me Milk,* Spain *great Employments gave.*
Rome *gave me Death, and here* Caet' *a Grave.*

This Castle standing upon a Promontory overlooketh the Town, and thirty Miles of Sea. In the end of the Town, towards Land-side, for this Town is a pure *Peninsula,* I saw the Cloven Rock, which Tradition here holds to have been thus cloven at our Saviours Death. The long Stairs going down between the two Mountains in the very open gash, and rendring you to a neat Chappel below, strike you all the way long with a sacred Reverence. And are able almost to rend also a Stony Heart in two, with the thoughts of our Saviour's Passion. *The Cloven Rock.*

Upon the top of all this *Promontory* there is an antient *Monument* of *Manutius Plancus* an old *Roman,* with a great deal of old *Latin* upon it; but my riding Boots put me out of all reading Humour, and I was very willing to let *Plancus* lye quietly in his Monument above, so I could but recover again our Boat and there sit still. Of this Town was the famous Cardinal *Caetanus,* of St. *Thomas Aquinas* his Name, Order, and almost Learning. This Town was built by Æneas, in honour of his Nurse *Caeta* who died here.

Returning again to *Mola,* we went after Dinner to see *Cicero's Grotte,* and so away. *Cicero's Grotte.*

We had not ridden three hours but we came to the Ferry of *Carigliano,* near to which I saw the fair Rests of an old *Amphitheater* standing alone in the Fields, with the Rests also of an *Aqueduct.* I wondered at first to see an *Amphithea-* *The Ferry of Carigliano.*

ter standing alone, and far from any great Town: but upon enquiry, I found that here had stood once a noble Town called *Minturna*, but now so ruined that not one Stone of it appeareth. Indeed we are often at this fault in *Italy*, and look for Towns in Corn-Fields. *Luna, Populonia, Cuma, Baiæ*, and *Minturna* cheat thus our Expectations, and leave us no Monuments of themselves, but a pure *Fuit Ilium*, which though it be Travellers loss, yet it's Mans comfort, that Towns do die as well as he: hence *Rutilius*,

Minturna.

> *Non indignemur mortalia Corpora solvi;*
> *Cernimus exemplis oppida posse mori.*

Having passed over the River in a Ferry-Boat, we entred upon the Meadows, in whose *Fens* (called the *Fens* of *Minturna*) *Caius Marius* lay hid a while, and there with his stern looks and manly Voice, saying, darest thou kill *Caius Marius?* So terrified the Slave sent there to kill him, that he let him escape to his Ship, and so into *Africk*. He may speak big that speaks for his Life; and any looks become a Man when he looks to himself well in dangers.

Plutarch.

While we rode along these Meadows we saw before us the Mountain of *Garo*, anciently called *Mons Massicus*, famous for excellent Wines; as well as the Country thereabout, which was called *Ager Falernus*, so famed by Poets for its *Vinum Falernum*.

Passing thus along, we came at Night to *St. Agatha's*, and the next Morning betimes we entred into *Campania Felix*, so surnam'd because of it's admirable Air, wonderful plenty of Corn and Wine,

Campania Fœlix.

Part II. A Voyage through Italy.

Wine, and pleasant Prospects on all sides, which makes an Ancient call it, *Certamen Cereris & Bacchi*, the strife of *Ceres* and *Bacchus*. It was this Country which, with its delights broke *Hannibal's* Army; which neither Snow could cool, nor *Alpes* stop, nor *Romans* vanquish, saith *Seneca*. Indeed the pleasantness of this Country made us a full mends for all the ill way we had before: Nature having set that scurvy way there on purpose that we might like her Favourite *Campania* the better after it. I call this Country Natures Favourite, in imitation of *Pliny*, who calls it *Opus gaudentis naturæ*, that is, a Country made by Nature when she was in a good humour. It's an Heathen that speaks, and you must pardon him.

We intended that day to have gone to *Capua* to Dinner; but when we came thither, we did not find it at home. For this Town now called *Capua* is two Miles distant from the place where old *Capua* stood. Indeed the old *Capua* was a Town of Importance; for it was either the second or third in the World; and stood in Competition, as *Carthage* did with *Rome*. Nay it demanded of *Rome* to be used like a Sister, not like a Subject; and stood high upon it, that one of the Annual Consuls should always reside here. But that *Capua* is vanished with its vanity; and this *Capua* hath no reason to be so proud, being famous for nothing but that action of many noble Women here, who to avoid the Insolencies of the *French* Soldiers (received into the Town friendly) leapt into the River *Vulturno* to save their Virginity and Honour, from their lewdness: an action rather wonderful, than warrantable.

Capua.

See St. Aug. l. 2. de morib. Eccles. And St. Thom 2.2. qu. 64. an. 5.

There

eth up notably the Interest of *Spain* in the Court of *Rome*: And it squeezeth it self now and then into huge Sums, four millions of Crowns, to send Tribute into *Spains* Coffers. For this Kingdom is a Thousand five Hundred Miles in Compass, four Hundred and Fifty wide. It hath in it twenty Arch-Bishops Seats; an Hundred and twenty five Bishops Seat? A Thousand five hundred Bourghs; two millions of Souls: Ten *Principalities*; twenty three *Dutchies*; thirty *Marquisats*; Fifty four Counties; and about a Thousand Baronies, whereof four Hundred are Ancient: It can raise an Hundred and fifty Thousand Foot, and an hundred Thousand Horse. It's ordinary Squadron of Gallies are but twenty. *It's greatness. It's Strength.*

As for the Town it self of *Naples*, if it be the third of *Italy* for greatness, it is the first for strength and neatness; and therefore deservedly surnamed *La Gentile*, the Gentile. It hath *Campania* on one side of it, and the *Mediterranean* Sea on the other: So that it's fed by Natures best Dugs, Sea and Land. Its Air was always esteemed so pure; that the great Men of *Rome* had either their *Villas*, in *Naples*, or hard by. It's well built, well paved, well furnished with excellent Provisions, well filled with Nobility, and the Nobility well mounted. The chief street is *Strada di Toledo*, Paved with Freestone, and flanked with noble Pallaces and Houses. We entred into some of them, and others we saw which had not recovered their *empompoint* since they had been sick of *Mazienello's* Disease: Their very looks shewed us that their Sickness had been *Convulsion-Fits*. The chief Palaces are these: The stately Palace of the Viceroy, that of *Gra-* *The Town of Naples.*

vina,

vina, Caraffa, Ursino, Sulmone, Toledo, &c. Most of the Houses of *Naples* are made flat at top, to walk upon: A most convenient thing to Breath upon in the fresh Evenings, and easy to be imitated by other Countries.

I saw here also the several publick places of Assemblies of the Nobility, according to their several ranks. These places are like open walking places, rail'd about with high Iron Rails, and painted within.

The Molo. Then the *Molo* running a quarter of a Mile into the Sea, and affording great refreshment to the Towns-Men who walk here in the Evenings in Summer, where they are sure to cool their Lungs with a sweet *Fresco.* At the end of the *Molo* stands mounted the high *Lantern*, to direct Ships home safe in the Night; and a fine Fountain of fresh Water.

The Churches of Naples. As for the Churches here they yield to none in *Italy.* The *Domo* is antient, and therefore out of the mode a little: Yet it hath a modern Chappel which is very Beautiful: and is one of the finest in *Europe*, both for Brazen Statues, and rich Painting. The *Cupola* was painted by the rare hand of *Domenichino.* In this Chappel is the Tomb of St. *Januarius*, Bishop of *Benevent*, and now Patron of this Town; whose Blood being conserved in a little Glass, and Concrete, melts and grows liquid when it is placed near to *Baronius* his Head, and even bubbles in the Glass. A *& Brevia-* *French* Nobleman, Count of *La Val*, was con- *rium Rom.* verted from *Calvinism* to the Catholick Religion upon sight of this Wonder. On the Left-hand of this Chappel without, lies Buried Pope *Innocent* the IV. who ordered first, that Cardinals should

Part II.   A Voyage through Italy.   167

should wear red Hats. The Verses upon his Tomb told me this. In the Sacristy are kept many precious gifts of Princes, and divers Relicks of Saints enchased in Gold and Silver. *Petrus à St. Romualdo in his Treas. for. Chro ad an. 1604.*

The *Annunciata* is both neat and devout: The Cupola and Roof are well painted and guilt. The two Infants of *Bethlehem* with their several Wounds, one in the Head, the other the Body, are shewn here. The Hospital is joyning to it, and is of great reception: It maintains two Thousand Sick and Decrepid in it; besides above eight Hundred Orphans and poor Children. *The Annunciata.*

Near the great Hospital stands St. Peters Church, and before it the Altar upon which (as the Inscription saith) St. *Peter* said Mass at his first coming to *Naples*.

The *Theatins* Church called St. *Pauls*, is very neat; and if you saw it with its best Hangings on, you would think it one of the neatest Churches in *Italy*. The Roof is curiously painted and guilt. Here I saw the rich Tomb of *Beato Coetano* a holy Man of this Order, and the Tabernacle of the high Altar, both very Rich. In the Sacristy they have as rich Ornaments as in any Church of *Italy*. *St. Paolo.*

The Jesuits Church here is the best they have in *Italy*, if it be not a little too wide for its length. In the Sacristy I saw the richest ornaments for the Altars, and the best Silver Candlesticks that I have seen any where else. It's rich in Painting, Sculptures, and Marble. The High Altar was not yet finished, but promiseth Wonders. *The Jesuits Church.*

The *Franciscans* Church, called St. *Maria Nova*, is very trim, with its neat Chappels and Tombs, and guilt Roof. Here I saw the Tomb *St. Maria Nova.*

Ll 4   of

Part II. A Voyage through Italy.

Marchese di Piscara, surnamed the Thunderbolt of War. The words upon this Tomb are so ingenious (that though I profess not to set down many Epitaphs in this my Voyage) I cannot but strive to carry them into other Countries. They are these.

Quis jacet hoc gelido sub marmore ? Maximus ille
   Piscator, belli gloria, pacis honos.
Numquid & hic pisces cepit ? Non.   Ergo quid ?
   Urbes,
   Magnanimos Reges, oppida, regna, Duces.
Dic quibus hæc cepit Piscator retibus ?   Alto
   Consilio, intrepido corde, alacrique manu.
Qui tantum rapuere ducem ?   Duo Numina, Mars,
   Mors.
   Ut raperent quidnam compulit ? Invidia.
Nil nocuere ipsi ; vivit nam Fama superstes,
   Quæ Martem & Mortem vincit, & Invidiam.

The Church of St. *John Carbonare* is considerable for it self, but much more for the stately Tomb in it, of King *Robert*. In the Church of the Nunnery which stands at the foot of the Hill, as you go up to the *Carthusians*, I saw a most curious Tabernacle upon the Altar, of precious polished Stones. Its one of the richest I have seen any where, but that of *Florence* described above.

Then we mounted up that winding Hill of the *Carthusians* Church and Monastry, called St. *Martin's*. It's the most sumptuous thing in all *Europe* for a Monastry, whether you regard it's situation, or it's fabric. It's situated upon an high Hill under the wing of the Castle St. *Elmo*, to put

The stately Monastry of the Carthusians.

put Castles in mind, that they ought to defend and protect Religion. The whole Quadrangle, or Cloister of this Monastry, is of pure polished white Marble, paved with Marble squares, and adorned round with a Baluster, and white Marble Pillars. Then entring into an open Gallery, we had as fine a Prospect as *Europe* can afford, *Barcly. Irem* not excepting that of *Greenwich*, thought by *Bar-* *Animarum.* *clay*, the best Prospect in *Europe*. For here I saw all *Naples* under me, with the perfect sight of the two other Castles, with the Haven, the *Molo*, the *Arsenal*, the Ships, the Country round about *Naples*, Mount *Vesuvius*, *Pausilipus*, the Ships at Sea, the Promontories of *Misenum* and *Minerva*, the Isle of *Caprea*, with a world of other delightful sights. Then I was led into the apartment of the *Padre Visitatore*, where I saw most neat Rooms, and some good Pictures. Then going to the Church, I found it to exceed the Cloyster, which before I thought to have exceeded all other things. It's all of Marble, gilding and painting. The Pavement is all of curious red and white Marble squares as also the Sacristy. The Chappels and Pictures match the roof, and the Pillars with their particular Graces. The Sacristy is absolutely the richest I ever saw. The great Cupboards are of such a rare *Mosaic* wood work, inlaid into Pictures, that it disputes hard with the Quire of *Dominicans* in *Bologna*. Here they shewed me a great Crucifix of Silver, which had been fifteen years in making. The *Remonstrance* to expose the B. Sacrament in, is made like a Sun, whose Beams are mingled with Silver and Coral. The great Candlesticks of Massive Silver, and the great Flowerpots are curiously wrought. Then

Part II.   A Voyage through Italy.   171

Then I went to see the three Castles; That
of St. *Elmo*, which is hard by the *Carthusians*, was built by *Charles* the V. It stands well upon its own Guard, by reason of its high situation: But I doubt whether it can offend any enemy, except *Naples* it self, which is under it. *Castle St. Elmo.*

The Castle *Vovo* was built by *William* the third of *Normandy*, upon a rock in the Sea; and from its oval form, is called *Castel vovo*. There is a digue leading unto it from the Land. *Castle Vovo.*

The *Castle Nuovo* was built by *Charles* of *Anjou*, designed King of *Naples*. It stands near the *Molo*, and level with the Town and Sea, as if it could defend and offend both. *Castle Nuovo.*

These three Castles are guarded by natural *Spaniards*; and well furnished with great Cannons, by whose language (which is *ultima ratio Regum*, Kings last Arguments) the *Neopolitans* are either Catechised into duty, or threatned into obedience. Indeed, such a People and Town are not easily bridled: Such a wanton Courser as *Naples*, is not to be ridden with Snaffles; it hath often plunged under the King of *Spain*, but could never fling him quite out of the Saddle, *merce a gli tre Castelli*.

Then I went to see the Markets here, and found them most admirable, especially those of Fruit, which *Campania* sends hither: And were but the Taxes taken off, or reasonably moderated, *Naples* would be the cheapest and richest place in the world. But the Kings Officers, if they suck in *Milan*, and fleece in *Sicily*, they fley in *Naples*, which usage drove the People some years past, into such a desperate humour, that they took up Arms, under the command of *Mazainelo* *The Markets.*

Some of the famous Men for Learning of this Town, were old *Statius*, rare *Sannazarius*, Alexander ab Alexandro*, and *John Baptist Marini*: three excellent Poets, and one Antiquary. *Naples* hath furnished the Church with eighteen Popes.

Learned Men.

Having thus seen the Town it self of *Naples*, I was most willing to see the Wonders of Nature, which are near unto it. Horsing therefore betimes one Morning, we went with a Guide to see *Vesuvius*, the burning Mountain, some seven miles distant from *Naples*; Our honest Guide had studied the History of this Hill, and could tell how often it had broken forth into Flames, since the beginning of the World, that is, twenty times. *Xiphilinus* the Epitomist of *Dio*, relates at length, one that happened under the Emperor *Titus*. But the last which happened in the year 1631. he remembred very well, and related it to me as we went along, with a sad Preface, of

The Mountain Vesuvius.

Infandum Peregrine jubes renovare dolorem,

because he could also say,

———————— *Et quorum pars magna fui*,

having been an Actor in that Disorder. For he was Son to a rich Husbandman here, and with much ado, *Æneas* like, he had rescued his old Father from the Ashes of *Vesuvius*, which overwhelmed and buried whole Villages. Here said he, pointing to the place, stood a great Vineyard, one of the best of the Country; but now three fathom deep in Ashes. Here stood a Village full of of rich Husbandmen and goodly Houses; but now ruin'd by the Stones shot at it from *Vesuvius*. Here stood once a pleasant *Villa*, beautified with curious Walks, Orange-trees, Fountains and Arbors, but *Jam cinis est ubi villa fuit*. In a word, above Two thousand People were burnt, lamed or stifled in this Eruption. Then he shewed me the vast Stones, which overcharging the Stomach of *Vesuvius*, he had vomited up, with such a boaking, that *Naples* thought the day of Judgment had been at hand. Then he shewed me a Channel, where a River of fiery green matter, mingled with Brimstone, Allom, Iron, Water, and Salt-Petre, had run from that spewing Hill. The manner of its breaking out was thus: The Hill began first to smoke more vehemently than before: Then it flamed and cast out a Cloud of Ashes, which, had the wind stood toward the City, had cover'd all *Naples*, and buried it in those Ashes: Then it began to roar, as if Madam Nature her self had been in Labour; Thunder was but Pistol-crack to this noise: And the mouth a Cannon a full mile wide, must needs give a great report. It bellowed and thundered again: *Naples* trembled: The Ground swelled: The Sea it self shiver'd for fear, when the Hill tearing its Entrals with huge violence, was brought to Bed of a world of vast Stones, and a flood of Sulphurous Matter, which ran from the top of the Mountain into the Sea, for the space of three Miles. All this he told me, and this he shew'd me afterward, in a public Inscription, upon a fair Marble Stone erected hard by. And all this made me but the more desirous of seeing this Mountain. Wherefore spurring

Part II. A Voyage through Italy.

ring on, we came soon after to the foot of the Hill; where leaving our Horses, we began to crawl up that steep Hill for a good mile together, to the mid-leg in ashes. At last, with much ado, we got to the top of the Hill; and peeping fearfully (remembring *Pliny*'s accident) into the great hollow, from the brink of it, found it to be like a vast Kettle, far greater than those Hell Kettles, near *Dislington*, in the Bishoprick of *Durham*, made by Earthquakes. For the Orifice of this Kettle is a Mile or two wide, and very nigh as deep. In the bottom of it, is a new little Hill, rising out of the hollow of the old, and fuming perpetually with a thick Smoke, as if it also would play tricks too in it's turn. Having gazed a while at this Chimney of Hell (for *Tertullian* calls Ætna and *Vesuvius*, *Fumariola inferni*) we came faster down than we went up. He that is not content with this my short description of the burning of this Hill, let him read *Julius Cæsar Recupitus*, who hath made a little Book alone of it, called, *De Vesuviano incendio Nuncius*.

See Baker's Chronic. in Henric. 2.

Hell's Chimneys.

Having recovered our Horses again, we came back to *Naples*; and the next Morning, taking a new Guide, we went to see the wonders of Nature about *Baia* and *Puzzuolo*.

Horsing then again betimes in the Morning, we passed by the Castle *Vovo*, and soon after to *Margelino*, to see the Tomb of *Sannazarius* the Poet, who lies buried in the Church of *Santa Maria del Porto*, which was once *Sannazarius* his own House, which dying, he left to be made a Church of, under that Title: So that in his Testament, he wrote *de Virginis partu*, as well

Our journey to Puzzuolo.

Sannazarius's Tomb.

a3

say here that it is a full Mile long; but I thought it scarce so much. We rid some forty paces by the light of the wide Entrance; but that vanishing, we were left in the Dark a good while, till we came to the half way, where there hangs a burning Lamp before the Picture of our Saviour in the B. Virgins Arms. The light of this Lamp was very grateful unto us; and I am confident a Puritan himself, were he here, would be glad to see this Lamp and Picture, and love them better for it ever after. All the way of this *Grotta* is very even and level, but hugely dusty; as a Room must be that hath not been swept these sixteen Hundred Years. The People of the Country meeting here in the Dark, know how to avoid one another, by going from *Naples* on the right hand, and returning on the left; that is, by keeping on the Mountain side going, and returning on the Sea-side: And this they express by crying out often; *A la Montagna*, or *a la Marina*; *to the Mountain-side, or to the Sea-side,* to give notice whether they come, or go. Our Guide understood the Word, and he gave it unto me, and I to my next Man, it ran through our whole *Brigade*, which consisted of a dozen Horsemen in all. Almost all the way we rid in it, we shut our Eyes, having little use of them; and our Mouths and Noses too, for fear of being choaked with the Dust: So that our exterior Senses being thus shut up, our Interior began to work more freely, and to think of this odd place. My thoughts, coming newly from *Sannazarius* and *Virgils* Tombs, fell presently upon Poetry, (for all this Country is a Poetical Country) and I began to think whether this were not *Polyphemus* his Den, because *Homer* makes it to have been near the Sea-side, as this is, and capable of holding great Herds of Sheep, as this also is. Sometimes I thought that it might have been here, that *Jupiter* was hidden from his devouring Father, *Saturn*, who came into *Italy* for certain; as also because *Sophocles* makes mention of *Jupiter Pausilipus*. But at last I concluded that this was the place where merry Gods and Goddesses, after their jovial Suppers, plaid at Hide and Seek, without being Hood-wink'd. By this time we began to see the other end of the Grot a far off, by a little Light which grew grater and greater, till at last we came to the Issue of it.

Grotta del Cane. Being got out of this *Cymmerian* rode, we began to open our Eyes again to see if we could find one another; and our Mouths too to discourse upon this exotick place. Thus we rid discoursing upon this Wonder, till we came to the *Grotta del Cane*, a new Wonder.

Arriving there we presently had a Dog ready (though for the most part the Dogs here run whining away when they see a troop of strangers arrive) and I saw the Experiment of that famous *Grotta*, which being but three yards within the side of the Hill, may be seen without entring into it. The Experiment is this. A Man takes a Dog alive, and holding down his Head with a wooden Fork to the Ground, the Dog begins first to cry, and then to turn up the white of the Eyes, as if he would die. Then letting him hold up his Head again, he recovers. And having thus twice or thrice shewed us the Experience of this infectious place, he puts down the Dogs head again, and holds it down so long, till the Dog seems

seems to be dead indeed. Then taking him by the stiff Leg, and running with him to the Lake *Agnano*, some forty Paces off, he throws him into the shallow water of this Lake, and presently he begins to recover, and to wade out. They would make us believe, that as it is the nature of this *Grotta* to kill, so it is the nature of this Lake to revive dead things again. But if the Dog were dead indeed, all the water of *Agnano*, tho' it were *Aqua Vitæ*, would not recover him: He is only astonished with the infectious Vapor which breatheth out of this *Sulphurous* ground below. The Pestilent nature of this *Grotta* was shewed us plainly by a lighted Torch, which as long as it was high from the Ground, burnt clearly: But as it was approached by little and little near to the Ground it grew dimmer and dimmer, till at last it burnt blew, and being held close to the Ground, it went quite out.

Then we were shown hard by, the Stoves of St. *Gennaro*, which by a natural sulphurous Vapor issuing strongly from low causes, put a Man presently in a Sweat, and are excellent Remedies for the *Neapolitan* Disease, called by some Authors, *Campanus Morbus*: *Nature*, an *Indulgent Mother*, thinking herself bound to afford a Remedy to the disorders which she her self hath enclin'd the *Neapolitans* unto.

The Stoves of St. Gennaro.

Then fetching about the Hills by a narrow unfrequented way, we came to the Convent of the *Capucins* standing there where St. *Jannarius* was Beheaded. In a little Chappel on the Right-hand as you enter into the Church, they shewed us the Stone upon which he was beheaded; the Blood is still upon it.

The Capucins.

The Sul-phatara.

From hence we descended down into the *Sulphatara*, where the burning *Sulphur* smokes out perpetually from under ground. This *Sulphatara* is a kind of Pit, environed on all sides with Banks, and it is about fifteen Hundred Foot long, and a Thousand broad. We rid down into it on Horse-back, and it sounded hollow under our Horses Feet, as if we had been riding over a wooden Bridg. There are divers *Spiracula*, or vents round about it, out of which the thick Smoak presseth furiously, as out of a Furnace; and makes Poets and Potters find matter enough; those for their Fables calling it, *Fornum Vulcani*: These for their Medicinal Pots, which they make of this Brimstony Earth.

Near to *Sulphatara* stands a round Pool of black, thick Water, which always boileth; and whatsoever you throw into it, it comes out boiled indeed, but not entire; something or other of it being always diminished, saith *Leandro Alberti*. One putting in four Eggs in a long Ladle, pulled out but three again: I wonder Poets feigned not this Lake to be that part of Hell allotted to punish Usurers, seeing it takes use for every thing that's put into it.

Descending from *Sulphatara* to *Puzzuolo*, we wondered to see the very High-way smoak under our Horses Feet, when yet we found not them so fiery under us; but I found the Smoak to come out of little chinks of the dried ground: which shewed us that the whole Country was on Fire under us. Before we came to the Town we saw the remnants of a fair *Amphitheater*, and *Cicero's* Academy.

Immediately after this we came to *Puzzuolo*, so called, either from the multitude of Springs about it, or else a *Putore*, from the smell which this Brimstony Country affords. The Town is but little, yet anciently a Bishops Seat. Taking Boat here presently, we passed over the Creek of the Sea to *Baia*, which is three Miles from hence; and as we row'd along, I admired the wild design of *Caligula*, who built a Bridge from *Puzzuola* to *Baia*: Some of the Arches yet standing on both sides, shew us that his folly is real: And I believe *Suetonius* meant this work when he taxeth the *insanas substructiones*, and made buildings of this Emperor. That which contributed much to the bold attempt; was the nature of the Sand of this Country, which made into Morter, and let down into the Water, grows hard and solid, even to petrify there at last. *Puteolanus pulvis, si aquam attigit saxum est.*

Puzzuolo.

Pliny and Vitruvius.
Baia.

Reaching the other side of the Bay, and leaving our Boat to attend us, we rambled for an hour and an half among the Antiquities of this ruined Paradise of *Baia*: For you know, *Nullus in orbe locus Baiis praeluxit amoenis.*

First we were led to the *Mercato di Sabato*, looking still like a Street with ruins of Houses on both Sides.

Mercato di Sabato.

Thence we went to the *Elizian* Fields, which are much beholding to Poets for their Fame: Otherwise they are but a very common Plat of Ground without any gracefulness at all; except only that if *Baia* were a Town still a Man might make a fine Bowling-ground here. But Poets who have Power and Licence to erect *Iibacum* in-

The Elisian Fields.

to a Kingdom, have out-poeted it here, by erecting this little spot of Ground into a Paradise.

Piscina Mirabili. Thence we came presently to the *Piscini Mirabili*, a vast building under ground born up by forty or fifty great square Pillars, long an Hundred and fifty Paces, forty wide, and thirty high. We descended into it by many Steps, and it's so well walled with Stone, and Lime on all sides, that Water cannot sink through. And all this was only to keep fresh Water in, either for the *Roman* Gallies that used to lie hereabouts, in this Harbor; or else for the *Romans Gusto*; who having their curious *Villa's* hereabouts, had no mind to drink of the Springs of this Bituminous Country. At the top of this *Piscini Mirabili*, I espied some Spouts of Stone yet remaining, by which they used to let the Water from above into the vast Reserver.

Promont. Miseni. Mare mortuum. Cento Camerelle. Returning again, we were shown the Promontory of *Misenum* a far off; and the *Mare Mortuum* hard by.

Then we went into the *Cento Camerelle*; so called from an Hundred little Rooms that were built together like Chambers within one another, to keep Slaves in, who served the Gallies.

Going again towards our Boat, we were shown the place where *Agrippina* should have been drowned by a false-bottomed Boat; but that failing, her Son *Nero* caused her to be Stabbed here. Indeed Breasts that had turn'd their Blood into Milk, to give Suck to such a Monster, could expect nothing else but to be emptied of a'l their Blood; but she was design'd to this ill usage long before. For being foretold, when

she

she was with Child of *Nero*, that she had in her Womb a Son, who should be Emperor, but withal, who should kill her, she cried out: *Occidat, modo imperet: Let him kill me, so he be but Emperor*; and she had her Wish. It's said also that this *Parricide* (for, *Nero nunquam sine publici paricidii prefatione nominandus est*, (saith *Valerius Maximus*) after his Mother was kill'd, would needs have her ript up, that he might see where he had lodged nine Months together: And I believe that nothing hastened more the Conspiracy of the *Romans*, against him, than that they could now no longer endure him, who could not endure his own Mother. Hard by the Shoar stands yet the Tomb of that unfortunate Princess.

Then taking Boat again, we rowed by the ruins of *Marius*, and *Cæsar's Villas*, and divers other scraps of Antiquity, and all along in the Water (in a clear day) you may see the Foundations of *Baiæ*, and some Arches, and the Pavement of the very Streets; all now in the Sea. *Omnia fert ætas*; and Time, which in all other places is called *Edax rerum*, may here be called *Bibax rerum*, having sup'd up here a whole Town. *Agrippina's Tomb.*

Rowing on still by the Shoar, we came to the Foot of *Nero's Pallace*, near to the ruins of which, stands mounted a strong Castle, built *à la moderna*, upon a high Hill. Leaving here our Boat again, we were wished to put our Hands into the Sand of the very Sea which we found to burn under the cold Water.

Then we went hard by to *Cicero's* Baths, a great square place, where antiently were written over Head in old Letters, the names of the Diseases which these Waters Cured: Which *Cicero's Baths.*

Letters

Letters some Physitians caused to be defac'd, pretending that they were superstitious Characters, when indeed they were unwilling Men should be cured by any thing, but the strange Characters in their *Recipes*.

The Baths of Tritola.
Near these aforesaid Baths, are those of *Tritola*, where we were led into the long *Grotte*, and presently put into a Sweat by a stifling heat that met us violently in that long entry. I followed my Guide, and finding the steam to be Choaking, I stooped down low behind the Guide, to let him break the hot Air before me. As I thus stooped, I found out by Experience what others find by hearsay; that the nearer the Ground a Man stoops here, the cooler he finds himself. Thus *Antæus* like, fetching now and then succor from my Mother Earth, I found Humility to be a safe Remedy. In the middle of this long, narrow Entry there's a place for those that stand in need of Sweating, to stand on stradling wide, and so sweat abundantly. They told me that at the end of this *Grotta*, there are Baths of Sovereign Virtue; but I being well without them, had no mind to be choked in seeking out Health.

Lacus Avernus.
Returning from hence we had a huge walk of it to the *Lacus Avernus*, made by the River *Acheron, i. e. sine gaudio*: a fit name for the River of Hell. This Lake is famous for it's stinking Air which was observ'd to kill Birds as they flew over here. On the farther side of it was the Temple of *Apollo*.

The Grotte of Sibylla Cumæa.
Leaving this Lake on our Right hand, we made towards the *Grotte* of *Sybilla Cumæa*, so called from the City *Cume*, which stood not far off. This long *Grotta* was once a *Subterranean*
passage

Part II.   A Voyage through Italy.

passage to the City of *Cuma* (as that of *Pausilipus* is yet to *Naples*) and the *Sybills Grotte* is that little dark Entry which strikes out of the long *Grotte*. This leads you to the Chamber of the said *Sybille* and her Baths. It's a fine retiring place for a chast Maid, that fears as well to see as to be seen: *Tam timet videre, quam videri*, and such the *Sybills* were; who for their Virginities sake, had the gift of Prophecy given them, saith St. *Hierome*. This *Sybilla Cumæa* Prophecied very particularly of our Saveour's Birth, and for that reason *Julian* the *Apostate* burnt her Prophecies saith *Ammianus Marcellinus*, an Heathen Historian of those times.   *Tertul.*

As we returned again from hence to our Boat, we gazed upon a great Mountain called *Monte Nuovo* because it was cast up in one Night (on *Michaelmas* Night, *Anno* 1536) by a Earthquake, which the Philosophers call *Brasmarichus*, that is, when the Earth is thrown up, and Mountains are formed. Some hold this Mountain to be three Miles high, but I think it enough to give it a full Mile. It cover'd (at its rising up) a great part of the old *Lacus Lucrinus*, which was quite sucked up by this great sop.   *Monte Nuovo.*

Then taking our Boat again, we returned to *Puzznolo*, and at night to *Naples*; where we staid but one day more, as well to rest our Horses, as to see the Silk-shops, where they make curious Silk Wastcoats, Stockings, Scarfs, &c.

He that desires to know the History of *Naples*, let him read the Book called, *Il Compendio dell Historia di Napoli, di Collennccio.*   *The History of Naples.*

Having thus seen *Naples*, we returned again towards *Rome*, the same way we came, without
any

Take heed of the Gabellers of Fundi.

any danger of *Banditi*, but not without some trouble caused us by the Officers of the *Gabella* at *Fundi*, who met us a quarter of a Mile out of the Town, and stopt us upon the Road to search us, and see whether we had any thing liable to the *Gabella*; or more Money of the Country, than the Law allows Men to carry out. For my part, I had taken care of all this afore hand, and had nothing liable to the greatest rigor. But some of our Company, that did not believe the rigor to be so great, found it. For to some they pulled off their Boots, searched their Pockets, Breeches, Doublets; nay, even their Saddles, Horses tails, and the very Horses feet. From one Gentleman they took four Pistols of Gold, because he carryed so much more than was allowed: Though with much ado we got the Gentleman his Money again; I have known divers that have not escaped so well, having been stripped in the open Fields, even to their Shirts, &c. their Watches taken from them, though they had brought them with them to *Naples*, and not bought them there. This is to learn my Traveller to be inquisitive in all his journeys, of the Laws of the Country where he travelleth, especially such obvious ones as concern public Passages, Bridges, Ferries, bearing of Arms, and the like; the knowledge of which customs will make him avoid many inconveniencies, which I have known others fall into.

In another Voyage to *Naples*, in our return to *Rome*, we made little excursions, to take in some places about *Rome*, which he had not seen before, as *Arbano*, *Castel Gandulfo*, *Frescati* and *Tivoli*, which lay almost in our way.

Rising

Rising therefore betimes at *Veletri*, we crossed over the Hills, and came to *Albano* (anciently called *Longo Alba*) and now one of the seven Bishops Seats about *Rome*, which are given to the eldest Bishop Cardinals, that they may be at hand always, and ready to assist the Pope in his affairs of importance. The others are *Porto, Ostia, Frescati, Tivoli, Preneste, Veletri*. In *Albano*, I saw nothing of moment but an old Church, and some old Houses: Yet seeing it stands in so good an Air, I wonder the great Men of *Rome* have not built Houses here, where the Wine is so exquisitely good. Indeed this Wine makes this Town to be much taken notice of by all strangers, as being the best Wine that's constantly drunk in *Rome*.

Albano.

Hard by *Albano* stands *Castel Gandulfo*, the Popes Country House, in Summer. It stands very pleasantly, having on one side of it a Lake and Woods; and on the other, the *Campania* of *Rome*, and the City it self in view. I stept into this Castle but found nothing but bare Walls, it being unfurnished.

Castle Gandulf.

From hence we went to *Frescati*, called antiently *Tusculum*. This is absolutely one of the sweetest places in *Europe*. The Town is but little; but round about it, especially on the Hill side there are so many curious *Villas, Pallaces, Gardens, Fountains, shady Walks*, and *Summer delights*, that I wonder not, if Princes, Cardinals, and other great Persons, retire hither, in Summer. In a word, here *Cato* was born, here *Lucullus* delighted himself, and *Cicero* studied and wrote his *Tusculan* questions. The first place we went to see here, was the *Villa Aldobrandani*.

Frescati.

This

The Villa Aldobrandina Belvedere.

This *Villa* is also called the *Belvedere* of *Frescati*, because it stands so pleasantly; having the *Campania* of *Rome*, and *Rome* it self in sight on one side; and on the other, the Hill side all covered with Laurel Trees, curious Fountains, *Cascatas*, and other delightsome Water-works, which afford here a cool season, even in the Months of *July* and *August*. The variety of these Water-works, are so many and so curious, that I cannot but describe them.

The Cascata.

First then, the rare *Cascata* presents it self, and its made thus. At the turning of a vast Cock, the Water (which is brought through a great Hill, from a source five Miles off) spouts out of the top of two high winding Pillars of Stone, which stand mounted upon the head of an high pair of open Stairs, and then falling down upon the same Pillars again, it follows the winding bent of them, cut into Channels and little Gutters, and so warbles about these Pilars visibly, till it arrive at the foot of them. There finding issue, it falls upon the foresaid Stairs, and covers them all with a thin gliding Stream, which makes an open Stair-case of Water. Besides, this Water sets a number of little Fountains on work, which stand on either side of these Stairs, and descends by degrees with them: So that in a moment the whole Hill side is spouting out Water and filling the Air with a sweet murmur.

2. Then the Gardiner turning another Cock above, gives, at once, such store of Wind and Water to the great *Girandola*, below the Stars, *The Girandola.* in the *Grotta* of *Ælus*, that it imitateth perfectly Thunder, Hail, Rain and Mist.

3. By

3. By this time, the great Statue of the Centaure, with an Hunters Horn at his Mouth, windeth it duly, and in perfect measure. *The Centaure.*

4. *Pan* also plays on his Mouth-Organ tuneably. *Pan.*

5. Whilst the Lion and the Leopard fighting together, spit angerly in one anothers Faces, though all pass in cold Blood, because in cold Water. *The Lion and the Leopard.*

6. These Waters also afford innumerable and inavoidable wetting places; as the false steps in the Stairs; the wetting place behind *Pan*; the o-wetting place behind the Centaure, and the little under-ground spouts on all sides.

7. Then the Hall of *Apollo* is opened, where he sitting upon Mount *Parnassus*, and the nine Muses under him in a Circle, with several wind Instruments in their Hands, strike up altogether melodiously, whilst an untouched Organ underneath the Hill, plays a soft ground to the Muses Instruments. *The Hall of Apollo.*

8. During the Melody, a little round hole in the midst of the Room, bloweth out from below, such a cool and stiff Wind, that bears up a little hollw ball of Copper, a yard from the Ground. Over the Door is this distich.

Huc ego migravi Musis comitatus Apollo.
Hic Delphi, hic Helicon, hic mihi Delos erit.

Then being led to see this Hydraulic Organ, and to view what Fingers Art had lent unto Water; I found the Organ to be made thus. First, the Pipes are like other Organ Pipes of Lead, and set in a close frame, as the manner is, with *The Water Organ.*

stops

stops, and touches to them. Close to the stops the force of water turns a Wheel, made like a great Drum, and as long as the Organ. This Wheel hath in it, here and there, divers pieces of Brass, about the thickness of an half Crown piece, and just as broad as the stops of the Organ. These Brass pieces sticking out just so far, as to reach the stops in their turning about, and to press them down as the Organists Fingers do, and being placed here and there, in that Musical distance, as to strike their note in tune, as they turn about leisurely, they altogether compose a perfect and sweet Harmony; the Wind-pipe of this room (mentioned even now) serveth sufficiently for Bellows to this Organ, as well as to the wind Instruments of the Muse; and all is caused by force of Water. But as we were taken with these Water-works, which make this Organ play in tune, we were suddenly overtaken with another Water-work, which playing terribly upon us, put us quite out of tune: So seldom doth Wind come without Water.

A terrible wetting place.

Villa Ludovisia.

Having seen this Garden and Pallace, we went to the *Villa* of Prince *Ludovisia*, which is hard by. The House is but little, but the Garden is both large and adorned with store of Waterworks; so that if the Gardiner befriend you not, you cannot escape without being soundly wet. One thing I observed in this Pallace here, that the Curtains of the Beds are wrought with little holes of Needle-work, that the Air may enter by them, but not the Gnats.

Monte-dragone.

From hence we went to the *Villa* of Prince *Burghese*, called *Monte-dragone*, from the Dragon in his Arms. It stands a mile and an half from

Part II.   A Voyage through Italy.   201

from the *Beluedere*, and the way to it, is through curious walks of Laurel-trees. The House is stately, and capable of lodging a King, with his whole Court. The Chambers are neat and fit for both Seasons, Winter and Summer. I saw divers good Pictures in them. The last Supper is of *Alberto Dures*'s Hand, and hugely esteemed. The story of *Polyphemus* is of the Hand of *Lanfranco*. But that which pleased me best, was the Hall below, full of the true Pictures of famous Men, both for Learning and Arms. Its an excellent School, where a Man may learn much true skill in Physiognomy, and see how Worthies looked. This Hall lets you out into the little neat Garden, where you find Waterworks, wetting sports, and a pretty *Girandola*.

Having thus seen *Frescati*, we went to *Tivoli* *Tivoli*. some fifteen Miles off. This is an antient Town, standing upon an Hill some fifteen Miles distant from *Rome*, and in sight of it. It was anciently called *Tyber*, and held by the *Romans* for a delicious place. We saw here the old Temple, and *OldTyber*. the House of *Sibylla Tyburtina*. Then we saw the *Cascata*, much admired here by those that never *The Cascata*. were in *Swisserland*, or at *Terni*. This here is made by the River *Anio*; which falls suddenly down a stony Rock, and foams for anger, to see its bed grown too short for it. Indeed it makes such a murmuring complaint against nature, to the stones below, that it almost deafs, like the *Catadoups* of *Nilus*, all its neighbors.

Thence we went to the *Villa* of Cardinal *d'Este*. *Villa d'* It stands high and overlooks the *Campania* of *Este*. *Rome*. But the Gardens of this *Villa*, is that which

which is here most looked after. They lie upon the side of an Hill, and are placed in four rows of Gardens, with four degrees in the descent, all furnished with *Cascatas*, *Grottas*, and other admirable Water-works: The Water is let in hither from the River *Anio*, which runs behind this Hill. For they have tapt the very Hill, and bored the Rock quite through to the River; so that the Gardiner hereby turning a great Cock, can let in as much Water as fills the Fountains, the *Cascatas*, the *Grottas*, the *Girandola*, and the other rare Water-works. Hence is made the great Fountain of *Leda*; the Stairs of Water; the long walk of two Hundred paces, set all along with little stone Fountains and Basins, purling in your ears, and casting out little tets of Water as you walk along them. And here you shall see as rare things for sight and delight, as the World can afford in this kind. Here a perfect representation of old *Rome* in a Perspective: Where you see the *Capitol*, the *Pantheon*, the chief *Triumphal Arches*, the *Circos*, *Theaters*, *Obelisques*, *Mausoleas*, and even *Tyber* it self: Here curious groves of Trees making a green spring in the midst of Winter: Here cool *Grottas* and Fountains, making a cold Winter in the midst of Summer. Here false birds chirping upon true Trees, every one according to his true nature; and all of them chattering at once at the sight of a false Owl, appearing and howling in a Tree. Here curious *Grottas*, especially the *Grotta* of Nature, adorned with Nymphs, Shells, Statues, and unavoidable wetting places, and Organs playing without any Man touching them: There a fearful *Girandola* of the Dragons, thundering

Part II.   **A Voyage through Italy.**   203

dering as if they would set Heaven on Fire with cold Water, and pelt *Jupiter* from thence with Hailstones. But I wrong these things, which are rather to be seen than described: And my Traveller will wrong himself much, if he stay not here three or four days, to view *munitamente*, these wonders of Art. Having seen these famous places, we returned to *Rome* again; where we saw its chief rareties over and over again; for *Romam juvat usque videre*, and all Men that have seen *Rome* only once, desire to see it again: Hence the *Romans* taking leave of a stranger departing from *Rome*, after his first Voyage, say jesting to him, *a Riveder ci*; that is, Farewel till I see you again; knowing that every Man who hath seen *Rome* but once, will desire to return again. For my part, I confess I was of this sentiment in my first journey; but now having seen it five several times, I took a long leave of it, and began to think of returning homeward by the way of *Loreto* and *Venice*. And that we might be sure to be at *Venice* at the great solemnity of the *Ascension*, we left *Rome* the first week after *Easter*.

We set out of *Rome* by the *Porta del Populo*, all along the *via Flaminia*, which reached as far almost on this side of *Rome*, as the *via Appia* did on the other; that is from *Rome* to *Rimini*. Its called *Flaminia*, because the *Consul Flaminius* made it by his Souldiers, in time of peace, lest they should grow idle and have their strength to seek when the War should break out. The rest of the way from *Rimini* to *Bologna*, was paved by *Æmilius Lepidus* the Collegue of *Flaminius*, and from him called *via Æmilia*.

Via Flaminia.

N n   This

Ponte Molo. This *via Flaminia* led us first to *Ponte Molo* (*Pons Milvius*) a good Mile distant from the Gates of *Rome*, where *Constantin* the Great overcame *Maxentius* the Tyrant, and drove him and his Men into the River. Here it was I saw *Tyber* first; and I wonder to find it such a small River, which Poets, with their Hyperbolical Ink, had made swell into a River of the first rate.

Tyber.

Following on the way, we passed by *Castel Nuovo*, *Civita*, *Castellana*, *Utricoli*, and so to *Narni:* so called from the River *Nar*. It was anciently called *Nequinum* (wicked Town) because of the Inhabitants, who being pressed with hunger in a Siege resolved to kill one another, rather than fall alive into the Hands of their Enemies. They began with their Children, Sisters, Mothers, Wives, and at last fell upon one another; leaving their Enemies nothing to triumph over but bare Walls and Ashes. This Town is an ancient Bishops Seat, and St. *Juvenalis* (whose body lyeth in a neat low Chappel in the *Domo*) was the first Bishop of it. A little out of the Town are seen high Arches, belonging anciently to an Aqueduct.

Narni.

From hence we went to *Terni*, a Bishops Seat too. It was called anciently *Interamna*, because of a world of little Brooks here. This Town stands in a most pleasant soyl, and is famous for being the birth-place of *Cornelius Tacitus* the great Historian. Arriving here betimes, we went four miles off, to see the famous *Cascata*, in the Mountains, which far excells that of *Tivoli*.

Terni.

From *Terni* we went to *Spoleto*. This is a neat Town, which giveth denomination to the Dutchy of *Spoleto*. Anciently the Country hereabout

Spoleto.

Part II.   A Voyage through Italy.

about was called *Umbria*, but in aftertimes it was called, the Dutchy of *Spoleto*, upon this occasion. The Emperor *Justin* having called *Narses* (the great General) out of *Italy*, he sent *Longinus* with the Power and Title of *Exarch*, in his place. This *Longinus* settled himself in *Ravenna*, and governed the rest of *Italy* by his Captains and Officers called *Duces*, or Dukes. Hence *Rome* lost her Consuls, (*Narses* and *Basilius* being the two last Consuls) and was governed by a Duke too, as well as *Spoleto*. This Town hath been famous anciently, for holding out against *Hannibal*, even then when he had newly overcome the *Romans* at the Lake *Thrasimeno* near *Perugia*; in which Siege of *Spoleto*, happened that famous Prodigy (which I may call, in a manner, a *Metaphysical transmutation*, rather than a *Metamorphosis*) mentioned by *Leandro Alberti*, who quotes *Livy* for it; of a Man in *Spoleto*, changed into a Woman in the time of the Siege. Surely it was some notable Coward, whom Nature disavowing, degraded him of his Breeches. Hence I remember that *Plato* saith, *Abjectori armorum Maxime conveniret, ut in Mulierem ex Viro translatus, sic puniatur: A Man that casts away his Arms in a Battle, ought to be punished, by being changed from a Man into a Woman.* This Town of *Spoleto* gives the name to the pleasant Valley of *Spoleto*, which lies near it. It's above thirty Miles in Compass, surrounded on all sides with Hills, and those Hills are clad with many fine Towns: People willingly dwelling here, where the Air and the Earth, our chiefest Nurses, are so purely good.

Plato *lib.* 12. *de Legib.*

The Valley of Spoleto.

Foligni.

Assisium.

Montefalco.

Tolentino.

From *Spoleto* we went to *Foligni* (*Fulignum* in Latin) famous for *Confectioners*. Not far from hence stands *Assisium*, famous for St. *Francis*, Founder of the *Franciscan* Order; the Convent here is stately, and much visited by devout Pilgrims: And *Montefalco* famous for the miraculous heart of B. *Clara*.

From *Fologni*, climbing up the *Apenins*, we came to *Tolentino*, famous for the Tomb and Relicks of St. *Nicholas Tolentinas*. Of this Town was *Philelphus* a learned and noble Knight, who desirous of possessing of the Greek Tongue in Perfection, was not only content to go into *Greece* in Person, and there visit the ruins of *Athens*, and the Tombs of the ancient Philosophers; but brought thence with him a *Grecian* Lady, whom he had married at *Constantinople*, by whose daily Conversation he might learn the pure Accent of the *Greek Tongue*. And this he did in such Perfection, that he triumph'd over the *Grecians* themselves in their own Language. Witness that dispute which he had with *Timosbeus*, a *Grecian*, about the Force and Accent of a *Greek* Word, where both of them growing hot, and betting at last their Beards, which they both wore then long, *Philelphus* won the others Beard; and caused it to be shaved off immediately, and kept it in his Family as a Trophy: Though the poor *Grecian* would have redeemed it with a considerable Sum of Money. Indeed they deserv'd both to lose their Beards, that could be so hot about such a Hairs matter, as the Accent of a Word. The Statue of this notable Shaver, victorious *Philelphus*, I saw here in the Town-house.

Part II.   A Voyage through Italy.   207

From *Tolentino* we went to *Macerata*, a neat Town of *la Marca*; and passing through *Recanata*, another handsome Town of the same Country, we came betime to *Loreto*.

Macerata.
Recanata.
Loreto.

Resolving but to stay here one day, we put out all our time to use presently, and spent that Afternoon, and the next day in viewing exactly this sacred place, which is so much frequented by the devout Pilgrims of all Christendom. This place at first was nothing but a plain High-way till the Chamber of our Blessed Lady (in which the Angel announced unto her the mystery of the Incarnation of our Saviour in her Womb) was translated thither miraculously by the Hands of Angels, about the year 1294, when Infidels and *Turks* over-spreading the holy Land, would otherwise have profaned that holy place, which even from the Apostles time had been turned into a Chappel. For my part, though this be no Article of Faith, yet when I remember what was said in this Chamber, by the Angel to our Lady, to wit, *Non est impossibile apud Deum omne Verbum*: *Nothing is impossible to God*, I easily believe that he who plac'd this great World it self in a place where there was nothing before, can easily place a House there where there was no House before; and that he who makes an Angel wheel the *Primum mobile*, and the vast Machines of the Heavenly Orbs, quite round in four and twenty hours, may easily make Angels translate this little Chamber of our Lady, from one part of the World to another. Now that it was so translated *de facto*, both ancient Records, solid depositions, constant tradition, and the belief of all, almost, of the Catholick Princes of Europe

See Truselinus his *History of the House of Loreto*

rope (who have sent rich Presents hither) do testify. Besides I can say this, that the Walls are of such a Stone as is not used in any House in all the Country about: A great Presumption, that this Wall is Exotic. Again, the holy House here having no foundation in the Ground (as we see plainly) it is not credible that it was built here by Men who would have given some little Foundation to Walls of that thickness, and to a House of that bigness, especially standing alone in the Fields, as it did at first, and exposed to all Weather. Add farther, that the very old Painting which is seen upon part of the Wall on the inside sheweth the high Antiquity of this House. In fine, the whole Country would have given the Lie to his tradition at first, or as soon as Men had begun to cry it up for an House brought thither miraculously.

The holy house of Loreto.

Now for the holy House it self it stands in the midst of a great Church which hath been built over it in latter times, for the better conveniency of the Peoples Devotion, and the Church Service: And round about it more immediately there hath been built a decoration of white Marble, which stands half a Foot distant from the holy House, that Men may see it was not intended so much for a Prop, as for a Decoration to it, as also to keep it from the hands of devout Pilgrims, who otherwise would have made no scruple to have been nibling at the Stones of the Walls here, and so in time have much defac'd the holy House with their Pious Thefts. This Decoration is set round with two rows of Statues of white Marble, cut by the rarest Workmen of *Italy* in those times, to wit, *Sansovino, Bandinelli,*

San

San Gallo, Monte Lupo, and others. The lower row of these Statues expresseth the figures of the ancient Prophets: And the other row above expresseth the Statues of the *Sybills,* who Prophecyed among the Gentiles, and Heathens, of our Saviours Birth of a Virgin, and his Passion, as you may read at large in *Lactantius.*

As for the matter and form of this House, I found it to be of hard, red Stone, like Brick, but far harder and bigger than our Brick: The form somewhat square, about the bigness of a reasonable lodging Chamber. There's but one Window in it, and anciently there was but one Door; but now there are three; one at either side, and one behind the Altar, for the Chaplains that have care of the Lights and Lamps, which are always burning here. Towards the upper end of the House there is an Altar, where the Holy Sacrifice of Mass is offered from four in the Morning, until one in the Afternoon. This Altar is of Silver, and was given by *Cosmus* II. Great Duke of *Florence.* Before it hangs a Lamp of Gold, as great as two Men could carry. It was the gift and Vow of the Senate of *Venice* in a Plague time. On either side of the Walls are fastened two great Candlesticks of pure Gold, made like *Cornucopia's* and neatly wrought, they were the gift of the great Dutches of *Florence, Magdelena d' Austria,* as her Arms upon them told me. On the Gospel side of the Altar, there's an old Cupboard within the Wall, in which are yet kept some little Earthen Dishes, which were brought hither with the House, and therefore Tradition holds them to have been our Saviours Plate, and our Ladies Vessels. Now this Cupboard is adorn'd with

with a door of Silver given (if I remember well) by a Duke of *Parma*. In the end of the holy House there is a Window, where it is imagined the Angel entred when he came Embassador to the *Virgin Mary* concerning the great Business of the Incarnation of his Lord and Master. This Window is now checked and enriched with Silver. Round about above, hang Silver Lamps; and on the sides of the Walls there remains yet some very old Painting, wherewith this Chamber was painted when it was first consecrated into a Chappel in the primitive times. In the very bottom of this Chamber, they shewed me, by a lighted Candle, how that it hath no Foundation in the Ground; but stands here just as if it had been let down from the Air, and set upon the plain Ground.

Close behind the Altar runs quite cross the Chappel, a great iron Grate, through which you see the Statue of *Cedar*, of our Blessed Lady, with her Son in her Arms. It's said to have been made by St. *Luke*, and was brought hither, together with the Chappel or holy House. It stands up high in the very farther end of the Chappel: It's about four Foot high, and adorned with a particular kind of Vail hung before it, looking something like a Womans Garment. They call these Vails here, *Vesti*, and they are of divers Colors and Stuffs; but all rich and glittering; witness that which I saw in the *Treasury*, which was given by the *Infanta Isabella* of *Flanders*, which is valued at forty Thousand Crowns. It's set thick with six rows of Diamonds down before, to the number of three Thousand; and it's all wrought over with a kind of Embroidery of

little

little Pearl, set thick every where within the Flowers with great round Pearl, to the number of twenty Thousand Pearls in all. Upon the Heads of our Saviour and our Lady in that Statue, are set two rich Crowns (close Royal Crowns) of Diamonds given by the Queen of France *Anne d' Aufriche*. Before the Breast of this Statue hangs a Royal *Tosone*, or Fleece of rich Jewels, given by a Prince of *Transilvania*: A Collar of Rubies, Pearls, and Diamonds, and a rich Cross hanging at it, all given by Cardinal *Sfondrati*. Round about the *Niche*, in which this Statue stands, there goes a close row of precious Stones of several sorts and Lustres, but all great, both in bulk, in value, and in number; being Seventy one, in all, and together composing a rich *Iris* of several colours. Between this Statue of our Lady, and the Iron Grate, hang a row of Lamps, (about twelve in all) of pure Gold, and all as big as a Mans Head, one whereof exceeds the rest in curious Workmanship; and it was the gift of *Sigismond*, King of *Polonia*.

All the rest of the Chappel, where those Lamps hang, is loaden with the rich Vows, and Presents of great Princes. These I yet remember: To wit, the Image in Silver of the eldest Son of *Ferdinand* the Third, Emperor, with a Chain of Diamonds about it. An Angel of Silver, holding out and as it were presenting to our Lady a Child of Gold in Swathing-Bands, upon a Silver Cushion. It was the gift of the aforesaid Queen of *France*, being brougt to Bed of the Dolphin, now *Lewis* the XIV. The Picture of this Prince of *Conde* in Silver kneeling, a vow of his Mother when he went first to War. The *Busto* of St. *Barbara* in Silver, set with Jewels ; the gift of an Arch Duke of *Austria*. Another *Busto* of St. *Girione*, set with Jewels also a gift of a Queen of *Bohemia*. The Statue of St. *Ladislaus* in Silver ; the gift of *Ladislaus* the IV. King of *Polonia*. A fine kneeling Stool or Pew of Silver, given by Cardinal *Colonna*, with a world of other Silver Presents, wherewith this place is filled. In fine, I saw there the very Chimney which was anciently in this Chamber ; its under the Statue of our Lady, and now adorned with Silver.

The Treasury. Having seen the Holy House or Chappel, we were led the next Morning into the *Treasury*, where many other rich presents are kept. This *Treasury* is a large Room forty paces long, and about fifteen wide, like a long Chappel vaulted and painted over head. On the left hand of this Room, stand great Cupboards, which opening above, have little Nets of strong Wyar before them, which let in Eyes to behold, but keep off Hands from touching the inestimable *Treasure* contained within them. Some of these presents were given by Popes, some by Kings, Queens, Princes, Cardinals, Generals, Ladies and Noblemen of several Nations. In one Cupboard they shewed us a whole service for the Altar, that is, Crucifix, Candlesticks, Cruets, Basin and Eure, and the foot of the Chalice, all of Amber. In another, such a whole service of Agate. Another such a Service all of *Lapis Lazuli*, given by *Count Olivares*. Another all of Coral given by the Arch-duke *Leopold*. In another, such a Service in Chrystal. In another such a Service of Silver, with Flower-pots neatly wrought, given

by

Part II.   *A Voyage through Italy.*

by *Don Thadeo Barberino, Prefect of Rome.* In another, a stately Crucifix of *Ebony* adorn'd with many curious Pictures in Miniature, given by Pope *Clement* the VIII. In another, the Spread-Eagle of Diamonds, the Gift of *Mary*, Queen of *Hungary*. Two Crowns of Gold enrich'd with Pearl; the Gift of a Queen of *Polonia*. A Crown of Gold set with great Rubies of extraordinary size; the Gift of a Dutchess of *Nevers*. In another the Crown and Scepter of Gold enamell'd, given by *Christina*, Queen of *Sweden*, at her first coming into *Italy*. In another, the enamelled Pigeon, with a rich Jewel in its Breast; the Gift of the Prince *Ludovisio*. The Heart enriched with Diamonds, with a great Emerald in the middle of it, of an excessive bigness; the Gift of *Henry* IH. of *France*, at his return out of *Polonia*. In another, the rich enamelled three corner'd Jewel, with the Picture of the Blessed Virgin in the middle of it; the Present of two *Bohemian* Counts and a Gentleman; who being thrown out of a Window in *Prague*, by the Calvinists, and recommended themselves to God's Protection, and our Ladies Intercession, fell down all three gently, without the least hurt: Their Names were Count *Martinis*, Count *Slavata*, and a Gentleman that was Secretary to Count *Slavata*, who being thrown out the last, and falling upon the Count his Master, cryed him mercy for his rudeness in falling upon him: A great argument that they were little hurt, when they could Compliment with one another. There are now three Pillars before that house in *Prague*, out of which these three Men were thrown. In another Cupboard I saw several great Chains of Gold,

Gold, given by great Men; and some of these by great Generals. In another, a great Heart of Gold, as big as both a Mans hands, enamelled with blew, and set on the outside of it, with these Words in pretty big Diamonds, JESUS, MARIA, and within it are the Pictures of the Blessed Virgin on one side, and of the Queen of *England*, *Henrietta Maria*, one the other; the Heart opening it self into two leaves. In another, a neat little Heart also, of Gold, enamelled and set with Jewels, the Present of Madam *Christina*, Dutchess of *Savoy*; and Sister to the foresaid Queen of *England*, with her own and her Sons Picture in it. In another, the Picture of our Blessed Lady, with her Son Jesus in her Arms, cut in a great Pearl, and set in Gold. In another Cupboard, I saw a Picture of our Blessed Lady, wrought curiously in *Indian* Feathers of several Colors, and cut short as Plush; which Picture changeth Colors as often as you change its Situation, or your own Posture. In another, a great *Custodia* of Chrystal, given by *Christina* of *Tuscany*. In another, a *Custodia* of *Lapis Lazuli*. In another, a Diamond valued at twelve Thousand Crowns, the gift of the Prince *d'Oria*, in *Genoua*. Another of almost equal price, given by a *German* Prince. In another, a curious Book of Gold covered with Diamonds, with the leaves of Gold, but rarely painted in Miniature, the gift of a Duke of *Bavaria*. In another, the *Samaritans* Well of Gold, with Pictures of our Saviour, and the *Samaritan* Woman in Gold also; the Present of Cardinal *Brancaccio*. In divers other Cupboards, I saw a world of Jewels of all sorts, which confounded my Memory as well

well as dazled my Eyes. In other great Cupboards, they shewed me excellent Church Ornaments, of most rich Stuffs, embroidered with Silver and Gold, but one there was (to wit, a whole compleat Suit for the Altar, Priest, Deacon and Subdeacon) so thick covered with an Embroidery of Pearl, and those no little ones, that I could not perceive the Ground of the Stuff for Pearl: All these were the Presents of *Catherine Zomoisky*, Wife of the Chancellor of *Polonia*; and they are valued at an Hundred and thirty Thousand Crowns. I know not whether this suit of Church Ornaments, or that described above in the Popes *Sacristy*, be the Richer.

On the other side of this Room, are great Windows, betwixt every one of which, are set upon long Tables, divers great Towns, so precisely expressed in Silver, with their Walls, Ramparts, Churches, Steeples, Houses, Streets, Windmils, &c. That whosoever had once seen these Towns, would easily know them again in their Pictures here, they were all Vows and Gifts, and all ingenious *German* Work, as well as *German* Towns.

This is all I can Remember, though not half I saw in this *Treasury*. And having thanked the civil Priest that shewed us this fine place, we went out again into the great Church; where I observed upon the great Pillars that make the Isles of this Church, the History of the Holy House engraven in Stone, or written in Parchment in a fair Text-hand, in twelve or thirteen several Languages, for the use of the Pilgrims who flock hither from all Countries.

Going

Going out of the Church, I saw before the Church door the Statue in Brass of *Sixtus Quintus*, and a stately Fountain.

From hence we went to see the Cellar of the Holy House, which furnished with Wine, not only the Governors House, the Canons and the Church-men, the College of the *Penitentiaries*, the Convent of the *Capucins*, the *Seminarists*, the Hospital and all those that belong to the Church any way; but also furnish'd all Pilgrims, yea even all Princes, Cardinals, Bishops, Ambassadors, and great Men of known quality, with Wine, as long as they stay here upon Devotion. For this reason there belong large Revenues to this Church; and this Cellar is absolutely the best I saw in *Italy*. The Vessels are hugely great, and not to be removed from hence. They have a way to take out a piece of their broad sides, and so to make them clean. They are all hooped with Iron, and some of them are so contrived, that they can draw three several sorts of Wine out of one Vessel, and by the same tap. The Experience is pretty, but the Wine is better. Now whether these Vessels be too many, or the Revenues of the Holy House too great, you may easily conjecture, when so many Persons are fed daily, as I mentioned above, and so many Thousand Pilgrims pass so frequently that way. *Turselinus*[*] writes, that between *Easter* and *Whitsuntide*, there have flock'd thither, sometims, five, sometimes six Hundred thousand Communicants; and in two days space in *September* (about the Feast of the Nativity of our Blessed Lady) there have appeared Two hundred thousand Communicants, most of which were Pilgrims.

[* *In his Hist. of Loreto, L. 3. c. 25.*]

Having

Having refreshed our selves in this Cellar, we *The Apothe-*
went to the Apothecaries-shop, belonging to the *caries-shop.*
holy House also; and furnishing Physick to sick
Pilgrims for nothing. There we saw those famous Pots, which make even Physick it self look
sweetly, and draw all curious strangers to visit
them. For round about a great inner Shop,
stand Pots of a great Size, painted by *Raphael
Urbin's* own Hand, and therefore judged by *Virtuosi* to be of great Value. Witness those four
only, on which are painted the four *Evangelists*,
for the which were offered by a *French* Embassador in his Kings name, four Pots of Gold of the
same bigness, and were refused. Brave *Raphael*,
whose only touch of a Finger could, *Midas* like,
turn Galli-pots into Gold. *But as Phydias* his
Statues of Clay were as much adored antiently,
as his Golden ones; So *Raphaels* Hand is as much
admired in the Apothecaries Shop of *Loreto*, as
in the *Vatican* Pallace of *Rome*. These Pots were
given to the holy House by a Duke of *Urbin*,
whose Subject *Raphael* was, and for whom he
had made them with more than ordinary Art.

He that desires to know more of *Loreto*, let
him read *Turselinus* his History of *Loreto*. For
my part, my time being out, I must be gone.

Taking therefore Horse again, we made towards *Venice*, and saw these Places in our way.

Ancona, the Capital Town of the *Marca*, and *Ancona.*
one of the best Havens in the *Gulph*: Corresponding with *Slavonia*, *Greece*, *Dalmatica*, and many other Countries. Its built upon a Promontory, and back'd up Land-way, with a good Castle. The Haven was built by the Emperour *Trajan*, whose Triumphal Arch is yet seen here,

and

and is the chief Monument of this Town. Here is a *Molo* striking two Hundred paces into the Sea. *Pius* II. whilst he stayed here to animate in Person, the great expedition against the *Turks*, which he had zealously given beginning to, died. In the Vaults of the great Church, are kept many Saints Bodies and pretious Relicks. Its called St. *Ciriaco*'s Church, and it is the Cathedral.

Senegallia. From *Ancona* we went to *Senegallia*, all along the Sea side. This Town is so called from the *Senones Gallia*. Its a very neat and pleasant Town, standing in a sweet Air. Its a Bishops Seat. Here began anciently *Gallia Cisalpina*.

Fano. From hence we went to *Fano* (*Fanum fortuna*) because of the Temple of Fortune built here in memory of a Battle won by the *Romans*, near the River *Metaurus*, hard by where *Asdrubal*, *Hannibal*'s Brother was slain. Here's an antient Triumphal Arch yet standing. Not far from this Town also, *Narsetes* overcame *Totila*; Its an Episcopal Town.

Pesaro. From hence we went to *Pesaro* standing also most pleasantly by the Sea side. Its called *Pesaro*, and *Pesaurum* in Latin, from the weighing here of the Gold which the *Romans* besieged in the Capitol, sent hither to be payed to the *Gauls*, saith *Servius*. It once belonging to the Dukes of *Urbin*, but for want of Heirs Male, fell to the Church by right. From the Bridge of Stone, which is here, begins the *Marca d' Ancona*. The Air is here thought by *Uranoscopists*, to be the best in *Italy*; as are also the Figs here.

Catholica. From hence we passed by *Catholica*, a poor Village, adorned with nothing but a stately *Name*, and an Inscription upon the Wall of the Chappel,

pel, rendering you the reason why this Town is called *Catholica*, which was this. When the Emperour *Constantius*, a fierce *Arian*, used violence to the Fathers that had been assembled in the Council of *Arimini* (a Town not far off) and would not suffer them to depart (their business being done, which they came for, to wit, the Catholick Faith of the Council of *Nice* being here asserted and confirmed) till they had complyed with the Emperour's faction, consisting of *Arians*; Many of them too weakly (being weary of so long a stay from their Seats) fell to an unworthy compliance with the *Arian* Party. Which the zealous *Orthodox* Fathers seeing, left *Rimini*, and came into this little Village, because they would not Communicate with the *Arians*: Whereupon this Village got the Name of *Catholica*, because the true Catholick and Orthodox Fathers retired hither. If you ask me then, whether this Council of *Rimini* were good or no; I answer you, that the Council was good and Orthodox, and confirmed the Faith of the *Nicene* Council against the *Arians*; which was the business it was called about. And what happened afterwards when the Council was ended by the oppression of the Emperour, is not to be imputed to the Council, but to some weak Fathers, as an error of Coversation, and a too unworthy Compliance.

From *Catholica* we went to *Rimini*, called *Ariminum* in Latin, this is a pretty Town, in which the foresaid Council was kept. In the Market place I saw the Stone (set now upon a *Pedestal*) upon which *Cæsar* stood when he made a Speech to his Souldiers, to make them resolve to

Rimini.

O o   march

march up to *Rome*. Hard by, in the same Market place, stands a little round Chappel, famous for a miracle wrought there by St. *Antony* of *Padua*, in Confirmation of the real Presence. The History is too long, but seen here painted round the Chappel, with a cast of an Eye.

Cesena.
Forli.

From hence we went through *Cesena* an Episcopal Town; and *Forli, Forum Livii* another Bishops Seat; in the way before we came to *Cesena*, we saw an old Inscription in Stone, set up by a little River side, which I found to be the very Decree of the old Senate of *Rome*, forbidding in general, any Officer or Souldier whatsoever, to pass over the *Rubicon*, upon pain of being judged an Eenemy to his Country, and guilty of high Treason. By which Words I gathered, that this little River here now called *Pisatello*, was *Rubicon*, mentioned in the Decree of the Senate; and that this Decree pointed at *Julius Cæsar* and his Army. Yet *Cæsar* being resolved to march up to *Rome* with his Army, made a Speech to his Souldiers; and finding a compliance in their resolutions, passed over *Rubicon*, crying out: *Jacta est alea:* We must either Sink or Swim, and so passed on to *Rome*, which he soon possessed himself of, and then of the World. When once powerful Men draw their Swords, they throw away their Scabhards; and when once they have offended beyond Pardon, they strike at the very Throat of Authority; running upon that horrid *Maxime*, that *scelera sceleribus sunt tuenda*.

Rubicon.

Faenza.

From *Forli* we passed on the Right hand of *Faenza, Faventia* in Latin (leaving the way on the Left hand, which leads to *Imola* and *Bolognia*) *Faenza* is a neat Town, as all the others we had

Part II.   A Voyage through Italy.   221

had passed by before: But having no considerable thing in it, but white Earthen Pots, called Vessels of *Faenza*, we stayed not long in it, but made towards *Ferrara*. In the way I found little worth Observation, except only, that as we Travelled one Night somewhat late for Coolness, I saw Millions of little Flies in the Air, carrying a bright Light about them like Glow-worms. They continued all the way to our Inn for two hours after Sun set, especially upon the Corn Fields and high Grass. It was huge pretty me thought, to see Heaven upon Earth almost, and flying Stars conduct us to our Lodging. A Poet would have sworn by all the Cords of *Apollo*'s Harp, that *Jupiter* then was making *Vulcan* pave the Vault of Heaven with a *Mosack* Work of Diamonds, and that these were only the sparks that fell from him: Or that he was repairing the old Causey of the *Via Lactea* with fresh Stars, and that these were the old ones which he had thrown away. I catched some of these fiery Flies, to see where it was that they carried their little Lanterns and *Candles*, and I found it was in their Tails. The Country People call them *Lucciole*. And I believe, these are those Flies which *Pliny* calls *Cicindelas*, and *Aristotle* calls λαμπυρίδες.

Passing thus along we came late to a little Village, and the next Morning betimes to *Ferrara*. This Town of *Ferrara* was once the Seat of a Sovereign Prince of the house of *Este*, but for want of Heirs Male, after the Death of *Alfonso* the II. it fell to the Church, and *Clement* the VIII. took possession of it in Person, by an Entry and Ceremony, worthy of the Pen of Cardinal *Bentivoglio* who was there. The Town stands in a

Plin. l. 18. c. 26.
Arist. l. 1 de partib. animal. c. 3.
Ferrara:

Plain,

Plain, carrying above four Miles compass; it hath a good *Citadel*, strong Walls, Ramparts, Bulworks, and a good Garrison of Soldiers. Here are fair Streets, and very handsom Pallaces; but People are somewhat thin. The things which I saw here were these.

The Rarities.

1. The *Domo*, Ancient rather than Beautiful.

2. Over against it, two Statues in Brass, of the Princes of the House of *Este*; the one Duke; the other *Marquis*; the one Sitting, the other on Horseback.

3. Behind these Statues is the House of Justice, or Town-house.

4. The strong Pallace of the Dukes anciently, is in the middle of the Town, with a great Mote about it; the Court within is painted with the Pictures of all the Dukes of *Ferrara*: here the Popes Legate lyeth.

The Diamond Pallace.

5. The Diamond Pallace, as they call it, is of white Marble without, whose Stones are all cut Diamond ways, into sharp Points. Having seen it without, I longed to see it within, hoping that a Diamond Pallace without, would be all Carbuncle and Pearl within. But I was deceiv'd; for entring in, I found nothing worth the Pains of going up the ugly Stairs; and the poor Woman that kept the House told me as much, as well as the cold Kitchin. I wonder the Master of this House doth not keep it always lock'd up, that Strangers might value it by its outside only, which is admirable indeed.

Ariosto's Tomb.

6. The Monastery of the *Benedictins* is stately, in whose Church I found the Tomb of *Ariosto*, Author of the long *Poem* called *Orlando Furioso*. He was esteemed, in his Life-time, a great Poet, and

as

as such was Crowned *Laureat* Poet, by the Emperor *Charles* the V. but he was oftentimes seen, even in the Streets, to be too much transported with Poetick Fury, and to become *Ariosto Furioso*, while he was penning his *Orlando*. He had a rich Vein, but a poor Purse; and while his head was crowned with *Laurel*, his Breeches were often out behind, as well as those of *Torquato Tasso*, of whom *Balzac* saith, that though he were a good Poet, yet he had *des fort mauvaises chauses*.

7. The *Carthusians* Church is neat and full of good Pictures.

8. The Church and Convent of the *Carmelites* is also neat, in whose Library I saw a Manuscript of *John Bacon*, and another of Learned *Thomas Waldensis*, both *English-Men*, and both Learned Men.

Here's an Academy of Wits called *Gli Elivati*. *The Academy of Wits.* Of this Town was *Hyronymus Savonarola*, Author of the *Triumphus Crucis*; and *Baptista Guarini* Author of the *Pastor Fido*. *The Learned Men.*

He that desires to know the History of *Ferrara*, *The History.* let him read *Giovanni Baptista Pigna*, who hath written of it, *ex Professo*.

From *Ferrara* we went to *Padua* in two days, the Season being good and dry; otherwise in Winter, it's too deep a way to go by Land; therefore most Men embark at *Ferrara*, and go by Boat to *Venice*. The first day passing over the *Po* in a Boat at *Francalino*, we reached *Ruigo* the first *Ruigo.* Town of the *Venetian* State. This Town is built near where *Adria* (from whence the *Adriatic* Sea *Adria.* is called) once stood, and almost upon its ruins. It's governed by a *Podesta* and a *Capitano Grande*, as the other Towns of St. *Mark* are. Of this

Oo 3 Town

Town was *Cœlius Rhodiginus*, a Man of various Learning, as his Books shew; and *Bonifarius Bonifacii* another learned Humanist.

From *Rigo* we arrived at *Padua* betimes, but the desire of seeing *Venice*, made us hasten away the next day; deferring to see *Padua* till our return from *Venice*.

Embarking then betimes in the Morning at *Padua* in a *Piotta*, a neat little Barge, taken to our selves, and much more honourable than to go in the great Tilt-Boat, where all sorts of lousy Ruffians and idle People throng you up, we saw a world of stately Pallaces and Gardens, standing upon the Banks of the River *Brenta*, and shewing us that we were approaching to a great Town indeed.

Some five Miles short of *Venice*, we left the River and the Horses that drew us, and rowed through the shallow Sea which environeth *Venice* on all sides, for above five Miles space. This low Sea is called here *La Laguna*; and the Water is so shallow that no great Ships can come to *Venice*, little Vessels come by certain Channels which are well fortified with Castles, Forts and Chains, so that no Man can come to *Venice*, but with leave, or knocks. We arrived there betimes, and all the way we admired to see such a stately City, lying as it were at Anchor, in the midst of the Sea; and standing fixed where every thing else Floats.

La Leguna.

The Origin of Venice. *Venice*, at first was nothing but a company of little dry Spots of Ground, which held up their Heads in a shallow Sea, furnished by seven Rivers, *Piava, Sila, Livenza, Po, Adige, Brenta,* and *Tagliamento*, which run into it. To these little dry

dry Spots of Ground, Fishermen repaired antiently for their Fishing, and built little Cottages upon them. But afterwards *Italy* being overrun by *Goths*, *Huns*, and *Visigoths*, divers rich Men, from several parts of *Italy*, as well as from *Padua*, fled hither with the best of their Goods, to save them and themselves in these poor Cottages, unknown to those barbarous Nations: And finding by Experience this to be a safer place than any else, they began to provide against those frequent Disasters of barbarous Incursions, by building good Houses here. This many Men did and made at last a fine Town here, and greater than her Mother *Padua*. This happened twelve Hundred years ago, which makes *Venice* glory, that she is the antientest Republick in *Europe*. To which purpose I cannot omit to tell you here a pretty Story which was told me in *Paris* of a *Venetian* Embassador, who residing in the Court of *France*, and finding himself in a Visit, where there were many Ladies, was seriously asked by a grave old Lady, (who heard him speak much of the *Seignory* of *Venice*) whether the *Seignory* of *Venice* were fair or no? Yes Madam said he, one of the fairest in *Europe*. Is she great said the Lady again? Yes Madam said the Embassador, she is great enough. Is she rich said the Lady? Worth Millions replied the Embassador. Methinks then said the Lady, she would be a good Match for *Monsieur* the King's Brother: Yes Madam, replied he again, but that she is a little too old. Why how old is she I pray you, said the Lady? Madam, answered the Embassador, she is about twelve Hundred years old. At which the Company smiling, the good Lady perceiv'd

Est ello belle?

Est ello grande?

Est ello riche?

Quelle aisgé a elle?

her Error with blushing, and *Monsieur* was unmarried for that present. Indeed *Cosmography*, and *Topography* are hard Words; and as the old saying is, *aliquid Sceptrum, aliquid Plectrum*, a Looking-Glass is not the same thing with a Map.

Venice now. — As for *Venice* now, 'tis one of the fairest Cities in *Europe*, and called by the Proverbial Epethite, *Venetia la Riccha*, *Venice* the Rich. It's well nigh eight Milns in Compass, and in form something like a Lute. It hath no Wall about it to defend it, but a Mote of Water, that is five Miles broad, which surrounds it. It hath no Suburbs, but a world of little Islands close by it. The Streets of *Venice* are all full of Water; and for this Reason they use no Coaches here, but visit in Boats.

The Gondolas. — These Boats they call here *Gondolas*, and there are above twenty Tousand of them. For besides, that every noble *Venetian* or rich Man, hath two or three of his own; there are always a World of them standing together at several publick Wharfs; so that you need but cry out, *Gondola*, and you have them lanch out presently to you: These *Gandola*'s are pretty neat black Boats like our Oars, holding six Persons conveniently upon the Seats, which are covered over head with a thick black Cloath, with Windows at either side, which in Winter defends you from the Wind, and in Summer from the Sun. The multitude of these *Gondola*'s help to employ a great many poor Men, and to make a world of Mariners for publick Service, in time of need. Ordinary people here may go up and down the Town by little back Alleys, which they call here *Calle*; these by winding up and down, and deli-

Part II.   A Voyage through Italy.   227

delivering them over several Bridges, hugely
puzzle Strangers at first. Of these Bridges there
are above 1500 in *Venice*, all of Stone, and of one   Bridges in
Arch reaching from one side of the Street to the   Venice.
other, while the *Gondola*'s run under the Arch.
The greatest of these Bridges is called the *Rialto*, The Rialto.
built over the *Canal Grande*, all of white Marble.
This is one of the finest Bridges in *Europe*, because of the one Arch only, and of the vast
wideness and height of that Arch; the Channel
here being as wide as any Man can throw a Stone.
This Bridge bears upon its Back two rows of
Shops, and little Houses covered with Lead; and
lest this great weight should make the Foundation
sink, they built upon *Piloties*, that is, great Trees
rammed into the Ground, to the number of six
Thousand in all. In fine, this Bridge cost two
Hundred and fifty Thousand Crowns. It were
a fine sight to see, in an hard Frost, the streets of
Venice all frozen, and People walking up and down
upon Diamond Streets, or a Chrystal Pavement.
In the mean time it's no unpleasing sight to see
the Streets full of Water, and such stately Pallaces on either side: Especially the *Canal Grande*,
which runs quite through the middle of the City, and is hedged in on either side with stately
Houses; among which are counted two Hundred
Pallaces fit to lodg any King. The whole City
hath in it Thirty two Monasteries of Religious
Men, Twenty eight of Religious Women; Seventy Parish Churches; and about an Hundred and
fourscore Thousand Inhabitants.

    Having said thus much of the Situation of
Venice, I will now speak of the Government,
Strength, Riches, Religion, and Interest of this
Republick,

Republick, and then fall to the particulars I saw in it.

The Government. The great Council.

For the Government here, it's purely *Aristocratical*, by the *Doge*, and the Nobles. The great Council consists of two Thousand Gentlemen. This is the *Basis* of the State Government: Because that out of these are chosen all the other Magistrates, *Potestas, Generals, Capitani, Grandi, providetori Generali, Embassadors*, &c. This great Counsel assembles frequently in one great Room of the *Doge*'s Pallace, where there are Seats for them all, and where Businesses are voted by Baloting; that is, by putting in a close double Box of two Colours, a little Ball about the bigness of a Button, which is made so soft, that no Man can hear into whether part of the double Box the Ball falls. Every Gentlemen in this great Council hath two of these Balls given him, one white, and the other red: The one signifying the Affirmative vote, the other the Negative: So that they give their votes secretly, and without being known afterwards for what party they stood, or without giving example to others to follow them in their Votes, as leading Men would do; and so draw all into Faction and Cabals.

To run through all the Magistrates and Officers of this Republick, the *Pregiadi*, the *savi Grandi*, the *savi di Terra ferma*, the *savi de gli Ordini*, the *Consiglio de dieci*, &c. would be a work too long for a Traveller, and too tedious for my Reader. I will only speak of the Supream Magistrate here, the *Doge*, or Prince as they call him, who represents the Head of this Republick. He is now chosen by the whole Senate, and is for Life: Heretofore he was Hereditary, till the year 1032.

The Doge.

The

Part II.   A Voyage through Italy.

The manner of Baloting in choosing the *Doge*, is such a puzzle, that I had rather you should read it in *Sabellicus*, than I give my self the trouble of describing it. For the most part, they chuse a Man well stricken in years, and one who hath made his Circle of Embassies: That is, hath been fifteen Years Embassador in the chief Courts of *Europe*, three Years a piece in every one: And so acquired unto himself a perfect knowledge of all States, and State affairs. Being chosen once, he cannot stir out of the *Laguna* without leave. Nor at home can he do all things of his own Head; but with the advice of his Counsellers, who are six, chosen out of the most honourable Gentlemen of the City. These six sit with him in Counsel, and execute with him all Businesses, as to give Audience, read Letters, grant Priviledges, and the like: Which cannot be executed by the *Doge*, if there be not four Counsellers with him; and yet they can execute and act without the *Doge*; and it's they that have Authority to propose in the great Counsel, things of concern. In giving Suffrages, his Suffrage is no more than an ordinary Senators in the Senate; but he hath two Voices in the great Counsel. The *Doge* and these Counsellours are called *Il Collegio*, but then in main publick affirs there enter into this Counsel, Six *Savi grandi*, five *Savi di Terra Ferma*, five *Save de gli Ordini*, and Three *Capi de Quaranta Criminali*, This full College distributes Business to the other Magistrates to be handed, having been headed here.

The Habit of the *Doge* is ancient, and hath something of the *Pontifical* Habit of it His Pomp, Train, and Lodging are all Princely; and in public Functions he hath carried before him the eight

Silver

Silver Trumpets, the great *Umbrella* of Cloth of Tissue, the Coshion, the Chair, the gilt Sword, and a white wax Candle carried by a Child. All Letters of State are written in his Name, and Money is coyned in his Name, but the *Impronto*, or stamp of it, is always the figure of St. *Mark*, or St. *Marks* Lyon. For the most part the *Doge* is chosen out of those whom they call here, *Procuratori di* St. *Marco*. These *Procuratori* are of high rank and esteem in this Republick. Heretofore there was but one *Procuratori di San Marco*, whose Office was to have a care of all things belonging to St. *Mark's* Church, and the *Treasure*. But now there are Twenty five, most of which have made their Circles of Embassies in foreign Courts, and are fit Wood to make *Doges* of: Though some of them of late have been assumed to that dignity for Money; the State now making Money of all Men, as well as of all things.

Procurato-
ri di Sans
Marco.

As for the Strength and Power of *Venice*, i'ts very great, their Possessions in *Italy*, being full as great as the Pope's; and out of *Italy*, far greater. In *Italy* they hold fourteen Provinces under them. They are Lords of the *Gulph*, or *Adriatic Sea*.

Their
Strength.

They possess the Coast of *Dalmatia*, beyond the *Gulph*. They hold the *Iles* of *Corfu*, *Cephalonia* and *Zant*.

Candia, or the *Ile of Creta*, belongs to them by due. The Kingdom of *Cyprus* also is pretended to by them; and by it and *Candy*, whose two Crowns they shew us in the Treasury, *Venice* is stiled *Serenissima*. The Kingdom of *Cyprus* came to the *Venetians* by *Catherine Cornaro*, who was made Heir of it by her Son, the King thereof, who died young and without Issue, about the year 1438. The story is is this, *Catharine* was Daughter of *Marco Cornaro*, and Neece of *Andrew Cornaro*, two Noblemen of *Venice*. *Andrew* was sent *Auditore General* into the Kingdom of *Cyprus*, in the time of *James* King of that Island, and helpt him to many thousand Crowns, whereby he settled his tottering Crown. One day as the King was talking familiarly with him, he let fall (whether by chance, or design) a little Picture in *Miniature*, of a very handsom Lady. The King curious to see it, call'd for it civilly, and viewing it well, fell hugely in love with the Original of it, which *Andrew* assured him to be far handsomer than the Copy; and withal added, that if his Majesty liked her, she was his Neece, and that therefore he offered her freely to him for his Wife, with all the Money he had already lent him, and an hundred thousand Crowns more. The King bit willingly at these two Baits, Beauty and Money, and was not quiet till he had married her. Of her he had but one Son, whom (dying) he left under his Mothers Protection, but he dying also not long after, left his Mother heir of the Kingdom; and she at her Death, left this Crown and Kingdom to the *Venetians* by Will and Gift. This whole History I saw Painted in the Pallace of *Cornaro* by the hand of *Paulo Vernose*. As for the strong holds which the *Venetians* possess in *Italy*, they are these: *Crema, Bergamo, Brescia, Peschiera, Chiosa,* and *Palma Nuova* in *Fruili*. This last is one of the best places in *Europe*. It hath nine Royal *Bastions*; Eighteeen Cavaliers, which command all the Neighbouring *Campagnia*: It hath ditches of Water about it, thirty Paces broad and twelve deep; Its Ramparts behind the Wall are high and covering, and they are always fringed with

Laschi in Compendo Hister.

Palma Nuova.

with an hundred pieces of Cannon, and ready to receive six Hundred more, which are always in its *Magazin*, ready upon all occasions. And for Men and Armour, as the great Arsenal in *Venice* hath always Arms in readiness for an hundred Thousand Men; so this State being peopled with three Millions of Men, would easily find three or four hundred Thousand Men of Service, and an hundred Gallies: Yet their ordinary *Militia* is but of fourscore Thousand Foot, and some six Thousand Horse; and about thirty Gallies.

Their Riches. As for their Riches, though their ordinary Revenues (before the late Wars with the Turk) exceeded not four Millions, yet now they spur themselves, and the Country up to excessive sums. Few die but they bequeath something to such a Christian Service as this War is. Besides this, the Taxes are much augmented, and seizures and forfeitures more narrowly looked into, to help publick expenses. In fine, besides this, the great trading which *Venice* driveth (*Aleppo* alone bringing in some years, four Millions of Gold) the *Venetians* have found out a very compendious way to raise, in one quarter of an Hour, and by one dash of a Pen, fifty Hundred Thousand Crowns, to help themselves withal at a dead lift, and incommodate no Man. This they did, *Anno.* 1646 when fifty rich Families in *Venice* gave to the State an hundred Thousand Crowns a piece, to be made noble *Venetians*. The like course they took to raise Money, about an hundred Years ago, when they were set upon by most of the Princes of *Europe* at once.

Their Religion. As for their Religion, its *Roman Catholick*, and they have never changed it since the beginning of

Part II. A Voyage through Italy.

of their Republick. Hence Mr. *Raymond* in his *Mercurio Italico*, page 188. saith truly, that *Venice* hath this property above all other States; that she is a Virgin, and more, from the first infancy, Christian; having never yet fell from her Principles either in Government or Religion. It began to be built the very same year that St. *Augustin* died, as *Baronius* observes.

As for the Interest of the Publick, they are now well with the Emperor; not out with *Spain*, nor too secure of his Friendship; kind with the *French*, as long as they keep out of *Italy*; well affected to *England*, and just friends with the Pope. *Their Interest.*

Now for the particulars which I saw in *Venice*, they were these.

1. The Men themselves here, who looked like Men indeed: And as a Philosopher anciently said that when he came from *Corinth* to *Sparta*, he seemed to come from Horses to Men: So me thought, when I came from *France* to *Venice* I came from Boys to Men. For here I saw the handsomest, the most sightly, the most proper and grave Men that ever I saw any where else. They wear always in the Town (I speak of the Noblemen) a long black Gown, a black Cap knit, with an edging of black Wool about it, like a Fringe, an ancient and manly wear, which makes them look like Senators. Their Hair is generally the best I ever saw any where; these little Caps not pressing it down as our Hats do, and Periwigs are here forbid. Under their long Gowns (which fly open before) they have handsom black Suits of rich Stuff, with Stockins and Garters, and Spanish Leather Shoos neatly made. In a word, I never so many proper Men together, nor so

wise

wife, as I saw dayly their walking upon the *Piazza* of St. *Mark*. I may boldly say, that I saw there five hundred Gentlemen walking together every day, every one of which was able to play the Embassador in any Princes Court of *Europe*. But the misery is, that we strangers cannot walk there with them, and talk with them, but must keep out of their way, and stand a loof off. The reason is this: This state (as all Republics are) being hugely jealous of her liberty and preservation, forbids her Noblemen and Senators to converse with Foreign Embassadors, or any men that either is an actual Servant or Follower of an Embassador, or hath any the least relation to any Princes Agent, without express leave: And this upon pain of being suspected as a Traitor, and condignly punished. This makes them shy to all Strangers, not knowing what relation they may have to some Foreign States-man or Agent. For the same reason, they will not let their Wives visit the Wives of Foreign Embassadors residing in *Venice*, for fear of being suspected to commit Treason by proxy. They have in the Wall of the Pallace, in divers places certain wide Mouths of Marble Stone, over which I found written these words: *Denuncie secrete*, private informations, into which they cast secretly Papers of accusations, by which they accuse secretly any Officer or Nobleman, whom they durst not accuse publickly. This makes Men stand hugely upon their guard, and be wary with whom they converse, and what they say.

The noble Women of Venice.

2. As for the Women here, they would gladly get the same reputation that their Husbands have, of being tall and handsom; but they over-do it with their horrible *Cioppini*, or high Shooes, which

which I have often seen to be a full half yard high. I confess, I wondered at first, to see Women go upon Stilts, and appear taller by the Head than any Man; and not to be able to go any whether without resting their Hands upon the Shoulders of two grave Matrons that usher them: But at last, I perceived that it was good Policy, and a pretty ingenious way either to clog Women at Home by such heavy shoes (as the *Egyptians* kept their Wives at home by allowing them no shoes at all;) or at least to make them not able to go either far, or alone, or invisibly. As for the young Ladies of this Town, that are not marryed, they are never seen abroad, but masked like *Mascarades* in a strange Disguise, at the Fair time, and other public solemnities or shows, being at other times brought up in Monasteries of Nuns, till they be marryed.

3. Then I went to the Church of St. *Mark* the Evangelist, whose body lyeth here, having been translated hither from *Alexandria*, 820 and odd years ago; having ever since been one of the chief Patrons of this State, as his *Lion* hath ever since been the Arms of the Republic, and its Seal in all public writings. This Church is built *a la Thedesca*, as they call it, and as the best Churches built about those Times, were. Its neither great, nor high; but so rich for the materials, that nothing but Mosaick work and Marble appear in it. The Roof and the Walls a good way down, are curiously Painted with *Mosaick* Histories and Pictures; and the rest of the wall is rare marble. Among those *Mosaick Pictures*; there are to be seen in the vault of the Arch over the Door of the Treasury, two old Pictures the one of St *Dominick*, the other of St. *Francis*; both made before they Instituted their several

St. Mark's Church.

Orders, and yet both in the Religious Habits which those of their Orders wear; and all this out of the predictions of *Joachim* (Abbat of *Curacium*, and not of S. *Fleur*, as some wrongly call him) who lived before these Orders were instituted. The Picture also of the Pope, near to the Pictures of the foresaid Saints, is said to be a Prophetical Picture of the said Abbats describing; representing the last Pope that shall govern the flock of Christ, when all the world shall be of one Religion. The Pavement of this Church is suitable to the rest, being in some places composed of vast Marble stones, naturally representing the Waves of the Sea; in other places its curiously inlaid with stones of several colors expressing Flowers, Stars, Birds, Beasts and the like: Among which stones I preceived here and there some *Turky* stones of great value among us, but here not scorning to be trod upon. Thirty six Marble Pillars of a round form, and two foot thick in Diameter, hold up the roof of this Church. The high Altar is a rare piece, especially when you see the back of it open, as I did upon the Ascension Eve. This back of the Altar is richly adorned with divers rows of little enamelled Pictures, *a la Greca*, set in Gold, and enriched with brave Pearl and Pretious Stones intermingled every where between the Pictures. This most rich Ornament, or back of the Altar, was given by a *Doge* of *Venice*, and brought from *Constantinople*. Behind the high Altar stands the Altar of our Blessed Sacrament, where there are two transparent round Pillars, four yards high. In the Sacristy, which is hard by, I saw neat Mosaic work in the roof; and an admirable Picture of St *Hierom* of the same work also. Round about the inside

Baronius an. 1190.

Part II.   A Voyage through Italy.   237

side of the Church, over the Pillars, hang the *Scutcheons* of several *Doges*, in a large size. For the *Doges* at their Creation, cause three things to be made: First their Picture which is set up in the *Sala* of the great Council: Secondly their Arms or Scutchion, which are sometimes of Silver, and of an huge size, and are set up after the *Doges* death in the Church for ever. Thirdly they must make their Picture in the *Collegio*, or *Pregiadi*.

4. From the Church we were let in to see the Treasury of St. *Mark*, which joyns to the Church. It was shewn us by the special leave from above, and by two noble *Venetians*, who are always present when it is shewn. We were first shewn the Spiritual Treasury, and then the Temporal; that is, first the Relics and then the Jewels. The Relics were these principally. A great authentical piece of the holy Cross, above a span long. It is the greatest piece I have seen any where, except that in the Holy Chappel in *Paris*, and though some enemies of the very Cross of Christ, as well as of other Relics, do jeeringly say, that there are so many pieces of the Holy Cross shewn in the World, they if they were all put together, they would make a Cart load of Wood: Yet I dare maintain more probably, that all the pieces, any one Man can say, are shewn in *Europe* (and I have seen a good part of it) would not make so much of the Cross, as one of those parts on which our Saviours hands were nailed: Seeing the greatest part that we find of it, is no thicker than an ordinary mans Finger, and little longer than a Span; and that very part of it which I saw in the Popes own Sacristy in the *Vatican*, is no longer than a mans little Finger: And if the King of *France* (St. Lewis)

The Treasury of St. Mark.

The Spiritual Treasury.

P p 2

Lewis) in his two expeditions into the Holy Land, could get only so little a piece of it, as that which is shown in *Paris*, in the Saint *Chappelle*. And if the Pope himself could get no greater a piece of it, than mentioned above, I do not wonder, if in other places, they shew such little shreds of it, as altogether would not make two foot of Timber, much less a Cart load. We saw also here a finger of St. *Mark*. His Ring with a Stone in it, which our *Lapidaries* cannot tell how to name. Some of our Saviours Blood, gathered up in his Passion, with the Earth it was spilt upon. A thorn of the Holy Crown of Thorns. A Nail which nailed the two pieces of the Cross together. A Finger of St. *Mary Magdalen*. A piece of St. *John Baptist's Cranium*. A Tooth of St. *Mark*. A piece of St. *John Baptist's* Habit: Some of our Blessed Ladies Hair. An ancient Picture of St. *John Baptist*, enamelled in Gold. A piece of our Saviours white Robe when he was scourged. A very ancient Picture of our Blessed Lady, carried about anciently by *Constantine* the Great, who had it always with him. One of the Stones of the *Torrent*, wherewith St. *Stephen* was Stoned. And in fine, the Sword of St. *Peter*.

The Temporal Treasure. Then leading us to the temporal *Treasure*, in another Room, they shewed us (by Candle light, as they did also the Spiritual *Treasure*) these things. First, the twelve Crowns of Gold, and the twelve breast and back pieces (like Womens close bodies) of beaten Gold also, set thick, as well as the Crowns, with exquisite Pearl, both round and big: Twelve young Virgins used to wear them anciently upon a Feast day. Then three great Carbuncles, one whereof weigheth six Ounces, and is bigger than an ordinary Hens Egg: They value it

Part II.   A Voyage through Italy.

it at two Hundred Thousand Crowns. Then the two Crowns of Gold set thick with precious Stones; one being the Crown of the Kingdom of *Cyprus*; the other of the Kingdom of *Candy*. After this they shewed us the *Doge*'s Crown, called here, *il Corno*, because its made somewhat sharp and turning in at the top like a Horn. It's set round with a close row of excellent Pearl, each one as big as an Hasel Nut, with a vast Ruby in the front of it, worth a Hundred Thousand Crowns, say they, and one of the fairest Diamonds in *Europe*, in the top of it. Then they shewed us many other rich things, as the *Flower de Luce* of Gold, with a rich Diamond in it, given by *Henry* III. of *France*, at his passing by *Venice*, when he came out of *Poland*. The two *Unicorns* Horns, far less than that at St. *Denys* in *France*; but no less true. The two Crucifixes set with Pearl and rich Jewels, and in great number. The great Candlesticks and Thurible of beaten Gold, and curiously wrought, each one being almost as heavy as a Man can carry in both hands. The great *Chalice* of gold, as great as a man can carry in both hands. A *Saphyr* weighing ten Ounces. A cup or dish, as broad and deep as an ordinary Callote (or Cap, which we wear under our Hats) and all of one *Turky*-stone entire, and of huge Value; It was sent unto this Republick, by a King of *Persia*. A Vessel like a Tankard, of a rich *Cameo*; its Handel being curiously engraven with a Diamond. A little Vase of the roots of *Emeraud*. Another of *Sardonick*. A great cup of Agate. Another of *Roman* Agate, far finer than the former, and more transparent. A rich *Pax* of Mother of Pearl. A *Spanish* Embassador, once viewing this Treasure, took a Candle

Pp 3   and

and looked curiously under the long Tables, upon which these rich things are exposed; and being asked what he looked for, answered; that he looked whether this Treasure had Roots or no, as his Masters Treasure had, and therefore groweth yearly: Meaning the *India* Fleet of *Spain*, which bringeth home yearly to the King of *Spain's* Coffers and Treasure, twelve Millions.

The Doges Pallace.   5. Having seen this Treasure, and thanked the two noble *Venetians* that stood by, and requited the under Officers that shewed it; we went into the *Doge's* Pallace, which joyns to St. *Marks* Church; and mounting up the open stairs into the open Gallery, we saw the two great Marble Statues of *Mars* and *Neptune*, which stand at the Head of these Stairs, and signifie the strength of the *Venetians*, both by Sea and Land. They are excellent pieces, otherwise great *Sansovinus* would never have owned them by writing under them, *Opus Sansovini*. This open Gallery led us into a world of Chambers of Justice and Clerks Offices, all thronged with business and busy Men. Going up from hence into a higher story, we saw the *Doge's* Chambers of Audience, his *Anti-chambers*, his Dining-room, and the like. From thence we were led into several great Chambers of Council, all rarely well painted. After that we saw the great Chamber, or *Sala*, of the Senate-house, where the Nobles meet upon affairs, as great as the Chamber. For here they meet about the chusing of publick Officers, either for the governing of the City or Army: And sometimes they have been forced to stay there eight days (saith *Sabellicus*) not being able to agree about the Elections; they not being permitted to depart thence till they agree. This

Senate-

Senate-house or great Chamber, is above three-score paces long, and thirty wide. Its full of Seats for the Noble *Venetians*, to the number of two Thousand Men, who have right to enter here. It's painted on all sides by the rarest Painters that were in *Italy*, when this Room was made. Over the *Doge*'s Throne, is a rare piece of painting, covering the whole end of the Room above, and representing Heaven in a glorious manner. It's of the Hand of *Tintoret*. The great Pictures upon that side of the Room, which looks towards the Court of the Pallace, contain the History of Pope *Alexander* the III. and the Emperor *Frederic Barbarossa*. I saw also in this great Room, and in the next joyning to it, the true Pictures of all the *Doges* of *Venice*. In the other Chambers of this Pallace, in the Churches, and other Pallaces of this Town, I saw so many, and so rare pieces of painting, of *Titian*, *Tintoret*, *Bellino*, *Gentile*, *Castel*, *Franco*, *Bassano*, *Paolo Veronese*, *Perdonone* and others, that with Madam *Rome's* leave, I dare boldly say, that no place of *Italy* hath so many rare Pictures in it, as *Venice* hath; and perchance, you will be of my Opinion, if you read the curious Book of *Rodolfi*, who hath written the lives of the Painters of *Venice*, and the *Venetian* State, and sets down where their prime pieces are to be seen.

7. Having seen these Chambers of *Judicature*, *The little Arsenal.* we were led about to the *Sala* of the *Configlio de Dieci* (otherwise called, the little *Arsenal*) in the Pallace still. It's a curious sight, and therefore not to be omitted by my Traveller. There are Arms in it for a Thousand Men, ready upon all occasions of Sedition or Treason. The Muskets are always charged and primed, and every six Months they

ed to kill the whole Senate, while it was assembled; and make *Bajamante* Master of *Venice*. But the Plot was dasht in the Execution; because *Bajamante's* Brains were dash'd out by a poor Woman, who seeing him march under her window in the head of his rebellious crew, threw down from her Window, a great earthen Flower-pot upon his Head, and killed him dead. His party seeing this, retired, and were soon subdued: And his House was turned into a Shambles for Butchers; a fit disgrace for him who would have been the Butcher of his Prince and Countrimen. Here also, in this Arsenal, we saw the Sword and Arms of brave *Scanderbeg*, Prince of *Albania*, who won seven Battels over seven, the most illustrious *Bassas* the great *Turk* had, and died after all, peaceably in his Estates, in spite of *Amurath*. Its said, that the great *Turk* hearing how *Scanderbeg* with his Sword had cloven Men in two, sent to him; and desired him to send him his Sword, his cutting Sword; which he did: The *Turk* tried it upon his Slaves, and finding that he could not cleave Men as *Scanderbeg* had done, sent him word, that he had not sent him his true Sword; to whom *Scanderbeg* replied, that he had sent him indeed his Sword, but not his Arm. As for this Sword, which they call here *Scanderbeg's* Sword, its a broad thin Blade of a reasonable length, but light, and of as good Metal almost, as its Master. We saw here many other curiosities: As the Standard of the *Doge Zani*, who restored Pope *Alexander* the III. unto his Seat again; with his Sword, Buckler and Helmet. The Standard of the great *Turk*. The Standard of Horses hair belonging also to the great *Turk*, and which he hung out always before

fore Battle, as a signal of combat. It was taken by a *French* Man called *Ciotar*. The Statues of *Ludovico Sforza* Duke of *Milan*, and of his Wife *Viscomi*. The Statue or head of *Carara*, whom they call the Tyrant, but how truly I know not: The Statue or head in Brass of brave *Venerio*, General of the *Venetians*, in the Battle of *Lepanto*. The Head in Brass, also of brave *Bragandino*, flead alive by the *Turks* for his Countries Service. The Picture of *Santa Justina* in a great Case set with rich Stones. This Case was made for a great Looking-Glass which the *Venetians* sent unto the *Sultaness* of the great *Turk*; but the Ship that carried it, meeting in the way a Frigat which brought the News of a great Victory gotten over the *Turks* by the *Venetians* upon *Santa Justin's* day, it retured back again with the present; and the Senate caused the Glass to be taken out, and *Santa Justina's* Picture to be set in Place of it. Then we saw a rare *Carpet*, or rather a curious piece of Stuff with Figures in it, sent to the Reipublick of *Venice* by a King of *Persia*. The habits of two noble *Chinesi*, who were Baptized at *Venice*. The Armour of brave *Gatta Mela*, with the Picture of a Cat in his Head-piece. The Armour of some of the ancient *Doges* of *Venice*, who, to the number of Forty or Fifty, went to War in Person, and did such things there, as to make their very Armor to be Honourable. The Habit, Buckler, and Sword of a King of *Persia*; the Arms are set with rich Stones. The Armor of *Henry* the IV of *France*, with his Pocket Pistol. The Armor of the Duke of *Rohan*. The compleat Armour of a little Boy about ten years old, who was found dead in a Battle, fighting for the *Venetians* and his Country; and not known who

he

he was. Poor brave Child! Who being worthy never to have died, doest not so much as live in History! Indeed I did not think till then, that *Mars* had his Abortives too, dying before their time, and before they were named. Then they shewed me *Attila*'s Helmet, with the Head-piece of his Horse. A Cannon shooting seven Shots at once, as if Death, with his single Dart, went too slowly to work. Another Cannon shooting threescore Shots in ten Barrels. A Halbert with a Barrel within it, shooting fourteen Shots. Another Halbert shooting seven Shots. A Cannon of Iron carrying two Miles, and curiously wrought into Flowers with the points of Chizels. The Chollar of Iron of the *Paduan* Tyrant (as they call him here) *Carara*. The little Iron Cross-bow of the same Tyrant, with which he is said to have shot Needles a Span long, and killed many Men privately, who knew not how, or by whom they were hurt. Then the Devils Organs, or a Trunk of Leather, with ten Pistol Barrels in it, of a Foot and half long; and so disposed in order like Organ-pipes, that upon the opening of the Lock of this Trunk, all these Barrels being charged with several Bullets, should let fly at once; and so scattering wide, kill all those that should be in the Room. This Trunk was contriv'd by a revengeful Man, who having a Mind to be revenged both of his Enemy, and of his Enemies Friends at once, sent him this Trunk by an unknown Bearer (as a present from a Friend) while he treated his Friends at dinner. The holes through the sides of it, made by the Bullets, shew the devilish effect of this Trunk, and how well it deserves the name of the Devils Organ. The Box of *Bursargoes* here is just such another Invention. A Pi-

stol

stol in a Pocket-Book here is as bad as the others; which being Chargd and let off, would presently read your Doom. Swords and Daggers, with Pistol and little Gun Barrels running along their Blades, which being held drawn with the Broadside to a Man, appear to be only plain Swords and Daggers, and yet they discharge thrusts not to be parried by any fencing Guard. I saw also here a fine Tabernacle of Christal: A burning Lamp found in *Antenor*'s Tomb in *Padua*. A Burning-Glass, which burneth half a Mile off: A rare *Adam* and *Eve*, with the Serpent and the Tree, all cut out of one piece of Wood by the rare hand of *Alberto Dureo*: And in fine, the Picture of King *James* of *England*, the only Picture of any foreign Prince that I saw there.

The Piazza of St. Mark.

Having thus seen this Cabinet of *Mari*, we went out of the Pallace into the *Piazza* of St. *Mark*, upon which both the aforesaid Church of St. *Mark*, and the *Doge*'s Pallace look. This is one of the noblest *Piazza*'s that a Man can see in any Town. It runs from the Sea-side, up along the Pallace, to the Church of St. *Mark*, and from thence turning on the left hand, it spreads it self into a more large and longer open place, most Beautiful to behold; for the whole *Piazza*, even from the Sea-side to the farther end, is built upon Arches, and Marble Pillars; and raised up with beautiful Lodgings, fit to lodg all the *Procuratori* of St. *Mark*; all the rich foreign Merchants; a world of persons of condition; the *Mint*, and the famous Library. In that part of the *Piazza* which lies under the Pallace the *Nobili Venetiani* walk together, twice a day, to confer about business of State. This meeting here of the Noblemen is called the *Broglio*. And in the end

end of it, close by the Sea-side, stand two great Pillars of rich Marble, the one bearing upon it the Image of St. *Theodorus*, the other the Lyon of St. *Mark*; these two Saints, St. *Mark* and St. *Theodorus*, being the two Patrons of this City. These two Pillars were erected here by a *Lombard*, who required no other recompence for his Pains, than that it may be Lawful for Dice-players to play at Dice between these two Pillars, without being punished or molested; nay, though they played false play: Here also between these two Pillars they execute Malefactors, to shew that they deserve not the Protection of those two Patrons, who break the Orders of that Town which is under the Protection. It's pity that the *Lombard* himself was not whipp'd here, at least, for making himself the Protector of idle Rogues there, where the Saints are Patrons of honest Men. Over against the Pallace stands the *Mint*, in a place called *La Zeccha*, and from hence the Gold coined here is called *Zecchino*; a piece of Gold worth some seven Shillings and Sixpence of our Money. Hard by it stands the Library, famous both for the quality and quantity of the Books that are in it. *Petrarch* (once Canon of the Church of *Padua*) gave his Library to it; and *Bessarion* a Greek Cardinal of great Learning and Worth, gave as many great Manuscripts unto it, as cost him thirty Thousand Crowns, and yet by this Legacy, *Bessarion* was but even with the *Venetians*, who honoured him in such a particular manner, as to send out the *Bucentauro* it self to bring him into *Venice*, being sent thither *Legat* by the Pope.

8. Going from hence into the other part of the *Piazza*, which stands before the Church, I espied
upon

upon the very out corner of the Wall of the Church (as you come out of the Pallace) four Porphiry Statues of four Merchants embracing one another. Having enquired what those Statues were set for there, I was told by a grave old Gentlaman of *Venice*; that those whom these Statues represent, were four Merchants and Strangers, who brought hither most of the Jewels mentioned above in the Treasury : And that afterwards poisoning one another out of Covetousness, left this State heir of all. Just before the Church stand three tall Masts of Ships, upon curiously wrought Pedestals of Brass, & each Mast bearing, upon great days, a stately Flag, & Streamers. These three Masts signify the three noblest parts of the *Venetians* Dominions, to wit, the Kingdoms of *Cyprus*, and of *Candy*, and the state of *Venice*. In this *Piazza* I found always a world of Strangers perpetually walking and talking of Bargains and Traffick, as *Greeks, Armenians, Albanians, Slavonians, Polonians, Jews,* and even *Turks* themselves ; all in their several Habits, but all conspiring in this one thing, to sell dear, and buy cheap. Here also they have every night in Summer, a world of *Montebanks, Ciarlatani,* and such stuff, who, together with their druggs and remedies, strive to please the People with their little Comedies, Popet-plays, Songs, Musick, Stories, and such like Buffonery. It's strange to see how they find daily, either new fooling or new Fools, not only to hear them, but even they throw them Money too for such poor contentments. In this *Piazza* also stands the *Campanile*, or high Steeple of *Venice*, distant some fifty Paces from the Church of St. *Mark*. It's built forty Foot square on all Sides, and two Hundred and thirty six high. The

top

top of it is covered with gilt Tiles, which, in a Sun- *The high* shine day, appear gloriously afar off. The Foun- *Steeple.* dation of it is almost as deep underground, as the top of it is high above ground; a wonder, if you consider that it stands in *Venice*. From the top of this *Campanile* we had a perfect view of *Venice* under us, and of all its neighbouring Islands, Forts, Seas, and Towns about it; as also of the outside of St. *Marks* Church, its Frontispiece, its Cupolas, and the four Horses of Brass gilt, which stand over the Frontispiece. These Horses came out of the Shop, not out of the Stable of *Lisippus* a famous Statuary in *Greece*, and were given to *Nero* by *Tiradates*, King of *Armenia*. They were carried by *Constantine* the Great from *Rome* to *Constantinople*; and from thence they were transported hither. In fine, from the top of this Steeple we saw the compass of the great Arsenal of *Venice*, which looked like a little Town in our Sight. Indeed some make it three Miles about; but I cannot allow it so much. The sight of this *Magazin* of War afar off, made us hasten down from the Steeple to go see it nearer hand.

9. Taking therefore a *Gondola*, we went to the *The Arse-* Arsenal, where, after the ordinary formalities of *nal.* leaving our Swords at the Door, and paying the Porters Fees, we were admitted, and led through this great Shop of *Mars*. It's so well seated near the Sea-side, and so well built, that it might serve the *Venetian* Senators for a Castle, in time of danger: And in it there is a Well of fresh Water, not to be poisoned, because of the two pieces of *Unicorns* Horn set fast in the bottom of it. I confess I never saw any where such Oeconomy as is here observ'd. Fifteen Hundred Men are daily employed

ed here, and duly paid at the Weeks end, according to their several Employments and Works. The Expences of these Workmen amount to a Thousand Ducats every day in the Year: So that they make account that they may spend in this Arsenal four Hundred and thirty Thousand Crowns a Year: Enough almost to maintain a pretty Army constantly. Every Workman here hath Wine twice a day, and that very good too, but that it is a little mingled with Water. We were led through all the vast Rooms of this *Magazin*, Rooms like vast Churches: In one of them I saw nothing but great Oars for Gallies, seven Men going to one Oar. In another, nothing but vast Sterns. In another, nothing but vast Nails for Gallies and Ships. In another, they were making nothing but Salt-peeter for Gunpowder. In another, they were casting great Cannons, Morter-pieces, and Chambers. In another, they had nothing but a pair of vast Scales to weigh Cannons with. In another, Masts for Gallies and Ships, of a prodigious greatness and length; and yet of such a rare Timber, that one fillipping up one end of them, you hear it easily at the other end, by applying your Ear to it. Some of these Masts are worth fourscore Pounds. In other vast Rooms I saw store of Cannons of all sizes, both for Ships and Gallies; where also I saw some *Turkish* Cannons with words upon them in the *Turkish* Language. There I saw also one Cannon shooting three Shots at once: Another five; one great Cannon found buried in *Candy* full of Gold Medals: The great Cannons cast here while *Henry* the III. of *France* dined in this Arsenal. They had heretofore a prodigious quantity of Cannons here, but now these

Rooms are much emptied, by reason of this War with the *Turks*. In other great Rooms I saw huge heaps of Cannon-Bullets of all sizes, with some Ensigns won over the *Turks*. Then mounting up into the Chambers above, I saw in two vast Rooms, Arms for fifty Thousand Men. In another, Arms for twelve Gallies: In another, Arms for fifty Gallies. Here also I saw the suit of Armor of *Scanderbeg*: That of the *Doge Zani*; the Lantern of *Don John* of *Austria*'s Ship in the Battle of *Lepanto*: The *Lantern* of a *Turkish* Gally: The Armor of *Benjamante Theopoli*, and his complices, with one Arm only: Some Arms taken from the *Turks* in the Battle of *Lepanto*: Other Arms taken from the *Genuesi*; a great Cross-Bow shooting vast Arrows of Iron, above five quarters long: An Invention of great use, before Guns were found out. A Cannon-Bullet with four long Irons, like the tops of Halberts; which shut up close into it when they put it into the Cannon, but open again of themselves as soon as the Bullet is out of the Cannons Mouth: And so spreading into four parts, cut all they meet with strange Fury; a dangerous invention in Sea Battles, to spoil Cordage and Tackling. Here also they shew us the Description of the Town and Fort of *Clissa*, and how it was taken by the *Venetians* some twenty years ago. Then descending from thence, we went to see the places where they make new Gallies, and mend old ones. There I found a vast square Court three Hundred Paces broad in every square, and full of vast Penthouses, capable of holding in them, Gallies of fifty Paces long a piece. In the midst of this Court is a vast square pond of Water, let in from the Sea, where the new Gallies are tryed;

and the old ones are let into the Arsenal to be mended and rigged a new. Here I saw a world of Galleys, and a world of Men working about them most busily. There were heretofore divers of these great Courts full of Gallies, but now they are much exhausted; the Gallies being abroad in War. Hence it is observed that this Arsenal, before these Wars, could arm two Hundred Gallies, and two hundred Thousand Men. Here it was that they made a Gally, and set her out at Sea while *Henry* the III dined here in the Arsenal; which made that King say then, that he would give three of the best Towns in *France* (except his Parliament Towns) for such an Arsenal. Indeed the Arsenals of *Paris, Genua, Zurick, Naples,* and *Geneva,* seemed to me to be little Gunsmiths Shops in comparison of this. They were then making here two new *Galleasses* (when I was last there) of vast bulk and Expences. In fine, I saw here the old *Bucentoro*; and presently after the new *Bucentoro*. This last is the Galley of State, of the *Doge,* when he goeth forth upon the Ascension-day, accompanied with the Senate, to espouse the Sea as they call it here. This is a noble Galley, all gilt without, and wainscotted round about the Deck, with gilt Seats. There runs a Partition of Wood quite along the Deck of the Galley, with Seats on both sides, and with a low open roof of Wood to let in Air, and yet keep off the Sun; and all this is gilt and painted, and capable of five Hundred Senators, who in their scarlet Robes wait upon the *Doge* that Day. The *Doge* sits in the *Puppe,* in a Chair of State with the Popes *Nuncio* on one hand of him, and the Patriarch of *Venice* on the other, and a place for Music behind them. The Slaves are all under Hatches, and

and not seen at all; but their Oars, (twenty on each side) move all at once, like great Wings, which make the *Bucentoro* move most Majestically. And this is all that I can remember in this Arsenal, except the Cellar of Wine, and the great Rooms, (as I came out) where Women only are employed in mending old Sails; and Men (a part) in making great Cables: And indeed those vast Anchors which lye near the wooden Bridge here at the entrance, stand in need of Cables of the greatest size.

10. I happened to be at *Venice* thrice, at the great Sea Triumph, or Feast of the Ascension, which was performed thus. About our eight in the Morning, the Senators in their Scarlet Robes meet at the *Doge's* Pallace; and there taking him up, they walk with him processionally unto the Shoar, where the *Bucentoro* lies waiting them; the Popes *Nuncio* being upon his right Hand, and the Patriarch of *Venice* on his left Hand. Then ascending into the *Bucentoro*, by a handsome Bridge thrown out to shoar, the *Doge* takes his place, and the Senators sit round about the Galley as they can, to the number of two or three Hundred. The Senate being placed, the Anchor is weighed, and the Slaves being warned by the Captains Whistle, and the Sound of Trumpets, begin to strike all at once with their Oars, and to make the *Bucentoro* march as gravely upon the Water, as if she also went upon *Cioppini*. Thus they steer for two Miles upon the *Laguna*, while the Music plays, and sings *Epithala-miums* all the way long, and makes *Neptune* jealous to hear *Hymen* called up in his Dominions. Round about the *Bucentoro* flock a world of *Piota's*, and *Gondola's*, richly covered over head with sumptuous Canopies of Silk, and rich Stuffs, and rowed

The Ascension.

rowed by Watermen in rich Liveries, as well as the Trumpeters. Thus foreign Embassadors, divers Noblemen of the Country, and Strangers of Condition wait upon the *Doge*'s Galley all the way along, both coming and going. At last the *Doge* being arrived at the appointed place, throws a Ring into the Sea, without any other ceremony, than by saying: *Desponsamus te, Mare, in signum perpetui Dominii. We espouse thee, O Sea, in Testimony of our perpetual Dominion over thee:* And so returns to the Church of St. *Nicolas* in *Lio* (an Island hard by) where he assists at high Mass with the Senate. This done, he returns home again in the same State; and invites those that accompanied him in his Galley, to Dinner in his Pallace: The preparatives of which dinner we saw before the *Doge* was got home. This Ceremony of marrying the Sea, as they call it, is ancient; and performed yearly in memory of the grant of Pope *Alexander* the III. who being restored by the *Venetians* unto his Seat again, granted them Power over the Adriatic Sea, as a Man hath power over his Wife; and the *Venetians* to keep this Possession, make every Year this watery *Cavalcata*. I confess, the sight is stately, and a Poet would presently conceive that *Neptune* himself were going to be married to some *Nereide*.

The Corso at Murano. 11. Having seen this Ceremony in the Morning, we went after Dinner to see the Evening *Corso* at *Murano*, where we saw those fine *Gondolas* and *Piattas*, which he had seen waiting upon the *Doge* in the Morning, now rowing in State up and down the great *Canale* of *Murano*, to the sound of Trumpets; and with all the force of the brawny Watermen that row them. Sometimes meeting too thick in the Arches of the wooden Bridge here, they crack

Part II.   A Voyage through Italy.

crack one anothers *Gondolas*, break one anothers Oars, overturn their Boatmen, and are stopt for an hour together without being able to untangle. Embassadors themselves of Foreign Princes appear in *Corso* this Evening, with all their bravery (five or six *Gondolas* all in one Livery, as well as all the Gallants and Gentry of *Venice*, who appear here this Evening at *Corso*.

12. The next Morning no sooner appeared, but *The Fair.* new sights appeared also, and now upon land; and the Scene was St. *Mark's* place, where the Fair opening this day, and lasting for ten days, drew all the Gallants of *Venice* to come, and behold all the Gallantry and Riches that either Domestic or Foreign Merchants could set forth to sail. But the most part of the young Ladies that came to see the Fair, came in an odd dress, with a false Nose, and a little beard of black Wool, disguising their Mouth and Nose: So that they could see all the Fair, and be known to no body. Thus they go often to Marriages, and other Assemblies, when they have no mind to be known.

13. Having thus seen these foresaid sights, we *St. George.* went on with visiting the other things in the Town, and one day we went to the Island of St. *George Major*, where we saw a stately Monastery, Church, Cloister and Garden, which take up this whole Island. The Church is one of the best in *Venice*, and built by *Palladio*, the famous Architect. In the Church I was shewn the great silver Lamp, as great as two Men could carry. In a Pillar of Marble standing over a side Altar, I was shewn the Picture of a Crucifix, which was discovered, at the polishing of this stone, to have been naturally in the Vein of the Marble. In the

Refectory,

Refectory, I saw an admirable Picture of the Supper of *Cana* in *Galilee*, made by *Guido Rheni*. I visited it often, and could never satiate my Eyes with such a rare Piece. It takes up the whole end of the great Refectory.

The Pallace of Signore Nani.
14. From thence we rowed to the Pallace of *Procuratore Nani*, which stands in an Island beyond St. *Georges*. The Pallace is richly furnished with the true Pictures of many modern Princes and Ladies of *France*, *England* and *Germany*. This Pallace hath one strange thing belonging to it, beyond the Pallaces of *Venice*: To wit, a neat Garden, for Gardens in *Venice* are as wonderful things as Coaches: And I cannot remember, that looking upon the Whole City, from top of the high Steeple, I saw two places where there were any green Trees. But the best thing that I saw here, was the *Procuratore Nani* himself, the greatest Ornament of the *Venetian* Senate, whose learned Pen hath already given us an excellent History of *Venice*.

The Capucins.
15. From hence we walked to the *Capucins* Convent, which is in the same Island, and Church neatly built, and far above the rate of *Capucins*; but it was a vow of the Senate in time of the Plague; and they regarded more, in building it, their own Honor than the *Capucins* simplicity.

Madonna di Salute.
16. From hence, returning again towards the Town, we steered our *Gondola* to the Church of *Madonna di Salute*; a new round Church, vowed by the State in another plague Time, and likely to be one of the finest Churches in *Venice*, when it shall be ended. In the Sacristy I saw a rare Picture, of a Feast, by *Timtoret*; and others in the roof, by *Titian*.

17. From

Part II.   *A Voyage through* Italy.   257

17. From hence we went to the Church of the *Canon Regulars*, called *La Carita*, in whose Monastery Pope *Alexander* the III. lay hid privately like a poor Chaplain of this Church, unknown to the very Fathers of this place: Till at last he was discovered by a devout Pilgrim, who having seen him often in *Rome*, and hearing him say Mass here, discovered him to the Senate, and so he was both acknowledged by the Senate, and defended by them, as we said above. Over the entrance of the Quire, is seen the Picture of *Alexander* the III. receiving the Emperor *Frederic* to the kissing of his Feet, by the means of the *Doge* of *Venice*, who stands by: Here's also a good Picture of our Saviour's raising up *Lazarus* again to Life: Its of the hand of *Bassan*.

La Carità.

18. Another time I went to the *Dominicans* Church, called St. *Giovanne & Paulo*, where I found, among the Tomb-stones, that of the Lord *Henry Aubigni* (second Brother to the Duke of *Lenox* and *Richmond*) who died here in his Travels. Before the door of this Church stands the *Equestris* Statue in Brass guilt, of *Bartolomeo Colcono Bargamense*, a great Commander, to whom (as the words bear; *ob militare imperium optime gestum*) the Senate decreed this Statue to be erected. The Tabernacle and Altar are very stately. The Chappel of St. *Hiacinth*, and the miracles of this Saint are of the hand of *Bassan* and *Palmarino*. The Martyrdom of St. *John* and *Paul* is a Masterpiece of the hand of *Titian*. The Convent also of St. *John* and *Paul* is one of the most stately ones in *Italy*. The Refectory is famous for painting.

St. Giovanne & Paulo.

19. The Church of St. *Salvatore* is a fair Church, and well adorned with neat Tomes of divers

S. Salvatore.

Qq 4   *Doges*

Doges and great Persons. Upon the back of the high Altar is seen a Picture of the Transfiguration, of the hand of *Titian*. Upon an Altar on the right hand of the Wall, is a Picture of the Annunciation, under which *Titian* wrote these Words, *Titianus, fecit, fecit*, to assure Men by this double affirmative, that it was a good piece, worth his twice owning. There's another Picture of the last Supper, made by *Titian*'s Master. Upon the Epistle side of the high Altar stands a little Chappel, over whose Altar is the Tomb of St. *Theodorus* with his Body in it. He is one of the Patrons of this Town.

St. Chrysostome. 20. In the Church of St. *Chrysostome*, I saw, upon a side Altar, on the left Hand, the Statues in stone of our Saviour and his twelve Apostles, neatly cut, by *Tullius Lombardus*, whose rare Statues adorn also St. *Antonie*'s Tomb at *Padua*. His Statues are easily known by the neat Hands.

21. In the Church of the *Apostoli* I saw a rare Picture of St. *Lucy*, but now somewhat old.

22. In the Church of the Jesuits, I saw the Tomb of St. *Barbara*, Virgin and Martyr.

The Domo. 23. In the *Domo* (the Cathedral of *Venice*, but standing much out of the way) I saw little considerable, but the Tomb of St. *Laurentius Justinianus*, an Holy Man, a great Preacher, and the first Patriarch of *Venice*: The Patriarchal Seat of *Grado*, being removed hither in his Time.

St. Jacomo. 24. I saw also the Church of St. *Jacomo*, the first Church that was built in *Venice*, and built twelve Hundred years ago, in the Infancy of *Venice*, as an old Inscription here told me. Here are some good Pictures of *Lanfrancus* and *Maracus Titianus*, old *Titian*'s Nephew and Scholar.

25. And

part II. A Voyage through Italy. 259

25. And being in *Venice* upon St. *Georges* day *The Greeks* (the 23d. of *April*) we went to the *Greek* Church, *Church.* I mean to the *Greek* Schifmaticks Church, which is dedicated to God, in honour of St. *George*, and therefore this day was one of their greatest solemnities. Their Ceremonies and Service differed little from the Catholick *Greeks*: And if any one desire to know their Tenents, and how near they come to the *Roman Catholicks*, let him read a Book, in a thin *Folio*, Printed at *Wittemberg*, *Anno*. 1584. under tis Title, *Acta & scripta Theologorum Wittembergensium & Hieremiæ Patriarchæ.*

26. We went after dinner one *Saturday*, to see *The Jews* the *Jews* Synagogue. Among other things I heard *Synagogue.* here a Rabbin make a Homily to his Flock. He looked like a *French* Minister, or Puritanical Lecturer, in a short Cloak and Hat. The Snafling through the Nose, made all the edification that I saw in it: It was in *Italian*, but the coldest discourse that ever I heard in any Language. Indeed it was their Sabbath day; and they eat no other meat that day, but cold meat.

27. Another day we went to *Murano* again, to *The Glass-* see the Glass-houses which furnish almost all Eu- *houses at* rope with drinking Glasses, and all our Ladies Ca- *Murano.* binets with Loking-glasses. They utter here forth two hundred Thousand Crowns worth a year of this brittle Ware; and they seem to have taken measure of every Nations Belly and Humour, to fit them with Drinking-glasses accordingly: For the High Dutch they have high Glasses called *Flutes*, a foll yard long; which a Man cannot drink up alone, except his Man, or some other, hold up the foot of these more than two handed Glasses. For the *English* that love Toasts with their Drink, they

have

have curious Tankards of thick Chryſtal glaſs juſt like our Silver Tankards. For the *Italians* that love to drink leiſurely, they have Glaſſes that are almoſt as large and flat as Silver Plates, and almoſt as uneaſie to drink out of. And ſo for other Nations. In one Shop they were making a ſet of Glaſſes for the Emperor, of five Crowns every Glaſs: There were Drinking-glaſſes with high Covers made like ſpread Eagles, and finely gilt. Sometimes to ſhew their art, they make here pretty things. One made a Ship in Glaſs, with all her Tacklings, Guns, Maſts, Sails and Streamers. Another made an Organ in Glaſs three Cubits high, ſo juſtly contrived, that by blowing into it, and touching the ſtops, it ſounded muſically. A third made a perfect Caſtle, with all its fortifications, Ramparts, Cannons, Centry-houſes and Gates. Here alſo I ſaw them make thoſe vaſt Looking-glaſſes, whoſe brittleneſs ſheweth Ladies themſelves, more than their reflection doth. In fine, in *Murano*, you ſee the *Pallace* of *Signor Camillo Treviſano*, with the rare Garden and Fountains *a la Romana*.

The Shops. 28. After this we went up and down the Town of *Venice*, ſometimes a foot, to ſee better the Shops as thoſe of Silks, Cloths of Gold, of Books, and the Apothecaries Shops, where I ſaw them make their famous Treacle: Sometimes in a *Gondola*, to view over and over again, the *Canale Grande*, and the Brave Pallaces which hem it in on both ſides: Sometimes entring into the beſt of thoſe Pallaces, to ſee their rich furniture and contrivances. The beſt are, of *Juſtiniani, Mocenigo, Grimani,* *The Pallaces.* *Priuli, Contarini, Foſcoli, Loredano, Guſſoni* and *Cornaro*.

Part II.   *A Voyage through Italy.*   261

29. Then I enquired what learned Men had *The learned* adorned *Venice*, and I found these two to have been *Men.* chief, *Laurentius Justinianus, Hermolaus Barbarus, Petrus Bembus, Aloysius, Lippomanus, Paulus Paruta, Baptista Egnatius, Ludovicus Dolce, Paulus Manutius,* with divers others. I saw some years ago the noble and ingenious *Loredano,* whose witty Books make him famous over all the Academies of *Italy* and *Europe.* As also the *Procuratori Nani,* whose excellent History hath got him immortal fame.

30. Here's an Academy of wits, called *Incogniti,* *The Academy* and for their Arms, they have the river *Nilus* with *my of wits.* this this motto, *Incognito, & pur noto* ; unknown, and yet famous.

He that desires to know the History of *Venice,* *The Histo-* let him read *Andrea Morasini, Paolo, Paruta, Sabellico, Berdino Tomasino, Corido* and *Nani.*

Having thus seen all *Venice,* over and over again, in a months stay there, I was most willing to leave it ; having found it true of *Venice,* what *Socrates* said of *Athens,* that it was *melior meretrix,* *The defects* *quam Uxor ;* a fine Town for a fortnight ; but not *of Venice.* to dwell in always ; and this by reason of some stinking Channel, bad Cellars for Wine ; worse Water, and the moist Air of the Sea, not the most wholesome scarcity of Earth, even to bury their Dead in ; and little Fewel for firing. So that finding the four Elements wanting here in their purity I was willing to leave these polished *Hollanders,* and return to *Padua.*

Padua is the second Town to the *Venetian* State, *Padua.* though once the Mother of *Venice.* Its old enough to be Mother of *Rome* it self ; having been built by *Antenor,* whose Tomb is yet seen here. The Town is very great, and fuller of good Houses, than of
Men

Men of condition: Tyranny and too frequent Murders having much depopulated it, in point of Nobility. It stands in the *Marca Trevigiana*. The Walls about it are ſtrong, and back'd up with fine Ramparts. It lies near the *Eugenian* Hills, in a fertile ſoyl, and plain, which makes the Proverb ſay, *Bologna la graſſa, ma Padua la paſſa*. Its famous for the ſtudy of Phyſick, as many of our thrice worthy Phyſitians in *England* can teſtify. The chief things I obſerved in it are theſe.

Antenor's Tomb.
1. *Antenor*'s Tomb with *Gotic* Letters upon it: Which makes me doubt whether this Tomb be ſo antient as they make it.

2. The publick Schools called here *Il Bue*, or *Oxe*: What if the firſt Readers here came from *Oxford* as they did to the Univerſity of *Pavia*?

3. The Phyſick Garden, to acquaint the Student in Phyſick, with the nature of Simples.

St. Antony's Tomb.
4. The Church of St. *Antony* of *Padua*, whoſe Body lies in the open Chappel on the left hand; and this Chappel is adorned with curious figures of white Marble, repreſenting the chief actions of this Saints life. Under the Altar repoſeth his Body, and before it hang ſome twenty ſeven great Lamps of Silver, or Silver gilt. Over againſt this Chappel, ſtands juſt ſuch another open Chappel, called the Chappel of *San Felice*, which is rarely painted by famous *Giotto*, who made the *Campanile* of *Florence*. In a ſide Chappel on the right hand, is the Tomb of brave *Gata Mela*, whoſe true name was *Eraſmo di Narni*, of whom more by and by. The Tomb of *Alexander Contareno* General of the *Venetians*, and it is one of the beſt cut Tombs I have ſeen: Its faſtened to a ſide Pillar. The Quire of this Church is all of inlaid Wood.

In

In the Cloister of the Convent are seen many Tombs of learned Men: And in that quarter of the Cloister, which lies upon the Church, I found written upon a black Marble stone, these words: *Interiora Thomæ Howardi Comitis Arondeliæ:* The Bowels of the Earl of *Arundel,* late Lord Marshal of *England.* No wonder if his Bowels be enchased in Marble, after his death, who in his life time, loved Marbles *con todas su entrañas,* with his whole Bowels. His *Marmora Arondeliana,* commented upon by learned Mr. *Selden,* shew this sufficiently. This great Man died here in *Padua,* and yet in a manner at home; because he had made *Italy* familiar to him while he lived at home.

5. Going out of this Church, I saw the *Equistris* statue of *Gatta Mela,* the *Venetians* General, whose Tomb I saw even now in the Church. He was nicknamed *Gatta,* because of his watchfulness in carrying business.

6. The Church of St. *Justina,* is one of the finest Churches of *Italy*; and no wonder, seeing its Architect was *Palladio.* Under the High Altar of this Church, lies buried the Body, of St. *Justina.* The fine *Cupolas*; the curious Pavement of red and black Marble; the rich High Altar, all of *Pietre comesse*; the curious Seats, in the Quire, with the Histories of the old and new Testament cut in Wood in them; the fine Picture at the end of the Quire, over the Abbat's Seat, containing the Martyrdom of St. *Justina,* by the hand of *Paolo Veronese*; the Tomb of St. *Luke* the Evangelist; and that of St. *Matthias*; the Well, full of Relics; and the Tomb of St. *Prosdochimus* St. *Peter's* Disciple, and first Bishop of *Padua,* do all make this Church very considerable. Before this Church and Monastery

St. Justina's Church and Monastery.

ry lies the *Campo Sante*, and a fair field, where they keep Monthly a *Mercato franco*, and where the Evening *Corso* is kept, by Ladies and Noblemen in their Coaches in Summer.

The Monastry here is one of the fairest in *Italy*, and the second of that Order. The painted Cloister, the neat Library, and the Picture of St. *Justina* in the Abbat's Chamber, made by *Paolo Veronese*, are all worth your Curiosity. The *Domo* is not so well built as it is endowed with rich *Prebendaries*. An hundred Thousand Crowns a year go to the maintainance of an Hundred Clergy-Men, and Officers belonging to it. The Prebends are twenty seven, and ordinarily Gentlemen.

8. The Pallace of the *Capitano Grande* is stately without: Here stands the curious Library.

The great Hall.
9. The great Hall called here, *Il Palagio di Ragione*, is a vast Room 180 paces long, and forty broad, without Pillars. It hath four great doors to it, and over every door the statue of a learned *Paduan*. This Hall is also painted in the roof, with Astronomical figures, representing the influence of the Superior Bodies over the Inferior. At one end of it you see a round Stone, with these words written about it, *Lapis opprobrii, the stone of disgrace*; upon which whosoever will sit publickly, and declare himself not to be *Solvendo*, cannot be clapt up in Prison for Debt. At the other end of this Hall stands *Livy*'s Head in white Marble, and out of a little Back-door there, joyning to the Wall of this Hall, stands *Livy's Busto* in Stone with this Epitaph under it in old *Gothick* Letters ; *Ossa Tui Livii Patavini unius omnium mortalium judicio digni, cujus prope invicto calamo invicti Populi Romani res gesta conscriberentur.*

10. The

Part II.   A Voyage through Italy.

10. The Picture of the High Altar in the Au-*St. Augu-*
gustins Church, made by *Guido Rheni*; and that *stino.*
of St. *John Baptist* in the Sacristy, of the same
hand, are both exquisitely well done.

11. The Ruins of an old Amphitheater are seen *L' Arena.*
hard by the *Augustin's* Church. There's now a
House built upon the place, yet the Court is oval
still, and carries the name of *Arena.* Here they
tilt, and use other sports of *Cavalry.*

12. In the *Dominicans* Church there is a very *St. Domi-*
stately high Altar of *Pietre Cometſe.* Behind the *nico.*
Altar (in the Quire) are the neat Tombs
of the *Carari,* once *Signors* and Princes of *Pa-*
dua, till they were put out by the *Venetians.*

13. In the Church of *San Francefco Grande,* I *St. Fran-*
saw a curious Altar of white polished Marble, *cefco.*
which pleafed me very much, and the Tombs
of *Cavalcante* and *Lengolio.*

14. In the little neat Church of the *Oratorians, S. Thomas*
called the Church of *S. Thomas of Canterbury,* lies *di Cantua-*
buried the Lady *Katherine Whitenhall,* in a Vault *ria.*
made on purpofe, and covered with a white Marble
Stone. She was Daughter to the late Earl of *Shrews-*
bury, and Wife to the Noble and Vertuous *Thomas*
Whitenhall Efquire. If you would know more of
her, read here the Ingenious Epitaph written upon
her Tomb, and made by her fad Husband. For
my part having had the honour to see her often
in her Travels, I cannot but make honourable
mention of her here in mine; She having so much
honoured my profeſſion of Travelling, by her
generous Humour of Travelling. *She was as*
nobly Born as the Houfe of Shrewsbury *could make*
her: as comely, as if Poets had made her. Her be-
haviour was such, that if ſhe had not been noble by
Birth,

Birth, she would have passed for such by her Carriage. Her good qualities were so many, that if they had been taken in pieces, they would have made several Women Noble, and noble Women happy. She was wise beyond her years, stout above her Sex, and worthy to have found, in the World, all things better than she did, except her Parents and Husband. Her only fault was that, which would have made up other Ladies Praises, too much Courage; which befel her with the name of Talbot. But whilst her only Courage baled her on to Journeys above her Sex and force (having seen Flanders, France, and Italy, accompanied by her noble Husband, and an handsom Train) in her return back, like a tall Ship, coming laden home, and fraughted with precious acquisitions of Mind, she sunk almost in the Heaven, and alas! Died.

The Academies of Wits.
The learned Men.

15. Here are two *Academies of Wits*; the one called *Gli Recoverati*: the other, *Gli Infiammati*.

The most famous Men of *Padua* for Learning were these, *Livy*, *Apponius*, *Paulus* the *Jurisconsult*, *Sperone Speroni*, *Antonius Querenchus*, *Jacobus Zabarella*: and *Tisian* the famous Painter.

The Historians.

He that desires to know the History of *Padua*, let him read *Angelo Portinari delle felicitade di Padua*: *Antonio Riccobono, de Gymnasio Patavino, & de ejus praeclaris doctoribus*: as also the Book called *Gl' Origin di Padua*.

Vicenza.

Having thus seen *Padua*, we steered towards *Milan* again, to make the compleat *Gyro* of *Italy*. The first days Journey was to *Vicenza*, a fine Town belonging to the *Venetians*, and standing upon the two Rivers *Bachilione*, and *Rerone*. Here we saw the neat Town-house and large *Piazza*: The House and fine Garden of Count *Valmarana*, with the curious *Labyrinth* in the Garden: the *Arcus Triumphalis*, made

Part II. A Voyage through Italy.

made by *Palladio* at the Towns end; letting you into a fair Field called the *Champo Marzo*, where Ladies and Cavaliers in great store meet at the *Corso*, in their Coaches, every Summer Evening: the admirable Theater for Plays and Opera's; it was made also by rare *Palladio*, and is capable of Three thousand People, who may all sit and see with conveniency. The fine Palaces here, and those full of People of Condition.

The Theater.

Here's an Academy of Wits, called *Gl' Olympici*.

The Academy of Wits.

He that desires to know the History of *Vicenza*, let him read *Jacomo Mazari*, and *Alfonso Loschi*.

The Historians.

From *Vicenza* we went to *Verona*, called *Verona la Nobile*; belonging to the Venetians also. It stands in excellent Air, and no Man ever saw it but liked it. Its watered with the River *Addesis*, which coming out of *Germany*, runs by *Trent*, and so to *Verona*. Hence this Town abounds with good Provision, Wine, and Rich Merchants, which makes me of Opinion, that *Verona* would be a better Summer-Town for Strangers to live in, than *Padua*. The things that I saw here, were these; the three Castles, which with the new Bulwarks, make this Town able to defend it self against any Enemy.

Verona.

2. The Cathedral, or *Domo*, antient rather than stately: In it is buried Pope *Lucius* the III. with this Ingenuous Epitaph upon his Tomb:

Luca dedit lucem tibi, Luci, Pontificatum
   Ostia, Papatum Roma, Verona mori.
Imo Verona dedit tibi Lucius gaudia, Roma
   Exilium, inter Ostia, Luca mori.

R r
3. The

3. The famous Tomb of the *Signori della Scala*, who once were Masters here, and from whom *Joseph* and *Julius Scaliger* pretend to have come: This Tomb is seen from the Street, and is much esteemed for its heighth and Structure.

4. In the Monastery of St. *George*, the rare Picture of St. *George*, made by *Paolo Veronese*, for which the late Lord Marshal of *England* offered Two thousand Pistols.

The Amphitheater. 5. The rare Amphitheater, built at first by the Consul *Flaminius*, and repaired since by the Townsmen, and now the most entire Amphitheater in *Europe*.

The Academy of Wits. Here's also an Academy of Wits, called *Gli Philormonici*.

The Learned Men. The famousest Men for Learning here, were these; *Zeno Veronensis*, an Antient Father, and great Preacher; *Cornelius Nepos*, *Pliny* the Second, *Catullus*, according to that,

Mantua Virgilio gaudet, Verona Catullo.

Fracastorius, Onuphrius, Paminus, Paulus Æmilius the Historian, *Francesco Pona, Aloysius Novarinus,* and *Paolo Veronese* the ingenious Painter.

Near *Verona*, upon the Plains, before you come to the Town, was fought a famous Battel, where *C. Marius* defeated the *Cimbers.* Near this Town also was fought a famous Battel between *Theodoric* and *Odoacer*, where the latter was defeated.

He that desires to know the History of *Verona*, *The Historians.* let him read *Torello Saraina*, *Girolamo di Corte*, *Compendio dell' Istoria di Verona*; and the *Antiquitates Veronenses* of *Onufrius Panvinus.*

From

From *Verona* we went to *Brescia*, by the way *Peschiera.* of *Peschiera* and *Disenzano*. *Peschiera* is a strong Fort belonging to the Venetians, and guarded by a constant Garison. It stands upon the *Lago* *Lago di* *di Garda*, *Lacus Benacus* anciently, and is almost *Garda.* surrounded by its Cryſtallin Waters. It's a most regular Fortification, with five Baſtions, and high Ramparts, which cover the whole Town.

Disenzano is a little Town upon the Lake of *Diſenzano.* *Garda* alſo. Here they have excellent Fiſh, and Wine; that is, rare *Carpioni*, and *Muſcatello*, which they call *Vino Santo*.

From hence after Dinner we arrived betimes at *Brescia*, another ſtrong Town of the Vene- *Breſcia.* tians. We ſaw here the Caſtle, the Town-houſe, neat Churches, the Ramparts and Walls of the Town; the Cryſtalline Brooks running through the Streets; and the Shops of the Gun-ſmiths, eſpecially that of Famous *Lazzarino Cominazzo*.

The beſt Hiſtorians of the *Breſcian* Affairs, is *The Hiſto-* *Ottavio Roſſi*, in his Book called *Memorie Bre-* *ry.* *ſciana*.

From *Breſcia* I went once to *Crema*, and *Ber-* *Crema.* *gamo*, two ſtrong Towns of the Venetians, and both Frontiers to the State of *Milan*. The firſt is very ſtrong, and Famous for fine Linnen made here. The latter is ſtrong too, both by its Ca- *Bergamo.* ſtle, good Walls, and its high Situation upon an Hill, which gives you a fair proſpect into the *Milaneſe* for twenty or thirty miles. In the Church of the *Auguſtins* lies buried *Ambroſius Calepinus*, Author of the excellent Latin Dicti-onary, which Learned *Paſſeratius* hath ſet out

R r 2   ſince

since with great additions. Its in six Languages.

From *Bergamo* I went to *Milan*, one days journey. Another time I went from *Brescia* to *Milan* by the way of *Mantua*, and *Mirandola*.

Mantua.

Mantua belongs to a Sovereign Duke, or Prince, of the House of *Gonsague*. It stands in the midst of Marshes, which are nourished by the River *Mincius*; so that there's no coming to it but by two long Bridges over the Lake. And yet this Town was taken some Forty Years ago: No Town being impregnable where an Ass laden with Gold can enter; or where Faction keeps one Gate. For about that time the Emperor's Army, by secret Intelligence, presenting it self before it, was let in; and sacked the Town. At the entrance of the Town Gates, they observe the Fashion of many other Towns in *Italy*, to make Travellers leave their Pistols and Carabins at the Gate where they enter, and not see them again till they meet them at the other Gate where they go out; giving them, for all that, a *Contrasegno*, or little Talley, whereof you keep one piece, and the other is tied to your Pistols, whereby you may claim and challenge them. This was an antient Custom in the *Romans* times, as I find in *Valerius Maximus*, who saith, it was the Practice of those of *Marseilles* (then a Roman Colony) *Ut hospitia sua, quemadmodum advenientibus humana sunt, ita ipsis tuta sint.* As for *Mantua* it self, its well built, and full of good Houses. The Duke's Palace was heretofore one of the richest of *Italy*. I was told that it had seven changes of Hangings for every Room in the House; besides a world of rare Pictures, Statues, Plate, Ornaments, Cabinets, an Unicorn's Horn,

Valer. Maxim. l. 2. c. 1.

Horn, an Organ of Alablaster; six Tables, each three Foot long, the first all of Emeralds, the second of *Turky* Stone, the third of Hyacinths, the fourth of Saphirs, the fifth of Amber, the sixth of Jasper Stone. But the *Imperialists* swept all away. The Origin of the House of *Gonsague* is from *Germany*. For a long time they were only Marquises of *Mantua*, till *Charles* V. made them Dukes. The Revenues of this Prince are about Five hundred thousand Crowns. His Interest (as that of the other lesser Princes of *Italy*) is to join with the stronger of the two Nations, *France* or *Spain*. And he hath been often forc'd to put now and then a *French* Garison, and now then a *Spanish* Garison into his strong Town of *Casal*; one of the strongest Places I saw in all *Italy*; having an excellent Cittadel at one end of it, a strong Castle at the other, and strong Ditches, Walls, and Ramparts every where. In fine, this Duke can raise about Fifteen thousand Foot, and Two thousand Horse.

The Duke's Family.
His Revenues.
His Interest.
Casal. Its Strength.

Of *Mantua* were these two Excellent Latin Poets, Old *Virgil*, and Modern *Baptista Mantuanus* a *Carmelite*.

He that desires to know the History of *Mantua*, let him read *Mario Aquicola*.

Its History.

From *Mantua* we went to *Mirandola*, being invited thither by its wonderful Name. It is a Principality far more ancient than great; and it is so called from three Children born here of a great Lady, at one Birth. The Story, as it is pretty, so it is related by good Authors, and therefore I will give it you here, in the end of this my *Italian* Journey, as a Farewell. And 'tis this; *Constantius* the Emperor, Son of *Constantine*

Mirandola.
Franciscus Pius Leander Albatus.

tine the Great, had a Daughter called *Eurjdis*; who being grown up in Years, fell in Love with *Manfred*, a Courtier of her Unkle *Canstantine*, an handsom well-bred young Gentleman. *Manfred* was both Courtier enough, and wise enough, to understand this to be no small Honour; and therefore embraced her Affection with a corresponding Flame. In a word, they meet often; talk of it; give mutual Promises; make all the Money they can, and Jewels, and flee away secretly. They come into *Italy*, land at *Naples*, from thence to *Ravenna*, and at last pitch upon this Country where now *Mirandola* stands. It was then a place overspread with Thickets and Under-woods, and furnishing some Pasturage for Sheep, and Cottages for Shepherds. Here then they chuse to live privately, and converse with none but Country Swains, and Shepherds. Blind Love, whither dost thou hurry Princesses, to make them prefer Cottages before Courts? At last, with their Money they buy Land, and *Manfred* grew soon to that Authority among his Neighbours, that they chuse him for their Head; and recur unto him upon all occasions for his Advice and Protection: In the mean time (having solemnly Married *Euridis* at his arrival in *Italy*) she brings him forth three Sons at once, *Picus*, *Pius*, and *Papazzo*; and *Manfred* grows far more considerable daily in these Parts. At last the Emperor *Constantius* coming into *Italy* upon his Occasions, and being Complimented by all the several Provinces thereof, this Province, among the rest, chose *Manfred* as their Ambassador to the said Emperor, to carry to him the tender of their Respects and Homage. *Manfred*

Part II. A Voyage through Italy.

fred accepted of the Employment, and carried himself so Gallantly in the Embassy, that the Emperor Knighted him, and upon further trial of his Worth raised him to high Favour. *Manfred* seeing the Realities of the Emperor, thought it now high time to discover himself to him. Wherefore casting himself one day at the Emperor's Feet, and begging his Pardon, he discovered himself unto him, and told him his whole Story and Adventures. At first the Emperor was a little troubled; but finding such Freedom and Gallantry in his Carriage, mingled with such humble Ingenuity in the Confession of his Fault; he not only pardoned what was past, but presently sent for *Euridis* and her Children to come to him, and live at Court with him. This done, he makes *Manfred* Count and Marquis of a great part of these Countries, and gives him leave to build Towns and Castles there: And for his Arms gives him the Black Eagle. In fine, in Memory of the three Children born so wonderfully at one Birth, he commands that the chief Town should be called *Miranda*. After the Death of *Constantius*, *Manfred* and his Lady returned with great Riches unto their old dwelling place, and there began to build *Miranda*; which in process of time was called *Mirandola*. This true Story, if it look like a Romance, you must not wonder, seeing Romances now a days look like true Stories.

The Prince of *Mirandola* receives yearly Fourscore thousand Crowns.

The greatest Ornament of this Country, was that Famous *Joannes Picus Mirandulanus*; whose Life Sir *Thomas Moor* wrote, and having written it, lived it.

Jo. Picus Mirandulanus.

From

From *Mirandola* I struck to *Parma*, and so to *Piacenza*, *Lodi*, and *Marigno*, described all above; and at last to *Milan* again, where I had been before, and where my *Giro* of *Italy* ended, as now my Journey and Description doth. I taking here a new rise from *Milan*, and crossing through *Swisserland* by the Lake of *Como*, and over Mount St. *Godart*, came to *Basil*; here Embarking upon the *Rhine*, I saw *Strasburgh*, *Brisac*, *Spire*, *Philipsburgh*, *Openheim*, *Coblentz*, *Hamerstede*, *Wermes*, *Francfort*, *Mayence*, *Cologn*, *Duffeldorp*, *Skinskonce*, *Rais*, *Wesel*, *Arnebem*, and divers other Rhinish Towns: Then having viewed *Holland* and *Flanders*; I came at last to *Calais*, and so home to my dear Country, *England*, by way of *Dover*.

FINIS.

THE

TABLE
OF THE
NAMES
OF THE
Chief TOWNS contained in this Second PARTS.

A

Adria	223	
Albano	197	
Amiclæ	143	
Ancona	217	
Assisium	206	
Averſa	174	

B

Baiæ	191
Bergamo	269
Breſcia	269

C

Caeta	160
Capua	163
Campania	172
Carigliano, *River*	171
Caſal	271
Catholica	218
Ceravalle	115
Caſena	220
Crema	269
Cuma	194
Cicero's Baths	193

D. Diſen-

The TABLE.

D.
Difenfano 269

E.
Elifian Fields 191

F.
Faenza 220
Fano 218
Ferrara 221
Foligni 206
Forli 220
Formiæ 159
Foffa Nova 157
Ferfcati 195
Fundi 196

G.
Gandulfo 195
Grotta dell Cane 200
Grotta di Pofilipo 189
St. Gannaro's Stoves 201

K.
Kindom of Naples 174
Kingdom of Cyprus 230

L.
La Laguna 224
Lacus Avernus 194

Lago di Gerda 269
Loreto 207

M.
Macerata 207
Mantua 270
Marino 157
Minturna 162
Mirandola 271
Mola 159
Mons Maffieus 172
Monte Falco 206
Monte Garo 172
Murano 254

N.
Naples 174
Narni 204

P.
Padua 261
Palma Nova 231
Paufilipus, Ms. 129
Peperno 157
Pefaro 218
Pefchiera 269
Puzzolo 191

R.
Recanata 207
Rimini 219
Rome

The TABLE.

Rome	3, &c.	Tivoli	201
Ruigno	283	Tolentino	206
Rubicon, *River*.	220	Tres Tabernæ	175

S.　　　　　　　　**V.**

Senegallia	218	Veletri	157
Spoleto	204	Venice	224
Sulphatara	189	Verona	267
		Vesuvius, *Mt.*	183
T.		Via Apia,	159
		Via Flaminia	203
Taracina	157	Vicenza,	266
Terni	204	Villa Ludovisia	200
Tyber, *River*.	204		

Books

Books Printed for Richard Wellington, *at the* Lute *in* St. Paul's Church-Yard.

THE next Week will be publish'd the History of *Polybius* the Megalæpolitan: Containing a General Account of the Transactions of the whole World. In three Volumes; the last never before Publish'd. Translated from the Original by Sir *Henry Sheels.* With a Character of the Author, and his Writings, by *John Dryden* Esq;

Familiar Letters: Vol. I. Written by the Right Honourable *John*, late Earl of *Rochester*, to the Honourable *Henry Savile* Esq; And other Letters by Persons of Honour and Quality. With Letters written by the most Ingenious Mr. *Tho. Otway*, and Mrs *K. Philips*. Publish'd from their Original Copies: With Modern Letters by *Tho. Cheek* Esq; Mr. *Dennis*, and Mr. *Brown*.

All the Histories and Novels written by the Late Ingenious Mrs *Behn*, entire in One Volume. *Viz.* I. The History of *Oroonoko*, or the Royal Slave. Written by the Command of King *Charles* the Second. II. The *Fair Jilt*, or Prince *Tarquin*. III. *Agnes de Castro*, or the Force of Generous Love. IV. The *Lover's Watch*,

Watch, or the Art of making Love; being Rules for Courtship for every Hour of the Day and Night. V. The Ladies Looking-Glass to Dress themselves by, or the whole Art of Charming all Mankind. VI. The Lucky Mistake. VII. Memoirs of the Court of the King of *Bantam*. VIII. The Nun, or the Perjured Beauty. IX. The Adventure of thee Black Lady. These three last never before Published. Together with the History of the Life and Memoirs of Mrs *Behn*. Never before Printed: By one of the Fair Sex. Intermixed with Pleasant Love-Letters that pass'd betwixt her and Min-Heer *Van Bruin*, a *Dutch* Merchant; with her Character of the Country and Lover: And her Love Letters to a Gentleman in *England*. The Third Edition, with Large Additions.

The Whole Works of that Excellent Practical Physician Dr *Thomas Sydenham*. Wherein not only the History and Cures of acute Diseases are treated of after a new and accurate Method; but also the safest and shortest way of Curing most Chronical Diseases: Translated from the Original Latin, by *John Pechy*, M.D. of the College of Physicians.

There is newly Publish'd, a new and easie Method to understand the Roman History. With an exact Chronology of the Reigns of the Emperors; an Account of the most Eminent Authors, when they flourish'd; and an Abridgment of the Roman Antiquities and Customs. By way of Dialogue, for the Use of the Duke of *Burgundy*. Done out of French, with very
Large

Large Additions and Amendments, by *Thomas Brown*. Very useful and proper to be read in Schools.

A Mathematical Companion, or the Description and Use of a new sliding Rule, by which many Useful and Necessary Questions in Arithmetick, Military Orders, Interest, Trigonometry, Planometry, Stereonometry, Geography, Astronomy, Navigation, Fortification, Gunnery, Dyalling, may be speedily resolved without the help of Pen or Compasses. By *William Hunt*, Philomath.

A Discourse upon the Nature and Faculties of Man, in several Essays: With some considerations on the Occurences of Human Life. By *Tim. Nourse*, Gent.

Ovid Travestie: Or a Burlesque on *Ovid's* Epistles, by Captain *Alexander Radcliff*.

Reflections upon Antient and Modern Learning. By *William Wotton*, B. D. Chaplain to the Right Honourable the Earl of *Nottingham*. The Second Addition, with Large Additions. With a Dissertation upon the Epistles of *Phalaris, Themistocles, Socrates, Euripides*, &c. and *Esop's Fables*, by Dr *Bentley*.

The Family Physician, being a Choice Collection of Approved and Experienced Remedies, to Cure all Diseases incident to Humane Bodies; useful in Families, and serviceable to Country People, by *George Hartman*, Chymist; Servant to Sir *Kenelm Digby*, till he died.

A General Treatise of the Diseases of Infants and Children, Collected from the most Eminent Practical Authors, by *John Pechey*, of the College of Physicians.

Contemplations Moral and Divine, in three Parts; Written by the Late Lord Chief Justice *Hales*, to which is added the Life of the Author, by *Gilbert* Lord Bishop of *Sarum*. The third Part may be had singly.

Cocker's Decimal Arithmetick; the Second Edition, very much enlarged, by *John Hawkins*, School-Master at St *George*'s Church in *Southwark*.

Vade Mecum; or the Necessary Companion; containing Sir *Sam. Moreland*'s Perpetual Almanack, shewing the Days of the Month for any Year, past, present, or to come. A Table of the Kings Reigns since the Conquest, compared with the Years of Christ. A Table wherein any numbers of Farthings, Half-pence, Pence and Shillings are ready cast up; of great use to all Treaders. The Interest and Rebate of Money, the Forbearance, Discount, and Purchase of Annuities. The Rates of Post-Letters, Inland and Outland. Account of the Penny-Post. The Principal Roads in *England*, shewing the distance of each Town from *London*; also the Market-Towns on each Road, with the days of the week the Markets are kept on; also the Hundred and County each Town stands in. The Names of the Counties, Cities, and Borough Towns in *England* and *Wales*, with the number of Knights, Citizens and Burgesses chosen therein, to serve in Parliament. The usual Rates and Fares of Coachmen, Carmen and Watermen. The Sixth Edition, much Enlarged.

Plays

Plays Printed for an fold by *Richard Wellington*, at the *Lute* in St. *Paul*'s Church-Yard.

Where you may be furnished with most Plays.

THE Impoſture Defeated: Or a trick to Cheat the Devil. A Comedy, as it was Acted by his Majeſties Servants, at the *Theatre* in *Drury-Lane*.

Innocent Miſtreſs
Unnatural Mother
Spaniſh Wives
Unnatural Brother
Plot and no plot
Younger Brother, or Amorous Jilt
Old Batchelor
Agnes de Caſtro
Rover, or Baniſh'd Cavilier
Relapſe, or Vertue in Danger
Rule a Wife and have a Wife
Country Wife
Rehearſal
Anatomiſt, or the Sham Doctor
Cyrus the Great, or the Tragedy of Love

Don *Quixot* in three Parts
Roman brides Revenge
The Marriage Hater Match'd
Country Wake
Neglected Virtue
Phyrrus King of *Epirus*
Very Good Wife
Womans wit, or Lady in Faſhion
The Gallants
Sullen Lovers
Humouriſts
Mackbeth
Timon of *Athens*
Oedipus
Ibrahim the 13th Emperor of the *Turks*
Canterbury Gueſts
Loſt Lovers

www.ingramcontent.com/pod-product-compliance
Lightning Source LLC
Chambersburg PA
CBHW032139230426
43672CB00011B/2395